Robert Macklin was born in Queensland and educated at Brisbane Grammar School, the University of Queensland and the Australian National University. He began his journalistic career at the *Courier-Mail* and subsequently wrote for *The Age* and *The Bulletin*, and was associate editor of the *Canberra Times* until 2003.

His 2016 biography *Hamilton Hume* revived national interest in Australia's greatest explorer, and the acclaimed *Dark Paradise* exposed the horror of colonial sadism in the penal colony of Norfolk Island. His history of Australia's Special Forces, *Warrior Elite*, is required reading in the fields of military security and intelligence. His bestselling biography of Rob Maylor, *SAS Sniper*, revealed in graphic detail the battles against Islamist fanatics.

Robert has won numerous literary prizes including, with Peter Thompson, the 2009 Blake Dawson Prize for Business Literature for their classic, *The Big Fella: The Rise and Rise of BHP Billiton*.

Robert is the author of 28 books including the biography of Kevin Rudd, four novels and a number of works of history. He is a graduate of the Australian Film and Television School and has written and directed documentary films in 33 countries in Asia and the South Pacific. Robert now lives in Canberra and Tuross Head and divides his time between his books and screenplays.

ALSO BY ROBERT MACKLIN

Novels

The Queenslander
The Paper Castle
Juryman
Fire in the Blood

Non-fiction

Seven Cities of Australia
The Jesus Delusion
Jacka VC
Kevin Rudd: The Biography
Backs to the Wall
War Babies
My Favourite Teacher
The Great Australian Pie
SAS Sniper
Redback One
SAS Insider
One False Move
Dark Paradise
Warrior Elite
Hamilton Hume

With Peter Thompson

The Battle of Brisbane
Morrison of China
Keep off the Skyline
Operation Rimau
The Big Fella: The Rise and Rise of BHP Billiton

Books of the Film

Newsfront
The Journalist
Glass Babies

Australia and China's shared history from the goldfields to the present day

DRAGON & KANGAROO

ROBERT MACKLIN

Published in Australia and New Zealand in 2017
by Hachette Australia
(an imprint of Hachette Australia Pty Limited)
Level 17, 207 Kent Street, Sydney NSW 2000
www.hachette.com.au

10 9 8 7 6 5 4 3 2 1

Copyright © Robert Macklin 2017

This book is copyright. Apart from any fair dealing for the purposes of private study,
research, criticism or review permitted under the *Copyright Act 1968*, no part
may be stored or reproduced by any process without prior written permission.
Enquiries should be made to the publisher.

National Library of Australia
Cataloguing-in-Publication data:

Macklin, Robert, author.
Dragon and Kangaroo: Australia and China's shared history from the goldfields to the present
day/Robert Macklin.

ISBN: 978 0 7336 3403 1 (paperback)

Chinese – Australia – History.
Chinese – Australia – Social conditions.
Australians – China – History.
Australians – China – Social conditions.

Cover design by bookdesignbysaso.com
Front cover images courtesy of National Archives of Australia (Mao Zedong and Gough Whitlam, 1973)
    and Dixson Galleries, State Library of New South Wales (*Ballarat, 1858* by George Rowe)
Back cover photograph courtesy of Christian Jensen/Mitchell Library, State Library of New South Wales
    (G.E. Morrison in Western China)
Text design by Bookhouse, Sydney
Typeset in 12/16.8pt Bembo by Bookhouse, Sydney

This is for Allegra

CONTENTS

Prologue ix

PART ONE   WORLDS COLLIDE   1

One   The first celestials   3
Two   Dynasties and druids   8
Three   Rise and fall of empires   14
Four   From opium to gold   20
Five   New gold mountain   26
Six   Conflicts with colonials   32
Seven   Christian conversion   38
Eight   Colonial suppression   45
Nine   Lambing Flat   49
Ten   The Chinese bushranger   55
Eleven   Serving the squattocracy   61
Twelve   Northern frontiers   68
Thirteen   Anti-Chinese policies   75

PART TWO   CHINESE HISTORY AND POLITICS   85

Fourteen   'Chinese' Morrison   87
Fifteen   An Australian in China   93
Sixteen   Australian Federation   98
Seventeen   The Boxer Rebellion   106
Eighteen   Changing Chinese history   112
Nineteen   Winds of change   121
Twenty   The Chinese revolution   128
Twenty-One   China's second revolution   136
Twenty-Two   A world at war   145

Twenty-Three	End of an era	153
Twenty-Four	Changing the Chinese guard	161
Twenty-Five	China in the 1920s	169
Twenty-Six	China in the 1930s	179
Twenty-Seven	Diplomatic changes	186
Twenty-Eight	One war ends …	195

PART THREE AFTER WORLD WAR II — 207

Twenty-Nine	Challenges and opportunities	209
Thirty	Mao's declaration	216
Thirty-One	Into the heart of communism	225
Thirty-Two	Fear of Communist China	236
Thirty-Three	The Cultural Revolution	243
Thirty-Four	Relations thaw	250
Thirty-Five	The fall of Whitlam	257
Thirty-Six	Changing times	264

PART FOUR AUSTRALIA AND CHINA TODAY — 271

Thirty-Seven	Tiananmen Square	273
Thirty-Eight	The end of White Australia	284
Thirty-Nine	The trade boom	292
Forty	Presidential visits	298
Forty-One	Rise and fall of Kevin Rudd	305
Forty-Two	New leaders, new troubles	314
Forty-Three	Ever closer ties	322
Forty-Four	A mature relationship	331

Acknowledgements	339
Bibliography	341
Endnotes	342
Index	348

PROLOGUE

Racism has defined our species ever since *Homo sapiens* confronted other primates on our undefined but unstoppable quest for world domination. But despite our total victory over all-comers, it remains, pulsing in our DNA like some perfect paradox of Greek mythology that drives its possessor ever closer to the sun until it becomes his undoing. And worse, it is an illusion. For today there is only one race. We are it, and the differences between us, as recorded in our individual genomes, are so utterly inconsequential that they rearrange themselves overnight in the ecstasy of conception. They tell us little to nothing about intelligence and even less about our inherent character. They do, however, permit us a remarkable insight into our past.

They have led us to the recognition that we all derive from a small group who arose in Sub-Saharan Africa; and that some of them departed – perhaps in several waves – for the Middle East between 100,000 and 80,000 years ago. There, we now know, they encountered the Neanderthal people, descendants of a much earlier departure who really were of a different race; in fact, a different species. But even they were still able to interbreed since most non-African human genomes today contain up to 4 per cent of Neanderthal mitochondrial DNA.

From the Middle East, one group turned north, and by about 28,000 years ago their skeletons were identifiably 'European' though their skin would not lose its dark pigmentation until about 12,000 years ago.

A second group headed to the northeast and by about 15,000 years ago they were identifiably 'Mongolian'. They multiplied and settled in the plains, foothills, rich river valleys and off-shore islands of eastern Asia. In time they would become known as the Chinese, Korean,

Japanese and Indo-Chinese nations. Some even became Mongolians! On their journey they had touched upon a mysterious group that is known today as the Denisovans from fossil fragments recently discovered in a Siberian cave. The effects – if any – of this exposure and interbreeding are unknown. All we do know is that they are almost unmeasurable.

A third group turned south and travelled for about 30,000 years down through the Indian Subcontinent and South-East Asia to New Guinea and eventually Australia, arriving about 50,000 years ago. They, too, had met briefly with the Denisovans. But by 15,000 years ago they had populated the Great South Land and – like the rest of our species – had become more 'gracile'. Indeed, they had developed all the common characteristics of the people we know today as Aboriginal Australians.

From then on, in the words of Colin Groves, Professor of Biological Anthropology at the Australian National University (ANU), there was 'a gentle rain' of immigrant DNA from visitors to northern Australia from Malacca and Indonesia which trickled down through the genomes of the original inhabitants.[1]

Similarly, the Europeans and the Chinese were touched at the fringes by visitors from other parts of the globe. Indeed, about 6000 years ago, waves of agriculture-bearing immigrants from the Middle East moved into Europe; and at the same time there was an expansion south and west of agriculture-bearing people from China. But generally it was a time of relative genetic stability, particularly in the southern continent.

Then in 1788 the British Captain Arthur Phillip berthed the First Fleet in the magnificent Sydney Harbour and landed his 1336 convicts and their overseers at Sydney Cove. Over the next two centuries they would be joined by immigrants from around the world.

But the British, like people everywhere, preferred their own kind, believing themselves to be superior in every way to both the local inhabitants – whom they treated as scarcely human – and their Asian neighbours whom they regarded with a combination of fear and contempt as members of a different race. To be fair, they were unaware of the singular nature of the human species. That discovery was not made until the 20th century; and its implications have still not penetrated the ancient fears and prejudices of many in the international human community.

So when gold discoveries brought an influx of Chinese prospectors to the British colony, the racial chauvinism of the day led to violence, forced removal and a blanket prohibition on Asian migration that endured for more than 70 years.

Fortunately, in the last 40 years, a more enlightened Australian government has withdrawn the geographical restrictions on immigration. And coincidentally, at the same time the Chinese people have transformed their country's fortunes and developed an outward-looking middle class. The transformation has come at great cost to living conditions in China's crowded cities; and the countryside has been ravaged by industrial waste. The authoritarian government which had made the transformation possible refused to share even the power of free expression with its people, let alone a legal and political system open to all. So Australia, with its small population, its enormous spaces, its undeveloped potential, and its free and open society, has become a magnet for Chinese immigration and investment.

However, in those intervening 200 years, Australians had been fed an unremitting diet of fear of the 'Asian hordes'. And indeed the Japanese attempted to isolate and invade our country in the 1940s; and without Chinese resistance to their imperial expansionism they might well have succeeded. But while we forgave the defeated Japanese and turned them into our principal trading partner, we then developed alliances with New Zealand and the United States aimed at defending ourselves against such political bogies as 'the downward thrust of Chinese communism'.

In the 'war games' practised by the Australian Defence Force, China took pride of place as the enemy. And as the United States came to regard China as a competitor for international leadership – particularly in the Asia-Pacific – they applied pressure on Australia to thwart Chinese influence. This rekindled a residue of suspicion and distrust within the Australian community and the potential for retaliatory attitudes and actions among the Chinese leadership in Beijing. Yet at the same time China has replaced Japan as our biggest trading partner; its people have become the third most populous of our immigrants; and more than a million of them annually come as tourists – easily the largest contingent from any single country. Yet the ingrained suspicion remains.

Thus have we arrived at a pivotal moment in the Australian story.

How did it come to this? What forces selected such a thorny path? Does the road we have travelled hold lessons that will guide us through the inevitable crises ahead? Are we heading for a happy ending? Or will the ancient racist fears win out?

As Shakespeare says, 'What's past is prologue'; but until now there has been no sustained attempt to tell the story of the relationship between the two countries and the extraordinary effect each has had upon the political, economic and social development of the other. Indeed, it is so little known that in the argot of journalism it would qualify as 'the hidden history' with both sides of the equation engaged in an unacknowledged - and perhaps even unconscious – conspiracy to keep it so.

No more.

What follows is a chronicle as unexpected to the writer as I expect it will be to the reader. For as we travel down this great sweep of history we will discover ourselves on a wild ride of unexpected turns and uncharted courses, of noble intentions and appalling misjudgements. The men and women who helped and hindered its navigation are some of the most exciting and remarkable people that both countries have produced – scoundrels and tyrants, fools and buffoons, heroes and martyrs. But together they form the cast of one of the most engaging human sagas the world has known.

And its denouement is upon us.

PART ONE
WORLDS COLLIDE

CHAPTER ONE
THE FIRST CELESTIALS

John Macarthur might have been the founder of the Australian wool industry but he was totally imbued with the British aristocracy's notions of class and race. He regarded the Aboriginal people as little more than vermin. Slavery was part of his 'natural order' and he looked askance at the 1833 legislation in Westminster that would end it forever. He was well aware that the next radical move from the bleeding-hearted emancipists would be to stop the transportation of convict slaves for his massive colonial land holdings.

The very idea was insupportable. According to his biographer Margaret Steven, 'His arrogance concealed an anxious insecurity that contributed to the pursuit of unscrupulous ends and eventually gained control of his tormented mind.'[1] Banished from public life by Governor Richard Bourke in 1832 as 'a lunatic with little hope of restoration', Macarthur died at his Camden Park home two years later. Thereafter his family and his fellow landholders would begin to agitate for some alternative to the convicts and in 1840 their fears were realised; transportation was outlawed and the labour force demanded decent wages.

The administration of the colony of New South Wales under Governor George Gipps was no help at all, so the squatters privately cast their eyes to China. They made contact with agents in the Chinese ports of Guangzhou (Canton) and Xiamen (Amoy). Spreading their net, they also used Alexander Johnstone's recruiting agency in Singapore and the good offices of the British East India Company in Calcutta. However, it was the Chinese 'coolie' that the squatters were assured would prove the most suitable because of his 'untiring industry, frugality and perseverance' which were 'the inherited instincts of their race'. According to the *Port Phillip Herald,* they were much to be preferred for the simple tasks of shepherding since 'the great bodily powers of British labourers would be a misapplication of strength'.²

In fact, Macarthur had been ahead of the game. The records show that he had employed at least three Chinese people on his properties as early as the 1820s. And it is highly likely that they had compatriots whose records have been lost to history. But either way, his family was at the forefront of the new push to engage 'indentured labour', a polite term for slave-like pay and conditions, in the 1840s. And in the second half of 1848 the first arrivals from Xiamen disembarked in Sydney from the *Nimrod* with others remaining on board for their subsequent destination: the southern settlement of Port Phillip.

The colonial press stilled the fears of its readers that they were about to be overwhelmed by the Chinese with the comment that, 'The cost of bringing these men to Sydney is said to be £12 per head – more than the average expense of bringing immigrants from England. This is sufficient guarantee that but a small number will arrive.' However, a Victorian landholder, Henry Moore, undermined that reassurance with the revelation that 'they are engaged for five years at £6 per annum' plus basic found, 'bringing the total for one man's hire to about £11 per annum, or less'.

Others were concerned that only men were being imported. *The Telegraph* warned that, 'This for obvious reasons is bad and must be prevented; it is contrary to the laws of nature and unless some means can be found to compel parties to bring a proportion of women, the social condition of the colony will be likely to be of a character calling for the most watchful attention of the Executive.'

By the time the ship reached Port Phillip there was a substantial British crowd on hand to gawp as the Celestials came ashore at the Geelong wharf. The *Argus* sent a reporter to cover the scene and the newcomers proved suitably exotic: 'Their heads were shaved with the exception of a patch on the crown about four inches in diameter from which depended a tail two feet long,' he wrote. 'A very few of them had the large conical hats which we are acquainted with, capital substitutes for umbrellas, being nearly three feet in diameter. Their dress appeared invariably black ... cotton, wide drawers and an upper dress like a sailor's duckfrock, but wide in the sleeves and rather larger. Their square-toed shoes were ornamented with silk on the uppers, and with soles an inch and a quarter thick.'

As to their manner, 'The celestials comported themselves with the self-possession of experienced travelers, very little impressed with the novelty of their position. They elbowed us out of the way and took especial care of their luggage.' When they crowded on to waiting drays which would take them to their new laboring positions, they seemed 'in a high state of delight and excitement'.

However, the correspondent for the *Geelong Chronicle* was also on hand and he brought a very different perception to bear. He saw 'cut-throat barbarians, waiting like so many wild beasts to be portioned off to their captors'. And 'impatient to action, they began fighting in an infuriated state of drunkenness'. Indeed, one of them 'jumped on the face and bowels of another coolie until the man's eyes protruded and blood gushed in streams from his nose, mouth and eyes'. The other 'savages' viewed the scene with 'delight'.

While it's hard to believe that the two men were present at the same occasion, their separate perceptions reflected the contrasting views of the community: wonderment on the one hand, contempt mixed with hostility on the other. It was a neat precursor to the opposing attitudes that would continue to animate the Australian community for the next 150 years.

As for the Chinese, some stayed for the term of their contracts then left for home; others absconded when the goldrush began three years later. Indeed, from the 3000 who arrived at the Port of Sydney on contract to the Macarthur family and their associates between 1840 and 1853, some became leaders of the Chinese prospectors and would be gradually integrated into the European community. Others would feel sufficiently comfortable in the colonies to continue their agricultural pursuits indefinitely, including 'Henry' Wang, a resident of Gulgong, New South Wales, who died at 105 years of age in 1911, having lived there since 1841.

The Chinese had left a country which continued to condone human bondage. When the last of China's ruling family dynasties, the invading Manchu – known as the Qing – had come to power in 1644, they possessed about two million slaves. But like previous dynasties they saw advantages in phasing the practice out and turned slaves and serfs into peasants. But by the mid-19th century the Qing's best days were behind them and the practice resumed. As the European powers forced themselves into Chinese territory and trade, the government and the country would soon go into sharp decline. The 4000-year role of the Middle Kingdom as an economic superpower was about to retire into the wings of the world stage.

There it would languish for more than a century to the chagrin, humiliation and frustration of its people. But then, in late 1978, a diminutive and unprepossessing emperor of the Communist dynasty, Deng Xiaoping, would release the bonds of enterprise and China would begin the extraordinary climb back to its former position in the first rank of the world's economic powers.

But the rocky road that the China–Australia relationship travelled in the two centuries since those first arrivals did not prepare either country for the powerful economic and social interaction that would develop between them virtually overnight. China was like a teenage boy suddenly aware of a new muscularity, awkward in yesterday's tight garb and unable to exercise its newfound wealth and power with the grace and finesse of its rivals. And Australia still struggled to find its own identity in its adopted home, so far from the European nation that spawned it and the great cousin across the Pacific with its promise of protection at a cost.

As the third decade of the new century approached, it was unclear whether either had the wit or the will to make the adjustment. China still had unfinished business in reclaiming its former lofty position among the global movers and shakers. Australia's situation was altogether more urgent and more problematic. The question posed by former prime minister Paul Keating remained unanswered: would Australia seek its security *in* Asia or *from* Asia? Had it matured sufficiently to relish the opportunities of its geographical good fortune, or would it redouble its efforts to reject its Aboriginal and regional inheritance in favour of its colonial tradition?

The kangaroo and the dragon struggled in awkward embrace.

CHAPTER TWO

DYNASTIES AND DRUIDS

While the colonial spectators gathered in fascination on that Port Phillip wharf, the Chinese arrivals were equally unfamiliar with the round-eyed British faces surrounding them. Apart from the occasional missionary or ship's crewman in the teeming cities, they had virtually no personal experience of pink-skinned foreigners. And the Chinese were no less racist than the European onlookers. They were, and remain, deeply proud of their history, customs and values which have produced a rich and impressive culture.

Their pioneering inventions of paper, printing (from woodblock to moveable type) and gunpowder are well known, but their inventiveness encompassed the whole spectrum of human activity, from civil service meritocracy centuries before the concept reached Europe, to the appreciation of the value of negative numbers a thousand years before Western academia suddenly ceased to scoff.

The Chinese used natural gas for fuel and light in 400BC, and the blast furnace to make pig iron in 300BC. They employed the belt drive between 53 and 18BC. They invented hot air balloons, man-lifting kites (with fatal results) and, in 132AD, they constructed a clever seismometer that indicated the direction and force of earthquakes. Then came exploding cannon balls and dental amalgam in the brilliant Tang dynasty of 618–907AD, and paper banknotes for good measure. While the British natives were still hunting and gathering, the Chinese were indulging themselves in splendid homes and palaces, dining on tofu, tea and stir-fry to the melody of tuned bells.

Indeed, China's history began long before the name by which the country and its people are known. Like most national histories, its beginnings are shrouded in myth and uncertainty. Even the origin of the name 'China' is controversial. It probably derives from the Qin (pronounced 'Chin') dynasty of about 200BC. Persian traders on the Old Silk Road referred to them as 'chin' and their homeland as 'chin-a'. Until the 19th century the Chinese themselves always referred to their country by the name of the ruling dynasty. The term Zhongguo (Middle Kingdom) which they then began to employ was a response to Western concepts of statehood and derives from their name for the Central Plains area where Chinese civilisation originally developed.

The first, half-legendary dynasty, the Xia, is dated from 2070BC; and its successor, the Shang, came to power in 1557BC. Its 'empire' was located on the northern Yellow River and occupied only a small fraction of what it would become. Much of what we know of the dynasty comes from archaeological studies of inscriptions on animal bones, turtle shells and bronze vessels that show peasants who were forced to leave their fields in time of war to accompany the nobles who fought their battles from horse-drawn chariots.

By then, the Britons had adopted or invented a Druid religion featuring human sacrifices and which had produced the remarkable and enigmatic Stonehenge. But very little is known about their mode of governance, much less their day-to-day lives, since the Britons left no written records. And for China's story of the time we rely on their first great historian, Sima Qian, the Grand Astrologer to the Han court, who compiled his massive documentary collection in about 50BC.

In those days, astrology was inseparable from astronomy and Sima Qian combined his duties with those of the imperial librarian. He reported that the Shang ritualised ancestor worship and claimed the 'Mandate of Heaven' for their rule. Under their banner, bronze casting became an industry, jade carving adorned the wealthy and – of particular pleasure to Sima Qian – their astrologers determined the length of a year as 365-and-a-quarter days.

The fall of the Shang in 1046BC began a pattern of conquest from the west and north by more vigorous and avaricious people who would gradually be absorbed into the Chinese culture, only to give way to the next wave of 'barbarians' beyond the borders. For the next 600 years China was divided into hostile forces. Battles slowly progressed from relatively short encounters restrained by a code of chivalry, to large-scale slaughters in a life and death struggle for supreme power. By the beginning of the 5th century BC, it would acquire the well-deserved label of the 'Warring States'.

This period encompassed the birth and death of Confucius (551–479BC), whose journeys took him through the central group of eleven states bordering the Yellow River which occupied the modern provinces of Shanxi, Hebei, Shandong and Hunan. It saw the rise of the Hundred Schools of peripatetic philosophers and oriental Machiavellis, Confucius among them, who attached themselves to the rival courts, each with his own schemes and strategies for good governance.

Confucius preached a return to the 'golden age' of Wu, founder of the Zhou dynasty, and he championed strong family loyalty, ancestor worship and a curiously negative version of the Golden Rule: 'Do not do unto others what you do not want done to yourself.' Though he was never able to find his ideal leader to promulgate his vision of the model society, Confucius's attitudes and aphorisms inspired an enduring, albeit intensely conservative, school of thought.

However, despite the continual warfare, it was a glorious age in the history of the Chinese intelligentsia, and in this it mirrored the contemporaneous Greek classical era. Both explored notions of moral authority and the great questions of the origin and purpose of the universe and humanity. But while the Greeks were testing the concept of democracy with its presumption that power rests with the people (or at least those permitted to exercise it), such a concept was no part of Chinese governance, then and now. In the oriental universe – as in most religions – authority flowed down from above.

One of Confucius's most prominent followers, Mencius (c.372–289BC), raised the issue of an appropriate relationship between the ruler and the people with a nod to the democratic principle but he made little headway. The people's only available prerogative was to take up arms against the leader when, through incompetence or cruelty, he surrendered the Mandate of Heaven. He would then be replaced by another who fulfilled the hopes of his subjects but whose successors, eventually and inevitably, fell prey to Lord Acton's iron rule that 'all power corrupts and absolute power corrupts absolutely'.

The year 221BC ushered in one of the most pivotal movements in Chinese history. It began with the conquest of the last feudal kingdoms by Shi Huang – meaning 'First Emperor' – who, after 37 years as king of the Qin, came to the imperial throne with a clear vision of the measures required to unite his domain. He demanded that the weapons of defeated states be sent to the capital, modern Xi'an, where they were melted down and transformed into works of art. During his eleven-year rule he would spread a common written language throughout the land, enforce a single code of laws, and standardise coinage, weights and measures. He began construction of the Grand Canal to join the Yellow River with the great Yangtse to the south; and at the same time, he linked earlier barriers against the 'barbarians' of the north into the Great Wall to ensure the security of his infant empire.

Alas, Shi Huang was as vulnerable to the fatal hubris of power as any other man and he suppressed free speech, burned all books that glorified the past and executed all who refused to comply (though he retained the works in his own private library). This roused his enemies and he became obsessed by fears of assassination. He let no one know which room in his many palaces would be his bedroom for the night. He sent envoys to the far corners of the land seeking elixirs of longevity, some of which undoubtedly shortened his life. But if he had to go, he determined that he would be well attended in the afterlife; so he built the tomb that contains the famous 8000 terracotta warriors. And once built, it was buried and booby-trapped to prevent looting.

When the first emperor died in 195BC, either by poison or overindulgence in yet another elixir of life, he was succeeded by his son Qin Er Shi who had none of the natural authority of his father. His only lasting contribution to humanity was the plaintive cry from his chief minister Li Si as bad news reached the emperor: 'Don't kill the messenger!' As the empire collapsed around him, Er Shi committed suicide and civil war erupted.

Of the two contenders to take his place, Liu Bang as king of the Han was from peasant stock and, despite receiving minor favours from the Qin dynasty, had raised an army in preparation for war. The other was General Xiang Yu of Jiangsu who captured Liu Bang's father and threatened to boil him alive unless the son surrendered. Liu Bang was undeterred: 'Send me a cup of the soup,' he replied. Liu Bang's bluff succeeded and as his forces surrounded the embattled Xiang Yu, the general committed suicide.

Liu Bang came to the throne as the Gaozu, first emperor of the Han dynasty, with the people in strong support and established his capital just outside Xi'an in 202BC. Under his rule the city became the terminus of the Silk Road and the political, military, cultural and economic centre of China. Its population rose to more than 250,000. Indeed, the great mass of the Chinese people adopted the Han as their progenitors and today refer to themselves as Han Chinese.

Despite – or perhaps because of – Liu Bang's humble background, education and culture became the hallmarks of the dynasty's imperial ruling class. But the extermination of the nobility meant that experienced administrators were in short supply and their roles were appropriated by opportunists to whom good governance came a distant second to the quest to enrich themselves and their families. Moreover, Liu Bang's family background meant that he and his successors would marry the daughters of their own subjects which created a rival family linking itself to the central power. And in short order the influence of the empresses would become a menace to the imperial house. Indeed, when Liu Bang died in 195BC, his empress Lu Zhi attempted to seize the throne for her family.

She murdered several of Liu Bang's sons born to concubines, and mutilated his favourite mistress and had her thrown into a latrine. She placed her own relatives in the top ranks of the army and the distant fiefdoms. A power struggle erupted. It would be fifteen years before a surviving imperial son finally wrested the throne back for the Liu family and became Emperor Wen. He then set about eliminating Lu Zhi's entire clan. And so began the process of dynastic rise and fall as the ruling families captured the Dragon Throne until their line exhausted the Mandate of Heaven to be replaced by yet another clan.

CHAPTER THREE
RISE AND FALL OF EMPIRES

In imperial China, every ruling family was attended by eunuchs within the imperial court. This cohort of sexually impotent males guaranteed that each child was sired by the monarch. Eunuchs also served as a firewall protecting the imperial family's very human foibles from exposure to the populace. On occasion they joined forces with a scheming empress or concubine in dark conspiracies to do away with the heir apparent in favour of her own son in the line of succession. But while the educated elite despised and denigrated them at every turn, eunuchs often provided the royal entourage with a valuable alternative to the corrupt and ambitious merchants and mandarins promoting their own special interests. They were affectionate to women and children and most of them kept small dogs as pets. Cai Lun, the inventor of paper, was not the only one of their number to bring distinction to his confederates.

No such gender-bending would have impressed the Britons of the day. Our first real glimpse of British life comes from the Roman general Julius Caesar, who led a major excursion to the island from Gaul in 55BC. He reported that 'the interior portion of Britain is inhabited by those [who] were born in the island itself: the maritime [coastal] portion by those who had passed over from the country of the Belgae [the Netherlands] for the purpose of plunder and making war . . . and continued there to cultivate the lands.

'All the Britains [sic] indeed, dye themselves with wode, which occasions a bluish colour, and thereby have a more terrible appearance in fight. They wear their hair long, and have every part of their body shaved except their head and upper lip.' As to their social customs, 'Ten and even twelve have wives common to them, and particularly brothers among brothers, and parents among their children; but if there be any issue by these wives, they are reputed to be the children of those by whom respectively each was first espoused when a virgin.'

The Romans suffered a brief uprising six years later when the warrior-queen Boudicca (sometimes Boadicea) rebelled, but it was easily put down and Britain would remain subject within the Roman empire for the next 350 years. Then came waves of invading forces from the northern European provinces with their Angles, Jutes and Saxons and from the Scandinavian raiders who settled in coastal towns and villages in the 7th and 8th centuries.

By then China had entered one of its glittering periods of high civilisation, the Tang dynasty. Its founder, Emperor Taizong, reigned for 22 years and was followed by Wu Zetian, one of his concubines, the first and only woman to seize the throne of China. Even before Taizong died, she had begun a secret liaison with his son Prince Li Zhi. And while at the emperor's death she was forced to follow custom and enter a nunnery for life, when Li Zhi mounted the throne as Gaozong he sought her out and she returned as Wu Zetian, the highest ranking of concubines of the second rank.

Using all the charms and wiles in her armoury, Wu Zetian manoeuvred herself into the total confidence of the emperor. Soon she was making all the major decisions of state and in 655AD was acknowledged as his full-time consort and empress. At his death she changed the state title to Zhou and thus became the Empress of Zhou in her own right at the age of 66 then ruled for fifteen years until a palace coup in 705.

Empress Wu's military leadership was outstanding and she extended the empire into Korea. She encouraged other women to take a role in cultural life. She founded an institute to produce the *Collection of Biographies of Famous Women* and was vigorous in support of poetry and the arts. Indeed, the Tang dynasty would produce three of China's most famous and enduring poets in Li Bai, Du Fu and Wang Wei.

Wu was not the only woman of the Tang to leave an indelible mark. The Emperor Xuanzong became so entranced with his son's wife, Yang Guifei, that he forced him to divorce her and took her as his favourite concubine. They were inseparable, and she used her influence much as Wu had done before her. But her judgement of men was fatally flawed. She patronised a Tartar buffoon, An Lushan, a former slave who, through her influence, rose to become commander of three military garrisons and governor of the Liaodong frontier province.

However, in 755 the court jester threw off his mask and led a rebellion that eventually overwhelmed the imperial capital Xi'an. The royal family fled to Sichuan but on the way their military escorts threatened the emperor's life unless he sacrificed the woman they blamed for their plight. Xuanzong was torn but finally he gave the order; and in what became known in poetry as 'the everlasting wrong' Yang Guifei was brought before the people in a village pagoda and strangled to death. When Xuanzong finally returned to Xi'an, he commissioned a painting of his beloved and spent many hours weeping before it. Like others of his imperial ilk, Xuanzong was ruled by his passions but he is also revered as one who put flesh on the bones of a great civilisation.

Eventually the Tang collapsed and was followed by the usual period of chaos and disunity until the next great dynasty, the Song, emerged. The Song again marked one of the high points of Chinese – and indeed human – civilisation. But it was under perpetual threat from nomadic groups from the north. The Song preferred diplomacy to war and the empire was halved in size before the entry in the 13th century of a new and terrible force: the Mongols under Genghis Khan who declared, 'The greatest joy is to conquer one's enemies, to pursue them, to seize their property, to see their families in tears, to ride their horses, and to possess their daughters and wives.'[1] His successors spread their savagery across the land until his grandson Kublai Khan claimed the throne in 1271 and ruled from Beijing. But instead of butchering the Chinese, he taxed them, and used the funds in an attempt to expand the empire north and south.

On the other side of the world, the Normans joined the list of British invaders when William the Conqueror was crowned king of England on Christmas Day, 1066. Anglo-French would become the *lingua franca* of the establishment and have a profound effect on the evolving English language. The ruling Normans thrived well into the 12th century until disputes over the succession of King Henry – and the English reluctance to see a woman take the throne – led to yet another civil war.

King John signed the Magna Carta in 1215, setting legal limits to his powers. However, he sought and received permission from the Pope to break his word as soon as the hostile nobles who had forced it upon him returned to their fiefs. Nevertheless, his successors were obliged to call the first 'parliament' to raise funds for their regal treasuries and this entrenched a principle unknown to the Chinese throughout their history – a legal framework for the people to express their will to those who would rule over them and eventually to change their government without resort to violence. But John's entanglement with the Church in Rome would become a divisive feature of English life and politics for centuries to come.

Meanwhile in the Middle Kingdom, the rapacity of Mongol rule brought about its own downfall as the Han people rose up and threw them off in 1368 in favour of a vigorous new dynasty from their own number, the Ming. Once again they would lead the world in science and civilised refinement. Emperor Yongle built a massive fleet of ocean-going ships – many of them 130 metres long. Then in 1405 with 27,000 men aboard, they embarked on a series of maritime expeditions traversing South-East Asia and the Indian Ocean as far as the Persian Gulf, before turning south to East Africa.

The fleet was commanded by a remarkable eunuch, Zheng He. Born to a Muslim family from Yunnan province, he was captured and castrated as a ten-year-old. Assigned to the household of Emperor Zhu Di, he spent his early life as a soldier fighting the Mongols in the north and received a sound education as a court favourite. He grew to the remarkable height of seven feet with a voice that was 'loud as a bell' – a valuable asset at sea. And for three decades as admiral of the fleet, he commanded the voyages that expanded China's knowledge and influence across half the known world.

Whether his ships touched upon the coast of the Great South Land remains controversial. The Chinese President Hu Jintao, in an address to the Australian parliament in 2003, said: 'Back in the 1420s the expeditionary fleets of China's Ming Dynasty reached Australian shores. For centuries, the Chinese sailed across vast seas and settled down in what they called "Southern Land" or today's Australia.' But despite claims of Chinese anchors and other artifacts being discovered on shore, the evidence remains elusive.

The Ming was also a dynasty of great literary achievement with the publication of *Romance of the Three Kingdoms*, a brilliant historical novel set in the final years of the Han in 169BC and ending with the reunification of the nation in 280. It is one of the four great classical novels of Chinese literature, with more than 800,000 words and 1000 colourfully drawn characters. It has retained its popularity to the present day.

Emperor Yongle died in 1424 and his successor Hongxi cancelled Zheng He's expeditions permanently, burned the fleet to the waterline and abolished frontier trade. China turned inward and so it would remain throughout the rest of the Ming dynasty until it was overwhelmed by its successor, the Manchu, in 1644.

A grouping of non-Han peoples related to the Mongols and other traditional enemies of China, the Manchu dynasty took the title 'Qing', meaning 'clear' or 'pure'. In 1683 they finally captured the last of the Ming princes who had retreated to Taiwan and returned them to the mainland, where they lived out their remaining days in quiet anonymity.

By then the greatest of the Qing emperors, Kangxi, was the undisputed ruler of the most formidable empire the world had known. With a population of 170 million and an area of 13 million square kilometres, it was an economic, ethnic and social powerhouse, utterly self-contained and so diverse geographically and historically that there was little interest among its rulers or its people in the world outside China.

In Britain, the Tudor line would mark the end of the Middle Ages. Their dynasty would rule England for 118 years. And when Henry VIII succeeded to the throne in 1509, he laid the framework for Britain's own 'golden age' under his daughter, the Virgin Queen, Elizabeth I. The polyglot nature of their migrating and invading peoples – Picts, Gaels, Romans, Saxons, Scandinavians and French – had combined to produce a vigorous, questing nation with a language of unparalleled breadth of complexity, expression and charm. During the 1590s the great names of the theatre, Christopher Marlowe and particularly William Shakespeare and his collaborators, began to produce a rollcall of literary masterpieces that still adorn the world's stages more than 500 years later.

The quest for empire soon followed and the British focus was on North America where their first colonial venture in 1584 was Virginia, named for the 'Virgin Queen'. By then their close allies the Portuguese had rounded the south of Africa, touched upon the Indian Subcontinent and continued east to the treacherous, pirate-infested straits of Malacca. There they made landfall and established a base before setting out across the new horizons of the South China Sea to the Middle Kingdom itself. The first tentative connections between two groups of *Homo sapiens* who had separated perhaps 70,000 years previously were slowly being established. And what a painful, confused and discordant process it would prove to be.

CHAPTER FOUR
FROM OPIUM TO GOLD

It started with a clash. In the 1590s the British had followed their Portuguese allies to the Orient and had emulated their violent piratical methods in seeking trade and commerce. The Chinese reacted by confining them to a single port – Guangzhou – where they could monitor their activities. Tentative trade began.

By the late 1700s, however, the increasing demand in Britain for Chinese silk, porcelain and tea was proving a serious problem for the British East India Company which held the Asian trading monopoly. The Chinese empire was self-contained. They wanted nothing the Europeans had to offer and would only accept silver in payment for their exports. The British government became alarmed as their silver reserves drained away to the 'Cohong' – the cartel of seventeen Chinese trading houses in Guangzhou. At the same time the East India Company was coming under pressure from its Indian colony where its traditional cotton exports to European mills were being undermined by a cheaper Egyptian product. The British solution to this dilemma was both ingenious and thoroughly immoral: they decided that in place of Indian cotton they would grow opium and use the drug, by fair means or foul, to pay for the Chinese exports.

Opium as a Chinese medicinal ingredient was well documented in texts as early as the Tang dynasty, but its recreational use was limited and there were laws against its abuse. By 1781 when British sales began, it was tolerated in much the same way that marijuana was accepted in other nations, as harmful in excess but of no great issue in the larger community.

Significantly, no less a colonial figure than John Macarthur became involved in turning the British opium into a massive drug-running operation into China. In 1808 in the wake of the Rum Rebellion that Macarthur masterminded against Governor William Bligh, he and his friend and neighbour, Walter Davidson, a wealthy young Scot, sailed together for England where they devised a plan to share in the drug bonanza.

In London, Davidson approached the trading house of Baring and Company who introduced him to the East India Company and by 1811 he had set sail for the Orient as a naturalised Portuguese. While Macarthur kept a low profile, his young associate worked as an agent for Baring until 1816 when he established his own trading house, W.S. Davidson & Company. And it is most likely that Macarthur's first Chinese employees in the 1820s were secured through Davidson who boasted that he was 'Portuguese in Canton [Guangzhou], and British everywhere else'.

Davidson later told a House of Lords inquiry into the East India Company's role in the drug trade: 'We were agents for all sorts of Indian produce but 90 per cent was cotton and opium. The Company knew I managed the opium trade. The arrangement was that every dollar I made from opium was mine and every dollar I made from cotton was theirs.'

By 1817 when the British strategy was fully developed, the drug began to take hold in China, particularly in the coastal cities, the riverine districts and among the wealthy Manchu. The Chinese government became alarmed as British ships brought their cargoes to islands off the coast where Chinese traders with fast, well-armed vessels took them to the mainland for distribution. Between 1821 and 1827 traffic increased fivefold. And just as the Qing dynasty sought funding from the treasury to put down a series of minor uprisings against their rule in the south, they found their silver reserves under pressure from payments for opium.

The situation took a turn for the worse in 1834 when the East India Company's monopoly was withdrawn and private entrepreneurs joined the drug-running cartels. American merchants with an eye for a quick buck introduced opium from Turkey. It was of poorer quality but cheaper to produce and the competition drove down prices as it increased the volume in a seemingly endless windfall of ill-gotten gains. The governments of Britain and the United States not only turned a blind eye to the drug-runners, they actively encouraged the practice as a means 'to open China to international trade' to the benefit of all.

The Chinese government was handicapped in their efforts to control the illegal trafficking as their officials were corrupted by the vast flow of cash passing through their hands. However, in 1839 the Manchu Emperor Daoguang appointed a viceroy, Commissioner Lin Zexu, to Guangzhou with orders to abolish the trade.

Commissioner Lin acted swiftly. The following year he confiscated 20,000 chests of opium (about 1210 tons) without offering any compensation to the traffickers. He then blockaded the port and confined foreign merchants to their quarters. He followed this with an open letter to the British monarch, Queen Victoria: 'Your Majesty has not before been thus officially notified, and you may plead ignorance of the severity of our laws, but I now give my assurance that we mean to cut this harmful drug forever.'

The British Superintendent of Trade in China, Charles Elliot, encouraged the traders to surrender their stocks of opium by promising compensation from the British government. In response, Lin said he would permit general trade to resume provided the merchants signed a promise to ban opium. However, when the British government considered Elliot's compensation plan, it realised there would be a storm of political protest at the idea of Britain 'kowtowing' to the Chinese and rescinded it. Negotiations quickly broke down and British naval ships opened fire on 3 February 1840. The Chinese responded but they were hopelessly outgunned and over the next two years British gunships blockaded ports, wrought havoc on coastal towns, took Guangzhou then sailed up the Pearl River and captured the emperor's tax barges.

This was a devastating blow to the Qing treasury. But worse was to come. British warships blockaded the mouth of the great Yangtse and took Shanghai; then a flotilla charged up the mighty waterway to Nanjing which quickly fell. China sued for peace and in the Treaty of Nanjing signed in August 1841, it agreed to open five ports to British trade and ceded the island of Hong Kong to Britain as a crown colony. It recognised Britain as an equal and under the notion of 'extra-territoriality' gave British subjects the right to be governed by their own laws in the treaty ports. Two years later, America and France concluded similar treaties. China's 4000 years of self-contained empire had been dealt the first of a thousand cuts.

Meanwhile, trouble continued to brew in China's southern provinces. The southerners fared little better under one dynasty than another, but during these times they were particularly aggrieved. The Manchus had never forgiven them for their fierce resistance to their assumption of imperial power and had reserved 50 per cent of all civil service posts for their own families, to the great resentment of the south where highly intelligent candidates were disaffected and estranged. And unlike their dynastic predecessors, the Manchus never relaxed the boundaries between conquerors and subjects to foster unity within the empire. Indeed, it was they who had forced all Chinese men to shave their scalps except for the pigtails that signalled obedience to their rule.

One alienated scholar, Hong Xiuquan, was so affected by repeated failures in the imperial examinations that in 1837 he fell ill and was bedridden for several days. In his feverish state he read a pamphlet he'd received the year before from a Protestant Christian missionary. It prompted a spiritual epiphany which convinced him that a fraternal bond had been forged between himself and the Jesus figure at the heart of the religion. So powerful was the experience that he felt compelled to launch his own mission against the imperial oppressors.

As the Westerners colluded with corrupt officials dealing in opium, Hong and his brothers roused the members of their extended family to found the God Worshipping Society, soon to be known as the Taiping. They were joined by Yang Xiuqing, a former firewood merchant from Guangxi who claimed to be a prophet in his own right, and an

American Baptist missionary, Issachar Jacox Roberts, who for a time acted as their spiritual adviser. Hong believed so totally in the eternal nature of the soul that the word 'death' was banned from the Taiping vocabulary; people no longer died but rather 'ascended to Heaven'.[1]

The Taiping's revolutionary manifesto declared war on 'grasping officials and corrupt subordinates', practised a form of equality in which women had the right to become state officials, outlawed foot-binding and opium smoking, and shared the land among the masses. According to the distinguished Chinese historian C.P. Fitzgerald, 'In essentials the Taiping creed was Protestant Christianity. [They] possessed the complete Bible as translated into Chinese by Dr [Karl] Gutzlaff, an early Protestant missionary, which they printed in Nanjing and distributed free to their supporters and converts. In matters of dogma, though not quite orthodox in some particulars, they held to the main tenets of Christian theology. During the early years of the movement, the opinion of foreigners in China was entirely favourable to the rebels. The Anglican Bishop of Hong Kong frequently asserted his entire conviction that the Taiping movement was a Christian crusade . . . The northern Chinese were not at first hostile but neutral, almost indifferent.'[2]

The crushing defeat of the imperial forces in the first Opium War confirmed the righteousness of Hong's cause. And as the Taiping took their fight to bandits and pirates who infested the south, their crusade took on all the elements of a guerrilla rebellion. The Manchu responded by persecuting their membership, but this only attracted new volunteers. And in January 1851 they began a full-scale revolt when their 10,000-strong rebel army soundly defeated an imperial force.

Coincidentally, that same year the colonial government of New South Wales lifted the ban on news of local gold discoveries. Until then they and their British masters had kept all finds secret, fearing a rush would cause social and economic chaos in the penal colony. But the 1849 Californian gold discoveries were attracting thousands of paroled and emancipated convicts. The colonial governor, George Gipps, responded with a £10,000 reward for the discovery of payable gold. It was quickly claimed and in August 1851 a rush began on the Victorian town of Ballarat. By then Victoria had just become a separate colony, headed by Lieutenant-Governor Charles La Trobe who visited the site where he witnessed five men uncover no less than 136 ounces of gold in a single day.

The Chinese had been among the first to sail across the Pacific to the discoveries in California's 'Gold Mountain'. Now news travelled swiftly to the southern provinces where the Taiping rebellion had resulted in battles that would eventually exact the terrible toll of 20 million casualties. Soon, increasing numbers of Chinese were joining the massive influx of prospectors from Britain, Europe and the United States to *Xin Jin Shin* – 'New Gold Mountain' – in quest of a lucky strike.

CHAPTER FIVE
NEW GOLD MOUNTAIN

By far the largest contingent of the gold seekers would come from the British Isles. Their destination was a colony that was less than 70 years old in a land whose habitation predated that of Britain. The Aboriginal people had reached the Australian continent at the end of their journey out of Africa at least 50,000 years previously. And by the time the first English explorer, James Cook, reached the east coast of *Terra Australis* in 1770, the Aborigines had populated the entire country as well as its southern island, soon to be known as Van Diemen's Land. They numbered between 500,000 and one million souls, the great numerical disparity the result of their leaving no written history but for the world's oldest art forms on the country's rocks and cave walls.

The Aboriginal people managed the land and its animal life, principally by a sophisticated use of fire and their largely nomadic lifestyle, with such skill that by the time the first British convicts and their jailers arrived eighteen years after Cook, their continent could properly be described as 'the biggest estate on earth'.[1] The living was easy, food plentiful, leisure abundant – at least among the males – and tribal boundaries sufficiently well-defined to keep armed conflict to a minimum. There was a proliferation of language groups but a shared culture that derived from a legendary 'Dreamtime' with creation myths no less sophisticated than those of either the Europeans or the Chinese.

Unfortunately, their isolation had denied them the advantages of multiple contact with human and domestic animal diseases that would have provided a broad autoimmunity. Nor did their relatively peaceful coexistence with tribal neighbours spark the need to develop mechanical or chemical instruments of war. So when the British began to arrive in their thousands, the original inhabitants were utterly unprepared to resist the invaders and deeply vulnerable to their diseases.

Captain Cook had 'claimed' the continent for Britain by hoisting a flag and a simple vocal assertion of his monarch's right to do so. And since the Aboriginals had built no permanent structures and possessed no army and no recognisable political system – much less a king with whom to negotiate – the newcomers simply took the country for themselves. Indeed, in 1835 the British government issued a proclamation of *terra nullius*, asserting that the Aboriginal people had no claim to the land. And while there were British laws available to protect them from harm, the colonial administration made little or no effort to prevent their massacre and dispossession.

By the time of the goldrush the Aborigines were a broken people; and though there were pockets of fierce resistance to British intrusions in Victoria and later Queensland, the longest continuous culture on earth had been effectively shattered. They would play only a marginal part in the Australia–China relationship for the next 125 years.

The colony was itself entering an extraordinary new phase of transition. Its role as a dumping ground for petty British criminals had been relatively brief. Explorers such as Charles Sturt, Thomas Mitchell, John Oxley and particularly the native-born Hamilton Hume, had uncovered seemingly endless tracts of potential farmland; and Macarthur's immigrant grazier and cropper successors expanded their domains over much of the arable land on the southeastern slopes and plains. The gold discoveries would inject a tremendous new burst of growth and development.

While the western half of the continent was mostly desert, where even the Aboriginal population was relatively sparse, the British had now succeeded in establishing its authority over the entire country. Various areas would follow the lead of Van Diemen's Land and Victoria to become separate colonies, but the government in Westminster had the final say in all matters. And the local administrators were thoroughly British in their perception of themselves as the heralds of empire.

These attitudes would soon be reflected in their response to the presence of Chinese miners.

European ship owners had profited greatly from transporting them from the South China ports across the Pacific to the Californian rush; and when they learned of the Victorian discoveries they set themselves for another bonanza on the north–south run. Indeed, they circulated pamphlets in the southern provinces – particularly Guangdong and Fujian – with news of the great discoveries. As well, the coolies in Australia contacted their families and friends, encouraging them to make the journey.

In 1852 the first advance party of young Chinese prospectors from well-connected 'good families' set out for the diggings; and the following year a score of them returned briefly with their golden booty to spread the news and buy goods and equipment to sell to their compatriots back on the fields. The Chinese rush to Victoria was on, though their numbers would always be far less than those from Britain, continental Europe, and even the United States. Only some 500 made the journey in 1852 and a similar number the following year.

While the gold was undoubtedly a great attraction, the Chinese were also motivated by the collapse of their provinces into civil war as Hong Xiuquan's Taiping rebellion swept the imperial forces before it. And by 1854 Chinese merchants had entered the shipping trade and were resuscitating old, poorly maintained vessels for the run south. Accommodation was spartan at best, with six to eight travellers crowded into each berth. Several ships were lost at sea while others were forced to put in at Manila and Singapore, but in the first six months they carried some 3000 eager prospectors and the following year the number rose to 11,500.

Some 70 per cent of the Chinese immigrants were, like the coolies before them, bound by contract or debt. Now their masters were Chinese businessmen or their own extended families who had sold their land or pooled resources to send the digger abroad. The businessmen had developed a 'credit ticket' system by which the digger would work exclusively to repay the debt during his first year on the field. Since their families were party to the agreement and liable for the debt, the digger carried the weight of filial responsibility on his shoulders. The result was an absolute dedication to the task. Moreover, the businessmen appointed a 'headman' to oversee their activities in the field.

Secret societies from the home bases flourished in the colony and provided some support for the newly arrived. According to J. Dundas Crawford, the deputy British consul in Shanghai who visited Melbourne at the time, 'They pass through the town in batches of six to ten, in single file but never singly, each coolie carrying his own bamboo pole brought from China, on which are slung baskets of clothes, a few humble necessaries, and perhaps a box of tea or preserved eggs to barter, carrying their loads straight to the place assigned to them – most to the camping grounds beyond the town [but] a select few go to the various accommodation houses representing branches of secret societies.'[2]

They were denied virtually all female companionship. Few Chinese families could afford to pay for wives to accompany the diggers, much less their children. Single women were an entrenched part of the family and in any case, according to Hong Kong Governor Dr John Bowring, there was 'an intensely strong sentiment that no female with any sense of propriety or modesty could consent to quit her native home'.[3] For most miners, their only social consolation was the occasional pipe of opium they had brought across the sea in their belongings.

Once at the diggings the Chinese usually lived and worked with their clans or societies who shared the same dialects, though some diggers with a smattering of English established their claims among the Europeans. Each Chinese settlement was overseen by its headman whose big tent, which flew a red flag, usually contained a range of merchandise for sale. The camps were active, bustling centres where the miners lived four to six to a tent. The lines were kept scrupulously clean and small areas were set aside for domestic shrines where the Daoist god of wealth featured prominently. Most of the larger camps also had a rough timber 'temple' for ritual and celebration.

They kept to themselves. This was hardly surprising given the language barriers and the clannish nature of their society. But it fed into the prejudice of 'difference' from the white diggers and their rambunctious ways. Indeed, the much larger areas occupied by the British, Europeans and Americans were by comparison roaring, riotous cesspools of every sin and iniquity known to man. Drunkenness, prostitution, theft, violence and gunfire abounded. The government set a miner's licence at £1/10/- a month for police to keep order on the field. But the diggers combined to thwart the licence inspectors. And when shafts began to lose their attraction as nuggets became harder to find, the diggers moved on to the next 'big easy'.

The first signs of open conflict between the Chinese and the Caucasians took place in Bendigo in 1854 when British and American miners held a meeting and declared that 'a general and unanimous rising should take place . . . for the purpose of driving the Chinese off the goldfield'. Local constables acted quickly, warning the ringleaders against taking any action, and for the moment further trouble was avoided. Instead, the miners turned on the government itself and threatened armed rebellion at the new twice-weekly 'licence hunts' by troopers on the fields.

The confrontation came to a head in October, following the murder of a miner at a Eureka grog shanty and the acquittal of the suspected government agent who killed him. A series of unruly mass meetings followed with threats to rebel unless the government agreed to the demands of their newly formed Ballarat Reform League. The Victorian governor Sir Charles Hotham appointed a royal commissioner, Robert Rede, to investigate conditions on the goldfields, but instead of taking submissions from the miners he summoned police reinforcements from Melbourne. And when the miners intercepted them, fighting broke out. On 29 November 1854, a meeting of 12,000 diggers resolved to burn their licences and take up arms. They created a Eureka flag that excluded the British Union Jack, and some of the Irish diggers whose country had been colonised by the British in centuries past rose to prominence.

The diggers trained for combat and were joined by 200 Americans under the banner of the Independent California Rangers. But when battle was joined at 3 a.m. on 3 December, with British army garrisons at the forefront, the rebels quickly fell beneath the weight of the government's forces. By 8 a.m., the second in command, Captain Charles Paisley, sickened by the carnage, saved a group of diggers from being bayoneted and threatened to shoot any police or soldier who continued the slaughter. The Eureka rebellion was over almost before it began.

CHAPTER SIX
CONFLICTS WITH COLONIALS

The Chinese played no part in the uprising, but that only confirmed the European diggers' view that they were no more than alien intruders, foreign opportunists who would undermine the very conditions they were fighting for. And as their presence increased to perhaps 15 per cent on some fields, they became the focus for the defeated men's anger and resentment. Early in 1855 they lashed out at the Chinese camps in an attempt to drive them off, and on occasion their attacks became full-scale riots. The constabulary could do little to control them.

The more enlightened members of the community attempted to take a stand. A Justice of the Peace on the magistrate's bench in the Victorian country town of Castlemaine asserted, 'All men here are equal, they come from all parts of the world in equality, and you have no right to drive any away because they do not work as you please.' But his words fell on stony ground.

One of the diggers' main complaints was that when they abandoned failing shafts and moved on, the Chinese miners took up the vacant claim and worked it out, content with the lower return even if it meant working around the clock. They also claimed that the Chinese misused scarce water resources in 'washing' the gold-bearing soil. But according to George Preshaw, a banker who plied his trade on the New South Wales goldfields, 'The water question had in truth as little to do with the riots as the writer of these lines; it was simply that the Europeans wanted, and would have, the ground occupied by the Chinese.'[1]

In 1855 the Victorian parliament passed the *Immigration Restriction Act* forcing the Chinese alone to pay a £10 per head tax on arrival. It also restricted the number of Chinese travellers per tonnage of shipping.

Both measures caused a slowdown in arrivals in Melbourne, from 10,000 between 1853 and 1855, to only hundreds passing through the port subsequently. Instead, they landed in Adelaide or the town of Robe in South Australia, which soon became the favourite sea terminus before a long overland trek to the Victorian goldfields. In the beginning, Chinese hopefuls would pay local guides who often abandoned them in the bush. But as more followed, the Chinese organised their own route. They even dug wells and established overnight lay-bys beside the bush tracks. However, that was just the beginning of their travail. When they reached the Ballarat and Bendigo fields, they were scorned and derided by the Europeans.

This descended into open violence in 1857 in the Buckland Valley between Mt Buffalo and Falls Creek when at least 100 white vigilantes led by 'Americans inflamed by liquor' attacked the 700-strong Chinese camp. According to *The Argus*:

> Carrying long-handled shovels, pick handles and crowbars, [the Americans] moved on the Chinese camp and ordered the occupants to quit. They were given an hour in which to pack their swags.
>
> They made the most of the time and without offering resistance they went to the next camp at Stony Point. The eviction was complete. The white men set fire to the tents and premises, burned the camp right out and, reinforced by other parties of Europeans, followed the aliens to Stony Point where the destruction of this camp also was effected.
>
> At the main camp lower down the river, the head centre of their operations on the field, a stand was made by the Chinese with a show of passive resistance. But the diggers had warmed up to the work at hand and their charge was determined. In a few moments they were in the midst of the horde of frightened foreigners, swinging their shovels and bars vigorously. Panic ensued.
>
> Indicating that they would evacuate without fighting, the Chinese gathered as much as they could of their portable belongings and left.

The camp was burned and to an accompaniment of wild wailings, the temple of their joss was consumed in view of the retreating Chinese. The white men, satisfied that the Chinese would not return, took possession of their claims and worked them.[2]

At least three Chinese were either drowned in the river or died of their injuries. The police arrested thirteen of the rioters, but the juries who heard the cases acquitted all of major offences 'amid the cheers of bystanders'. The Victorian government offered compensation and invited the Chinese to return but reportedly only 50 chose to do so. A commemorative monument was erected on the site by the Chinese Australian Family Historians of Victoria in 2007.

West of Bendigo, a party of Chinese prospectors in 1857 happened upon a rich field at the site of today's Ararat. They were able to work it for several months before any Europeans arrived; and when they did the newcomers were outraged that the Chinese had secured all the best ground. Trouble broke out immediately and by May that year rumours abounded that the government was planning to confiscate the Chinese claims and hand them over to the European diggers.

The government then demanded all Chinese in Victoria buy a 'residence ticket' without which they were unable to sue for recovery of a mining claim. But language problems meant that very few complied and when the British diggers demanded to see their tickets and none could be produced, they 'jumped the claims' of more than 60 Chinese miners, each worth at least £1000. The government then instituted an inquiry but the only compensation awarded the Chinese was for the equipment and timber struts used in their shafts.

Nevertheless, the Chinese diggers persisted and in some areas they flourished. According to local historian Kathryn Cronin, 'In Bendigo's Ironback Camp the Sheathed Sword secret society erected their large, three-roomed hall overlooking a small pond at the south end of the settlement, while at the north boundary stood the [Chinese] All Nations temple dedicated to Kuanti, the Daoist god of war.'[3]

New temples were dedicated with great pomp and ceremony, the processions often lasting late into the night. Roast pig, wine and other food were carried in tribute to the spirits while gongs and firecrackers echoed across the silent bushland. The temple custodians charged supplicants for their incense sticks and the privilege of saying their 'good luck prayers'. They were rarely short of worshippers.

The bigger camps became semi-permanent villages with tailor shops, herbalists, butchers and barbers. They planted vegetables; craftsmen among them made kites for sale and gold decorations; scribes wrote letters home. The Chinese ran their own travel service between the goldfields, and some of them joined the carting industry bringing food and equipment from Melbourne. Gambling saloons were open around the clock and there were travelling entertainments including the occasional Chinese opera company. A few made marriages with local colonial women, but most had to content themselves with the brothels that proliferated through the mining towns and even there they were not always welcome.

As a community the Chinese were by no means homogenous. They varied not only in provincial background and heritage but in language, education and class, from the poorest illiterate peasant to the wealthy scholar and merchant. And while a few certainly struck it rich via mining, by far the most successful Chinese of the goldfields were the shopkeepers, followed by the operators of the gambling saloons, and the headmen who made loans to the diggers and reaped a good living from the modest interest rates they charged. Some flaunted their newfound riches in colourful and extravagant national dress; others opted for the latest British fashion of black frockcoat, silk vest and patent leather boots.

It fell to the language groups and secret societies in Victoria – principally the See Yap from Guangzhou and the Sheathed Swords with its Tartar background – to minimise the frictions between their countrymen. They impressed upon their members 'the necessity which exists, to gain the favour of the white men by quiet, orderly conduct' and cautioned them to practise 'forbearance and patience' when they felt ill-used by the Europeans. And they backed their admonitions with fines (up to £2) or twelve strokes of a cane.

The societies also assisted in the miners' dealings with the colonial administration and took up injustices with officials. But when consultation failed to produce the required result, they were not above hiding their members from the police or spiriting them away before they were due to appear before the court. This was hardly surprising; the notion of the 'fair go' that would become so beloved of later generations of Australians was no part of the colonial vocabulary, and could never have been applied to the treatment of the Chinese.

Victorian police officers invariably used violence in arresting Chinese suspects, and special rules applied when issuing summonses. Instead of police swearing particulars to the issuing magistrates, the judicial officers would simply sign a number of blank summons forms which the constables would fill in when they chose an 'offender'. This was justified, they said, because the Chinese might run away and they would not be able to recognise them again 'in consequence of their peculiar similarity in personal appearance'.

The Chinese were not permitted to serve on juries, and when charged in court or called as witnesses they could not swear on the Bible. Indeed, hearings often threatened to become chaotic as they asserted their correct method of taking the oath by breaking a saucer or even decapitating a cockerel. Europeans accused of assaulting Chinese were invariably found not guilty and according to Cronin, 'Often on the same day, magistrates sentenced Chinese vagrants to eight to twelve months hard labour while European vagrants were imprisoned for little more than seven to fourteen days.'[4]

However, the societies would not condone actions that brought the Chinese community into ill repute. When in 1857 a society member, Hing Tzan, was implicated in the 'barbarous murder' of a prostitute, the Chinese community offered £100 reward for his capture. In Bendigo, some 200 Chinese joined in the hunt and delivered the offender – together with a suspected associate – to the authorities.

When differences arose between the Chinese societies, they sometimes took their disputes to the Victorian judiciary; but here they were treading a fine line since many of their operations – including smuggling, blackmail and 'protection' – were blatantly illegal. But their principal concern was invariably to bury their own differences and present a unified front to the colonists who threatened their safety and security. They asked only to be treated the same as the other people from around the world who came to find their fortunes in the Great South Land.

CHAPTER SEVEN
CHRISTIAN CONVERSION

Equality was not always a vain hope. In 1859, for example, a shipment of diggers from Guangzhou included a nine-year-old lad who would become a beloved figure and an ornament to his adopted country. Mei Quong Tart was in the care of his uncle when he and 50 of his compatriots passed through the New South Wales town of Braidwood headed for the nearby Major's Creek goldfields.[1] The local *Advertiser* referred to them as 'gentlemen of the long queue' suggesting that they were a relatively tolerant community. And young Quong Tart's subsequent life in the area supports the view.

However, the boy was understandably nervous in this utterly foreign environment. Soon after he reached the Chinese mining camp, he wandered away and was resting under a gum tree when he was suddenly confronted by a wild-eyed bearded stranger brandishing a gun. To Quong's astonishment, the bushman took aim at a boy sitting high in the branches above the Chinese lad's head and fired. As the boy stumbled down the tree, Quong screamed and ran for help. And when he reported the murder, a posse of miners set off immediately to find the killer. They quickly tracked the madman to his lair . . . only to discover that the 'boy' was in fact a possum.

It would become one of the adult Quong's favourite stories to recall when visitors from across the community came to enjoy his company and wet their whistles at his famous Sydney tearooms. He had a fund of them, for the Braidwood of the day was a glorious polyglot. According to the *Advertiser*, on the day Quong and his compatriots arrived, the Kentucky Minstrels in blackface were strumming their banjos and dancing a jig in the main street; a block away the more upmarket

Buckingham Family was busking a martial air before the Grand Hotel; while Mrs Badgery, a local innkeeper, was bawling from a balcony the mystic wonders of her latest headliner, The Wizard. Politicians trumpeted their wares on street corners; the Royal Mail coach galloped in from Nelligen on the Clyde River; jockeys in bright silks fingered their whips as they waited for the cart that would take them to the Braidwood racetrack; and drunken colonials, who had briefly struck it rich, wrestled in the dirt outside the sly-grog shop.

While he might have been nervous to start, the young Quong quickly found his feet. He was one of the few Chinese on the goldfield who could read and write and he put his knowledge to good and profitable use in writing letters home for the miners. Then his uncle found work for him in the store run by the Scotsman Thomas Forsyth and his wife at nearby Bell's Creek. Quong was soon speaking his own brand of pidgin English with a distinct Scottish Highlander burr. He would retain his unique accent for the rest of his life.

His duties at the store began as general factotum but according to his biographer Robert Travers: 'Under Mr Forsyth's fostering eye, little Quong learned the secrets of the account book, the journal and the ledger. He was able to absorb practical tuition in elementary geology, handling nuggets and pieces of ore until his keen eye and deft fingers could gauge the value of a sample to a pennyweight. He got to know how to judge men and in the everyday course of business studied the psychology of would-be debtors as Forsyth's keen Scottish gaze sorted the credit-worthy from the born losers.'[2]

However, Quong's real change of fortune arrived in the person of a frequent customer, Alice Simpson, whose husband Robert 'Percy' Simpson was a wealthy and well-connected grazier who owned a number of rich shafts in the Araluen district. Simpson employed more than 200 Chinese miners to work his claims, and quickly saw the value in having Quong as an interpreter, mounted on a pony, to accompany him on his rounds. And while he continued to work at the store, by the time of his eleventh birthday the Simpsons had taken him into their home.

Alice was the daughter of a Sydney solicitor, Randolph Want, whose clientele numbered among the city's leading citizens and though she had at least one son of her own she virtually adopted the young Chinese boy. She taught him to read and write English and he would retain the 'big round hand' of her classroom. She was also a devout Christian, and under her tutelage Quong happily converted to the Anglican faith.

Quong, like many of his countrymen, was a loyal hard worker and Percy Simpson rewarded him with a claim of his own. It produced a small fortune in payable ore and Quong reinvested in other likely claims. He went into partnership with his old employer, Thomas Forsyth, in a crushing plant that was extracting payable gold from the hills and creek beds of the district. According to his biographer, 'Quong Tart spent nearly twelve months slogging around Braidwood with the crusher. He often worked through the night. Nobody seems to have envied him his success, as he was well known in the district as an expert in seeking out the best reefs. He sought out abandoned claims, left to rot by miners who had either lost hope or could not afford the royalty demanded by the land owner.'

By eighteen, when the Simpsons departed for Sydney, Quong was a wealthy young man with a penchant for smart English clothes and a devotion to cricket. On his 21st birthday he applied for a certificate of naturalisation supported by the local justice of the peace and the clerk of petty sessions. And on 11 July 1871 he was granted his British citizenship as a loyal subject of Queen Victoria.

★ ★ ★

Mei Quong Tart's Christian conversion, while rare, was certainly not unique among the Chinese immigrants. Indeed, some of the more evangelical churches regarded their presence in the colony as a heaven-sent opportunity to attract the 'heathens' into the Christian fold. As early as 1855 a group of Bendigo enthusiasts built a mission church to teach the Chinese the gospel message. In Castlemaine, a Methodist began a weekly Chinese service complete with a convert from a Chinese mission to translate the lesson. The Anglican Bishop of Melbourne, Charles Perry, lamented that while the church 'has neglected the Aborigines – nay had perhaps destroyed them – now Providence have given us a race instead'.[3] They might well be 'deluded idolaters' but at least they were 'accessible to the light of civilisation and the gospel'.

Other churchmen contacted the non-denominational London Missionary Society (LMS) which was already active in China. With their trained Chinese missionaries, they envisaged colonial Chinese 'returning home with the Word of God in their hands and hearts' ready to preach in every city and town to which they may go. They would carry back 'to their debased and benighted countrymen the true principles of political freedom, mental elevation, social comfort and eternal happiness'.[4]

Aside from their presumption of superiority, the attitude and motives of the British church and state could hardly have been more disparate. The LMS was itself short-staffed but by chance one of their former alumni, the Rev. William Young, whose ailing wife needed a change of climate to recover her spirits, arrived in Sydney after surviving a shipwreck. However, the colonials were startled to discover that William was a Eurasian, the product of a Scottish father and a Malay mother. The Victorian cleric Rev. Richard Fletcher was aghast: 'Young's employment as an *English Minister* is certainly out of the question. He is so utterly unacceptable in that capacity that he could not gather a congregation and no one would have him . . . in New South Wales or Victoria.' Unless he could find employment as a missionary to the Chinese, Fletcher opined, 'there is nothing for him but starvation'.[5]

However, as more Chinese miners arrived in Victoria, Young found a position with a newly constituted mission supported by five protestant churches and backed by the LMS. They were headquartered in Castlemaine where they received a remarkable gift of 2000 Chinese-language bibles. The bibles had been sent two years previously by a

Manchester Sunday school and had been mouldering in the home of a friend of Rev. Fletcher. The local Chinese were not consulted; nor were they included in the mission organisation. As Fletcher later admitted, they began 'with no well-considered plan of work' but simply set up 'in an off-handed, extemporaneous style at one of the many goldfields'.[6]

Young was joined by two Chinese Christian scholars from the Hong Kong mission – Ho Ah Lo and Chu Ah Luk – and they worked from a tent where they held evening prayers and Sunday services. Soon they had some twenty regular attendees. But when the diggers discovered that worship of neither Jesus nor God brought them any additional nuggets from their claims, they drifted away. Indeed, word spread in some parts that preaching about Jesus would bring bad luck. Moreover, Young and his acolytes taught that it was sinful to worship their ancestors and their traditional rites made them 'servants of the devil and slaves of Satan'. And since the Christian colonists and miners reviled them, the Chinese doubted that they would be welcome within Christianity's ranks.

By 1858, Chu and Ho had abandoned the mission in favour of jobs as interpreters and after Young's wife succumbed to her ailments he departed for Melbourne. He later left the ministry and became an adviser to the Victorian government. But in this he was an unmitigated disaster. In 1868 he compiled a fanciful report that portrayed the Chinese as depraved drug addicts given to 'wholesale debauching of girls of tender years' and operators of a 'monster gambling establishment' calculated to corrupt young colonists.

Further attempts to evangelise the Chinese miners met with a similar fate. Indeed, the missionary zeal of Britain's Established Church would become one of the links between China and the British colony. But as with other national bridges it was compromised by racist impediments in both countries.

★ ★ ★

The most dramatic manifestation of this dissonance was taking place even then as the Taiping leader Hong Xiuquan was taking his rebellion, with its powerful Sino-Christian message, into the heart of the Manchu's southern strongholds. In 1853 he had captured the former imperial capital of Nanjing and established his court there. His next move was north towards the Manchu bastion of Beijing itself.

However, European powers – principally Britain and France – were engaged in their own imperial agenda. As they and their American compatriots were in the process of carving up the country, they calculated that it was in their interests to keep the weakened Manchu government in place. They sponsored an American mercenary leader, Frederick Townsend Ward, who raised an army of Westerners in 1860 to defend Shanghai against a Taiping advance. Then a senior British army officer, Charles Gordon, was placed in command of Chinese imperial forces in the so-called Ever Victorious Army to oppose the Taiping in battle.

At the same time, the foreigners initiated the second Opium War on the Manchu government, breaking down the final barriers to exploitation of the Chinese market. It culminated in October 1860 when a combined force of 18,000 British and French troops devastated the Manchu army and took Beijing. The emperor fled to Jehol and the British commissioner, Lord Elgin – whose father is best remembered for his appropriation of the marble statuary from the Parthenon – oversaw the looting and burning of the Summer Palaces. The foreigners then demanded a treaty that opened more ports to trade and exposed the Yangtse to British interests. And in a final humiliation they imposed a huge indemnity on the Manchu government to pay the cost of its own defeat. It would be drawn from the Chinese customs revenues which were henceforth controlled by foreign officers.

The British had refused to sell the Taiping arms while they happily supplied the Manchu with ships, arms and ammunition at extortionate prices; and with General 'Chinese' Gordon at its head, the Ever Victorious Army lived up to its name and took Nanjing in 1864.

Hong Xiuquan perished in the days before his capital collapsed in ruin. Gordon was honoured by both the British and the Manchu.

While many of today's historians regard the Taiping as an aberration, C.P. Fitzgerald saw the failure of their revolution as a turning point in the cultural history of China: 'The success of a great national religious revolution would have replaced the effete Manchus by a new dynasty, and a new cultural outlook, ready to accept the ideas of the west as a corollary of the new creed. As it was, they remained sunk in decaying despotism. For this tragic outcome the cynical policy of western imperialism in 1860 was mainly responsible.'[7]

CHAPTER EIGHT
COLONIAL SUPPRESSION

While the churches were engaging – however ineffectually – with the Chinese influx, the colonial government took direct action and established a Chinese Protectorate. It was a reprise of the system ostensibly designed to protect Aboriginals but in reality to document their destruction. In its new incarnation the Chinese themselves would finance their oppression. In addition to the £10 landing fee on all Chinese males, the government imposed a £1 annual 'protection fee' on the goldfields. Part of this levy would be used to quarantine the new arrivals in a 'sanatorium'; part would pay for the protectors and their staff; and anything left over would go into general revenue.

Governor Hotham's chief adviser on the plan was Scottish-born Joseph Anderson Panton. At 55 Panton boasted a military background and was widely regarded as 'an English gentleman of the old school'. After failing as a prospector he had been appointed a gold commissioner on several Victorian fields.[1] Under his draft legislation, a team of colonial protectors was established to supervise and administer all Chinese mining and other business on crown lands. It enjoined the governor and his executive to 'regulate their settlements and provide for their general management and good government'.

Panton's protectors were also former military or police officers and in each goldfield camp a protector was assisted by two police constables who were 'to be amongst the Chinese at all hours . . . for the efficient performance of their duties'. Other staff members included British and Chinese interpreters. Some of the protectors were conscientious in their duties, others less so. James McCulloch Hanley, for example, was dismissed and charged with 'obtaining money under false pretences', while some of the police constables ran protection rackets among the Chinese gambling houses, one sergeant reputedly reaping £2000 in bribes in less than two years. The Chinese rarely cooperated with them. As protector Captain Charles Standish complained, 'They utterly disregard the instructions which I occasionally transmit for their guidance.'[2]

The Chinese interpreters were recruited from among the miners with the offer of a steady wage. They were permanently on call, travelled with the protectors to outlying camps and officiated at all Chinese court cases. Their pay was barely adequate but they quickly realised that the position allowed them to protect the interests of their family, business partners and secret society members. It was also a handy route to naturalisation.

The protectors dealt mostly with the Chinese headmen in the camps. The government formalised these arrangements with regular payments and gave the headmen the responsibility of collecting the fees and other taxes from their compatriots. This was a recipe for corruption and soon miners in Bendigo, Ballarat, Castlemaine and Buckland complained of 'voracious, mercenary' headmen. And when lodging a complaint with their protector, individual Chinese miners were required to pay a further £2. On one occasion they attacked the Castlemaine occupant physically, beating him until police constables rushed to his rescue.

The military nature of the system was reflected in the insistence that all Chinese had to live in racially defined camps and villages where they could be observed and supervised. This meant that those working among the European miners had to relocate to exclusively Chinese areas. The effect was to alienate the two groups further. Moreover, the government continually increased duties and licence fees to exorbitant levels. In 1856, for example, Chinese protection and landing taxes raised £21,242 while total government spending on the system totalled only £9481.

At the same time, the British colonists were demanding ever more stringent restrictions on the activities of the Chinese people. The *Bendigo*

Advertiser caught the local flavour when it editorialised, 'It might be advisable to restrict the Chinese to a smaller portion of the ground than they at present take possession of, and let them understand that as soon as the ground on which they are working is required for leasing or other purposes, it will be taken possession of.'

However, the Chinese were not about to accept the blatant discrimination without protest. In 1859 the See Yap Society in Bendigo formed a United Confederacy 'to fight discriminatory taxes in every lawful manner' and thousands of Chinese flocked to its banner.

Their first political action took place on 11 May, when police arrested unlicensed Chinese miners at the nearby White Hills field. According to historian Kathryn Cronin, 'Gongs were sounded, fireworks shot into the air and hundreds of Confederacy supporters rushed to the scene. Several spirited Chinese fought with the police.'[3] They freed the prisoners but the police responded by firing their rifles and charging the crowd. The Chinese reluctantly surrendered the prisoners but then on cue hundreds gave themselves up as similarly unlicensed and followed the irascible troopers back to Bendigo jail where they demanded to be arrested. There they remained all day before quietly dispersing.

Two weeks later 3000 Chinese miners marched on Castlemaine demanding to be arrested. The Confederates imposed a boycott on all European goods and services. They also took to the law courts where they raised test cases in which they argued that Victoria's actions transgressed British treaties with China. They refused to pay their fines and crowded into the jails.

But the forces ranged against them were overwhelming. The magistrates dismissed the test cases and awarded costs against the plaintiffs. Conditions in the jails became insupportable. The rebellious confederacy lost momentum and by the end of 1859 it was no more. Some 13,000 Chinese paid their licence fees, depositing a massive £53,442 into the government coffers. The despairing miners recorded that 'the title Chinese Protector sounds somewhat like sarcasm'.[4]

Their protest was not altogether fruitless. By 1860 the Chinese camp system in Victoria was falling apart. At least half the former inhabitants were moving out in groups of between six and twenty and setting themselves up among the European miners. And while there was no particular welcome from the Europeans, the two groups worked together with little friction and a sense of shared experience. The government eventually discharged all Chinese headmen and most interpreters. European police constables were reassigned to general duties and the Chinese Protectorate faded into history. The government then suspended landing and residence taxes, as well as Chinese immigration quotas, for two years.

By then the rush to Victoria had faded and the damage was done. In the public mind, the Chinese were officially relegated to the outer fringes of colonial society. Their only consolation was that their homeland was ruptured by war and even more hazardous to life and limb. Those who remained would find work as shepherds, hawkers, market gardeners and fishermen on the eastern coastline. A few would become successful men of property or join with trading groups based in Hong Kong or Guangzhou.

However, those who travelled north to new finds in the Snowy Mountains, then joined the goldrush in New South Wales in the early 1860s, would find themselves on a racist battleground that would make the Victorian experience seem almost benign. Among the worst was in Lambing Flat, where the anti-Chinese prejudice would result in a racist insurrection that would distort and disfigure relations between China and Australia for more a century.

CHAPTER NINE
LAMBING FLAT

At Lambing Flat the gold was easily accessible and by August 1860 the nearby Yass *Courier* reported about 1500 miners from Britain and other parts of the colony had reached the diggings. A correspondent wrote, 'It is such a splendid-looking auriferous country for miles around. There are a great number of diggers flocking here every day.'

By October there were at least 6000 prospectors on the field. The *Courier* reported, 'The diggers continue to find new ground every day, and it is expected that the richest part of the neighbourhood has not yet been struck. Provisions are cheap and procurable in abundance.' The newspaper was also the first to report the arrival of 'a great many Chinese' and commented, 'the labour being light, this place is likely to become a favourite with them'. However, it soon became clear that the Chinese would come under fire from the Europeans who consistently outnumbered them by at least eight to one. And on 13 November 1860, they staged their first organised assault on the Chinese miners.

The Yass *Courier* described the terrible scene: 'Some 500 Europeans attacked a party of Chinese and maltreated them to such an extent as to cause the death of at least one of their number. We are informed that the "pigtails" of the unfortunate Celestials were cut off in so barbarous a manner as to detach the skin from the back of the head; and further that the brutality was carried to the length of cutting the ears off several.'

That was just the beginning. Despite the stationing of a gold commissioner and three mounted troopers on the field, the following month, another voilent conflict erupted. According to an official report, 'A vigilante group, to the accompaniment of a musical [German] band took it upon themselves to burn down some disreputable grog shanties and pour away the liquor which was allegedly drugged. They also drove off 50 Chinese, scalped two men and cut the ears off others. Police reinforcements arrived but no evidence of assault was found.'

The British prospectors formed a Miners' League which demanded the government 'control' the Chinese. Meantime, their 'riots' became a regular weekly event. One occasion was reported by a banker at the scene, George Preshaw:

> The mob numbered about 2000 men. They ascended Victoria Hill where about 300 Chinese were located; and a neater little canvas town could not well be found . . .
>
> On marched the mob and as they neared the encampment they made a run for it and, with yells and hoots, hunted and whipped the Chinamen off, knocking them down with the butt ends of their whips, galloping after them, and using the most cruel torture upon the poor defenceless creatures; in many cases pulling their pigtails out by the roots and planting their fresh trophies upon their banners.
>
> Not satisfied with this, their next step was to rifle all the tents of all the gold, then deliberately fire every tent in the encampment. In less than two hours, all that remained of the camp – the homes of some 300 Chinese – was a heap of smoldering ruins . . . The procession then reformed, the band struck up *Rule Britannia* and proceeded to the encampment at Back Creek . . . These were treated as badly (if not worse) than those at Victoria Hill. One poor creature, a Britisher who was married to a Chinaman, was maltreated by the mob and her infant narrowly escaped the wretches setting fire to her cradle. Scarcely had the Chinese been hunted away than these men jumped their claims.

The goldfields commissioners applied to the government for more police protection and the response was an addition of troopers, foot police and detectives. However, the attacks became more aggressive and the authorities were badly outnumbered. According to the *Courier*:

About two o'clock a large body came in from Stony Creek, headed by a brass band playing martial airs, with the Union Jack on either side floating over them. They came on horseback, on foot, and in vehicles, and the band occupied a 'jaunting car' drawn by two fine horses.

Soon after, a party from Spring Creek was led up the main street by a fine burly young fellow carrying the Union Jack, and by another beating a drum made out of a tin case, whose shouts gathered along with them all stragglers. The arrival of this last party was the signal for business.

Several boxes were placed together on a small hillock, with the Union Jacks on either side of them formed a platform around which the dense assemblage collected. The band opened the proceedings by playing a martial air, after which Mr. Charles Allen, storekeeper, of Lambing Flat, was universally appointed chairman.

The parties debated 'whether Burrangong was a European or a Chinese territory'. The answer was not long in coming and after a series of rabble-rousing speeches, the German band struck up. Having threatened to burn the police barracks if they interfered, the troublemakers advanced on the biggest Chinese camp. But the troopers intervened and the miners withdrew.

Police Superintendent Captain Henry Zouch summoned reinforcements from Yass and they arrived the following day. Nonetheless the miners rallied again two days later and, ignoring police threats and pleas, again attacked the Chinese, this time killing an unknown number and mauling scores more.

The police arrested eleven of the rioters and in the late afternoon 4000 miners gathered at the rough timber courthouse and demanded their release. Preshaw the banker again witnessed the scene: 'Captain Zouch proceeded to harangue the mob [from] the steps of the courthouse. He told them the prisoners would have a fair trial and could see their solicitors if they wished. The Riot Act was then read by Commissioner Griffin. This was received with clamour [and] not many minutes passed before the suspense was brought to an end by the mob firing several shots at the police, whereupon the foot police (sixteen in number under Inspector Sanderson) were ordered to fire.'

One man was killed and another injured. However, Preshaw said, 'Nothing daunted, the mob fired again and again. The mounted police then charged; the effect was instantaneous, the mob making a most ignominious retreat, helter-skelter down the hill and through the creek, leaving behind them a miscellaneous collection of hats, caps, sticks, guns etc. Many a foolish fellow will remember that retreat as long as life lasts.'[1]

The police took casualties with four seriously wounded; and after three days without rest, all the officers were exhausted and their ammunition spent. So after a brief conference they released the prisoners and beat a retreat to Yass, leaving the goldfield to the mercy of the mob.

Preshaw and his fellow bankers hid their cash and gold during the night and by morning the courthouse had been burnt to the ground. 'Fifteen thousand souls without a solitary policeman was a nice state of affairs,' Preshaw commented, 'yet strange to say there was very little crime during the interregnum.'

When news of the insurrection reached Sydney, the state's premier Charles Cowper decided to intervene. English-born, he had arrived in New South Wales as the two-year-old son of the colony's assistant chaplain, William Cowper, in 1809. He had farmed in the rich Argyle district and entered politics in 1843, becoming increasingly liberal in outlook and gaining the premiership in 1856. By 1860 his party was deeply divided on the issue of Chinese migration. Restrictive legislation had been introduced in the parliament in 1858 in the wake of Victorian and South Australian laws, but it failed to pass. The issue became more complex when the British and Chinese governments signed the Convention of Peking in 1860 which arguably gave Chinese citizens migration rights in British colonies and a new bill was even then being drafted as the attacks intensified.

Cowper's arrival provided a brief pause in hostilities and in March 1861 more than 150 troops with three 12-pounder field guns arrived in the encampment. However, the soldiers soon became very friendly with the British and European miners and the Chinese were restricted to Blackguard Gully. Meanwhile, a Gold Fields Bill, intended to separate the warring factions, lapsed when parliament was prorogued.

Regular British forays into the Chinese camps continued, yet on 24 May, two days after a violent confrontation, the troops departed. A rumour spread that 1500 Chinese had landed in Sydney and were bound for Lambing Flat and this prompted a 'roll-up' on 30 June that resulted in the biggest onslaught of all. More than 3000 miners armed with pick-handles, bludgeons, guns and whips assembled in a paddock beside their camp. The German band was again called to service and the miners advanced, waving British, Irish and American flags.

As they reached the Chinese camp, they surged forward and chaos ensued among the tents. The Chinese were vastly outnumbered and fell before the charge. An unknown number were bashed or shot, their bodies tossed down nearby mine shafts, and an estimated 250 were gravely injured. At least one European died and others were wounded in the fracas that lasted until the Chinese scattered and the entire camp was torched.

The police arrested several white miners and on 14 July about a thousand of their fellows laid siege to the jail in a rescue attempt. More shots were exchanged and at least one miner was killed outright. Once again the police departed for Yass and as they left the miners burned their quarters. Captain Zouch contacted the authorities in Sydney and Premier Cowper persuaded Captain Henry Carr Glyn of the British warship HMS *Fawn* in Sydney Harbour to detach 75 marines and become part of a force, replete with artillery, headed for the goldfield.

On arrival the strengthened force spread out through the fields, arrested a further five men and quelled the uprising. The prisoners were charged with affray and assault. The miners raised £400 as a defence fund and at their trial at Goulburn, four of the five men were acquitted. The miners celebrated; the servicemen returned to Sydney.

Thereafter the Chinese were restricted to designated fields by government decree and further assaults went unpunished since it was now clear to all that no colonial jury would convict their fellows. Four months later the New South Wales Legislative Assembly passed the *Chinese Immigration Restriction Act*.

When the dust settled, Premier Cowper decided to draw a symbolic line under the lawless uprising by giving Lambing Flat a new name. And what better, he decided, than that of the new governor of New South Wales, Sir John Young. It was so proclaimed in 1863. But the effects of the uprising, and the racist fires it kindled, would not be so easily extinguished.

CHAPTER TEN

THE CHINESE BUSHRANGER

The goldrushes of the mid 1800s led, not surprisingly, to the golden age of bushranging. Infamous felons reaped a harvest from the gold escorts throughout southern New South Wales in the first half of the 1860s. They included the notorious Frank Gardiner, Ben Hall and Johnny Gilbert, and Australia's only Chinese bushranger, the much less famous Sam Poo.

Sam was no Ned Kelly or Ben Hall. In fact, he was among the least successful highwaymen. He couldn't ride a horse and that put him at some disadvantage when being pursued by the mounted troopers of the day. So his career as a tobyman was not a long one. And it ended abruptly when he was charged with the murder of a popular police officer, John Ward, in February 1865. However, his trial and ultimate execution says much about the clash of cultures that bedevilled Australia at the time.

Sam Poo was not his real name – it has no Mandarin equivalent; it is either a slang rendering of similar syllables or more likely a derogatory nickname invented by the white settlers and adopted by the police prosecutors. The man himself was unable to communicate with them in English and his Chinese interpreter in the court proceedings didn't understand his southern dialect.

By the early 1860s Sam was prospecting, without much success, on the Talbragar River between present-day Dunedoo and Mudgee in New South Wales. He was a 'hatter', the term used for miners who worked without a partner to warn of the dangers from rock falls and unwelcome intruders. The term probably derived from 'mad hatters', the hat makers who used mercury in their trade which affected the nervous system causing trembling and antisocial behaviour. Sam's Chinese compatriots were quick to disown him once he was charged with the murder and claimed that he was a solitary character who practised firing his rifle at a tree stump near his camp.

The Chinese diggers in the area were scrupulously law-abiding and it was a shock to all when reports filtered in that a Chinaman had joined the bushranging outbreak that was sweeping the colony. Sam's modus operandi was to lie in wait for fellow pedestrians then leap from his hideaway, brandishing his pistols and demanding whatever gold, coin or other valuables they were carrying. Most of his victims were Chinese but colonials were not spared.

A report in the Sydney *Mail* said that Senior Constable Ward, 'a most efficient, intelligent and active officer' stationed at Coonabarabran, was returning home from Mudgee at 10 a.m. on 3 February 1865 when he met two men who told him an armed Chinese man was holding up travellers on the other side of a rise known as Barney's Reef. Constable Ward spurred his horse forward and spied the accused from the rise. The man apparently ran off into the bush where Ward easily overtook him. There was an exchange of shots and Ward was hit.

Soon afterwards local grazier James Plunkett and another police officer, Constable Todd, came upon the wounded officer who said a Chinese man had shot him. Plunkett took Ward to his Birriwa station where that night he was treated by Dr William King who had ridden 45 miles to reach him. However, Ward died the following day at about 4.30 p.m. without ever being able to identify his killer.

At the time the police troopers were enraged by the shooting of another of their number, Constable Sam Nelson, by bushrangers Ben Hall, Johnny Gilbert and John Dunn at the village of Collector. So, fourteen days after Ward's death, when three troopers led by Constable Edward Burns and a 'half-caste' black tracker named Hughes came upon Sam Poo in a gully near Cobbora, about 15 kilometres from Dunedoo, no mercy was spared. Again there was an exchange of shots and the Chinese fugitive was felled by a shotgun blast that clipped his neck and head. Then, according to the *Mail*, 'Constable Burns rushed to secure him; when the Chinaman raised himself from the ground and tried to fire again, Burns struck him on the head with the butt end of his gun, smashing the stock to pieces.' Sam suffered a fractured skull and was not expected to live.

But he lingered for several months and though the fracture left him mentally debilitated, by 9 October 1865 he was regarded as sufficiently recovered to stand trial for the 'wilful murder' of Constable Ward. He was arraigned at the Bathurst courthouse before a jury and defended by the court-appointed barrister, Joseph Innes, who would later become the colony's attorney-general. Innes pleaded him 'not guilty'.

The trial was farcical at best. Sam took no part in the proceeding since, according to the *Mail,* he had little or no understanding of what was occurring. 'The wretched man,' it reported, 'ever since his apprehension has been quite weak in intellect.' The Chinese interpreter was unable to communicate with the prisoner who spoke in a southern dialect unfamiliar to him. And it is highly doubtful that Sam had any real understanding of his situation.

The prosecutor, Edward Butler, who would precede Innes as New South Wales attorney-general, began by calling a Plunkett employee, John Clough, who said he saw Sam in the scrub the day after the shooting as he and his brother headed for home. 'He did not offer to molest us,' he said to Innes's questions. 'He had a swag with him and I asked him where he was going and whether he was lost. And I told him I would soon fetch somebody to shift him out of that . . . He was rather stouter than he is now.'

Then came one Elizabeth Golding, despite her having no knowledge of the events of the day. Instead, she claimed that Sam was the Chinese man who had earlier called by her house at Plunkett's station and made improper suggestions to her and her little girl. According to Golding, he said, 'If I cannot have my will of the girl, I will of you.' And he had a gun similar to the one shown to Golding in court. She had run to Plunkett's house with her child, and by the time she returned with her husband the Chinese man had left the scene. What this had to do with the shooting is a mystery. But in spite of the unlikely wording of Sam's alleged threat, it undoubtedly played on the most primitive prejudices of the all-white jury.

Equally irrelevant was James Plunkett's claim from the witness box to have seen the prisoner the night before the day of the shooting somewhere in the vicinity of a shepherd's hut on his property. More importantly, he said he had taken Constable Ward's statement that described his attacker as 'a short, cranky little man'. The statement was only admissible if it were a 'dying declaration' and Innes pointed out that since the policeman asked Plunkett to send for a doctor, he expected he might recover. But Mr Justice John Hargrave – who would precede Butler as the attorney-general – ruled against him.

Another witness, Thomas Morris, said he was droving some sheep on the evening of the 3rd when a man passed him riding a horse; he later heard shots and claimed to have seen 'someone' walking and carrying 'something' in his hand which might have been a firearm. He was between 250 and 300 yards away but the man was dressed in similar clothes to those presently worn by the prisoner. Then his droving mate, Alfred Smith, said that the man who passed after the shots were fired had something in his hand which he believed was a gun. However, since Ward had left Mudgee at 10 a.m. and Barney's Reef was no more than a three-hour ride, it would not have been 'evening' when the firing took place. Moreover, it was still daylight when Plunkett and Constable Todd came upon the wounded man.

The drovers were followed by Dr King, who said Constable Ward had suffered a gunshot injury to the pelvis and there were other small wounds. 'The case was a hopeless one,' the doctor said.

Then Sam's captor, Constable Burns, took the stand and gave his version of events: 'We met with the prisoner in the bush, our attention being drawn to him by his firing of a gun. He ran into the scrub which was very thick and we had to dismount to follow him. We fired after him and eventually brought him to bay and arrested him.

The prisoner was dressed as a Chinaman usually dresses: he had two jumpers on and the clothes he now wears [six months after the event].' He had a gun loaded with a bullet and slugs as well as a pistol, Burns claimed. That was when Burns smashed his rifle stock on Sam's head.

Dr King was recalled and said, 'The wounds I saw on Ward's body might have been produced by a bullet and slugs similar to the charge shown to me.'

The prosecution then rested its case and Innes asked His Honour whether there was anything to go to the jury on the charge of murder. His Honour responded that 'there was ample evidence to sustain an indictment for murder'.

Now was the opportunity for Sam to speak in his own defence. But that was hardly feasible since he did not know the language, was unable to communicate with his interpreter and had seemingly lost his senses in the police attack. Whether his testimony would have been helpful in any case is debatable, since the jury was out for only 'a short interval' before they returned with a verdict of guilty.

Two months later on 19 December 1865, Sam Poo was taken to the scaffold inside the Bathurst gaol. The *Mail* reported: 'In the absence of any of his countrymen outside the prison walls, three Chinese prisoners were brought out to see the end of Sam Poo; there were also about a dozen other persons present besides the police and officers of the gaol. The wretched man appeared perfectly unconscious of his fate, and until his arms were pinioned by the executioners, [he] stood at the door of his cell clapping his hands.

'The ceremony of pinioning over, he was led to the gallows without speaking a word, or even once lifting up his head. The rope was fixed, the bolt drawn, and Sam Poo ceased to exist.'

Clearly, Sam was headed for the hangman's noose whatever occurred in the Bathurst courtroom. No one placed him at the scene and not even the victim was able to identify him. No ballistic evidence was presented to suggest that Sam's weapon fired the fatal shot. And he was so mentally debilitated by the police attack that he was unfit to stand trial anyway. Three members of the legal establishment provided a respectable framework but it was in form, not substance. The jury was given no alternative, even in the unlikely event that they were open to one. Racial prejudice ruled the day; the result was a legal lynching.

It might have been passed off as a case of 'rough justice' at a time when frontier law was not as painstaking and sophisticated as today. But there is another dimension to the tragedy. Constable Ward's descendants, the people of the now populous district of Mudgee and indeed the entire New South Wales police force have elevated the trooper's death from a tragedy in the line of duty to a secular sacrament. His grave on Birriwa station has been transformed into a temporal shrine, beautifully laid out and opened in 2012. According to the current owners of Birriwa, a steady stream of visitors calls by to pay their respects to the English-born trooper described as 29 years old, with brown hair, blue eyes and a fair complexion.

Then, on 4 February 2013, the state's most senior policemen, the mayor, the local member of parliament and other dignitaries attended a memorial service 148 years after Constable Ward succumbed to his wounds. A dark photograph purporting to be Sam Poo – a vaguely oriental man in a hat – was supplied to the media.

CHAPTER ELEVEN
SERVING THE SQUATTOCRACY

Almost half the 3000 indentured Chinese workers who arrived in the southern states between 1848 and 1853 eventually made their way to the northern districts and what would become the new colony of Queensland in 1859. Others came directly from Xiamen to Moreton Bay, including 225 on the *Duke of Roxburgh* in 1851. The ship's owner was Robert Towns who would gain lasting notoriety as the driving force behind the Kanaka trade in South Sea Islanders for the Queensland sugar industry. He was a throwback to the British slavers and was in the market for Indian, Chinese and indeed any other human cargo that could fetch a price on the international labour market.

Towns wrote to the northern graziers directly, claiming the Chinese would be their 'salvation'. They would have 'the services of these men for five years at a rate not exceeding one-quarter you are obliged to pay your own countrymen,' he said, 'and I find I can get more work out of a Chinaman than a European, even in Sydney.' As an added bonus, Towns claimed, 'It will teach your other men a wholesome lesson that others are to be had if they persist in demanding such wages as you cannot pay.'[1]

By the end of 1852 more than 1000 Chinese had disembarked in Brisbane where a depot had been built to house them before distribution among their British 'masters' on massive sheep runs in the Darling Downs as well as the Burnett and Wide Bay districts. Many of the Queensland graziers referred to themselves as 'Pure Merinos', lineal descendants of the 'Exclusives' in New South Wales, led by John Macarthur, Gregory Blaxland and Samuel Marsden. And most of them treated the 'Celestials' with the same lordly contempt as their southern forebears displayed towards their convicts.

According to Queensland's first governor, Sir George Bowen, who toured the Darling Downs district, 'These gentlemen live in a patriarchal style among their immense flocks and herds, amusing themselves with hunting, shooting, fishing and the exercise of a plentiful hospitality. I have often thought that the Queensland gentlemen-squatters bear a similar relation to the other Australians that the Virginian planters of a hundred years back bore to the Americans.'

The graziers paid an initial £8 a head to import the Chinese for five years at an annual wage of between £4 and £7, plus two suits of clothes and rations. This compared with £20 to £25 a year plus found for a British shepherd, and provided the squatters with an excellent long-term bargain, particularly since the southern goldrush decimated the colonial labour pool.

Towns' ships were grossly overcrowded and conditions aboard so bad that dysentery swept through the passengers. With no latrines on deck the Chinese were forced to empty their bowels while hanging on chains over the roaring sea. According to one of the ship's captains, 'Several of these poor unfortunate wretches dropped from the chains, being unable to hold on from weakness.'[2]

On another occasion, Towns' barque the *Spartan*, designed to carry 153 men, left Xiamen with more than 260 aboard. The Chinese rebelled and several ship's officers were seriously injured, one fatally. The *Spartan* docked at Singapore where eleven Chinese men were found guilty of murder. But after the facts were revealed by a local newspaper, all but two had their sentences reduced to a few weeks in jail. On the next leg of the voyage, dysentery broke out and by the time the ship reached Sydney Harbour immigrant bodies were being thrown overboard.[3]

The Chinese passengers thereafter chose headmen from among their number to enforce discipline and act as spokesmen. They organised themselves into cooks, washermen and cleaners. They cared for their fellows who fell sick on the three-month voyage. Without this self-regulation, the casualties would have been much higher.

Once claimed by their new employers in Brisbane, the Chinese were outfitted with working gear and boots then loaded on to bullock drays for the long treks north and west to the sheep runs. As shepherds they would be allotted a minimum of 400 sheep per man; they would walk their flocks about the runs during the day and muster them into rough bush folds at night. They worked alone but each was allocated a couple of big, savage German collies to keep the dingoes away. The ration cart would arrive once a week and they would store their goods in an outstation hut occupied by a fellow Chinese who would take turns as a shepherd, or an overseer who regularly inspected the various flocks for disease or depredations by native dogs or Aboriginal people.

The Chinese had arrived in the latter years of a frontier war in country occupied by thousands of Indigenous tribal people who were being decimated by the usual European diseases of smallpox, measles, tuberculosis, influenza and syphilis. And according to local historian Margaret Slocomb, 'An untold number were deliberately poisoned with strychnine and arsenic, both in plentiful supply on all runs . . . Many of the leaders among them were shot or trampled to death by horses during the frontier war.'[4]

Indeed, the most egregious atrocity perpetuated by the squatters was the revenge taken for the killing of Gregory Blaxland, son of the explorer who first breached the Blue Mountains with Wentworth and Lawson in 1813. Blaxland junior had led a punitive expedition to avenge the death of two employees to Aboriginal spears and he effected 'heavy casualties' on the suspected tribe. In 1850 Blaxland's own mutilated body was found near the same place and within a week a 'huge force' was assembled, led by two of the more prominent district squatters who were duly sworn in as 'special constables' by the local commissioner for crown lands. The mob hunted down the suspects on Paddy's Island near the mouth of the Burnett River and there, it is reported, they carried out a massacre of up to 1000 Aboriginal people.

Two years later the shepherds were living and working in the same disputed territory and while the industry was becoming ever more dependent on the indentured Chinese, the graziers were reducing their conditions of service. As the southern goldrush caused a sharp increase in inflation, the clothing provision was eliminated and the rations reduced. And while their wages rose slightly to 12 shillings a month, not one of the more than 3000 labourers would have been able to pay his fare home at the end of his indenture. Moreover, they were not paid in silver as their contracts required but in a variety of coins unfamiliar to their Chinese financial system.

The Chinese were, in effect, trapped in a foreign clime, but they were not prepared to accept it meekly. On almost every station they protested volubly and on occasion threatened the owner with violence. When that didn't produce results, they were accused of training their dogs to molest the sheep in their care or walking off the job and leaving them to the fate of the Aboriginal people and the dingoes.

Relations soured and the station owners responded with corporal and other punishments that, at times, amounted to torture. The Chinese were frequently brought before the courts and only rarely escaped a two- or three-month jail sentence, whatever provocation they had endured. An overseer, B.J. Bertelson, for example, admitted that he had 'a private lock-up' on the property and had tied a Chinese man upright in a little meat safe by the throat, arms and legs and kept him without food and water for three days and nights. In 1852 the Chinese shepherds organised a mass walk-out in groups of seven or eight from properties in the north Burnett district in what the graziers charged was 'open rebellion'. The two-month prison sentence was applied to the offenders, except for the men on Bertelson's station where torture was proved.[5]

While the shepherding was monotonous, wearisome work, the Chinese proved themselves highly adaptable to station life and often acquired a range of skills, from milking to shearing. They seemed to have an inborn facility to grow vegetables and to prepare them for the table. So when they completed their contracts, they found a ready market for their skills. And since the Taiping rebellion had turned their homeland into a killing field, they had the choice of trying their luck on the goldfields or remaining in the districts they had come to know. Overwhelmingly they chose the latter and remained a substantial proportion of the population until the 1880s.

Towns' Chinese labourers expanded their activities into carting goods and gained a virtual monopoly of market gardening, supplying fresh fruit and vegetables at a fraction of the price of the imported equivalents, when and if they were available. In this they made a valuable contribution to the health and longevity of the pioneering community. Moreover, a substantial number of them found wives among the local European and Aboriginal women. As will be seen, more than a few of their descendants would become celebrated Australians in the late 20th and 21st centuries.

However, as Margaret Slocomb records, 'The main threat that remained beyond their power to overcome or even to manage was the growing political agitation against their presence in Queensland and, as plans for federation and nationhood advanced, throughout Australia itself.'[6] Also, the discovery of gold in the 1860s in areas from Wide Bay to Rockhampton brought some 3000 diggers to the various sites, including an estimated 1000 Chinese, mostly from Guangdong. Only a few of the agricultural workers were attracted by the lure of the lucky strike, though some might well have taken their carting and gardening skills to the goldfields.

There were anti-Chinese attacks on the first goldrush at Gympie but nothing of the size or intensity of the Lambing Flat uprising. In any case, major discoveries on the Palmer River near Cooktown in Far North Queensland intervened. According to Queensland historian Hector Holthouse, 'The trek out of Gympie became an exodus. Not only diggers but storekeepers, publicans, shanty-keepers, and a whole horde of gold-town hangers-on sold out or walked out and took ship north to the Palmer.'[7]

The remote river in Cape York Peninsula yielded more than a million ounces of extremely fine, rich alluvial gold, most of it between 1872 and 1874. While the miners from the southern Queensland fields were first to arrive, in the next three years the Chinese population exploded from 2000 to 19,500, overwhelmingly through migration direct from Guangzhou, Macao and Hong Kong. Indeed, the Hopkee Company ran a monthly service between Hong Kong and the port of Cooktown.

They arrived mostly in kinship groups then ran the gauntlet of fierce Aboriginal resistance as they made their way in single file from the coast to the diggings. According to one Chinese headman, Taam Sze Pui, 'The fear of such a fate kept one and all together and no one dare tarry behind to rest or to regain his breath.' They worked cooperatively and when beset by poor returns the less fortunate miners would be supported by the group.

A newspaper correspondent reported, 'The Chinese are everywhere and instead of only working the most likely spots, as is the case of Europeans, their perseverance is naturally rewarded with an occasional lucky find. There is an impression on the field that at least three-fourths of the gold falls to the lot of the Chinaman.' There were several early attempts to 'excite' the European miners to violent resistance, the reporter claimed, but no mass attacks ensued.

When a second, rich 'reefing' field was discovered on the Hodgkinson River to the south, the Europeans virtually abandoned Palmer to the Chinese. However, by 1877 the prospects of the Palmer field were diminishing rapidly, and there was little slackening in the number of arrivals. The Chinese persisted there until an alluvial field suddenly opened up in nearby Lukinville in 1878 and for the first – and only – time in the history of 'New Gold Mountain', Chinese groups fought with each other to lay claim to the new treasure. It was a bloody affair and the estimates of casualties range from four to 48 fatalities in battles between Macao and Guangzhou groups.

Meantime, the Hodgkinson field – in what became the Atherton Tableland – continued to produce payable ore. It had to be blown out with explosives then loaded on carts for transport to a crushing mill. Soon, lively small towns sprang up around the mines and a new port down from the range was established at Trinity Inlet and named Cairns after the then Queensland governor. The Chinese were attracted to the new settlements as shop and hotel keepers, butchers, carters and gardeners in the rich volcanic soil of the region. And as they developed its agricultural potential with crops of rice, corn, bananas and pineapples, it became at least as profitable as goldmining for the several thousand who remained. But as the gold ran out, most of their compatriots returned to China.

CHAPTER TWELVE
NORTHERN FRONTIERS

Meantime, workers on the Overland Telegraph Line from Adelaide to the Northern Territory had discovered gold at Pine Creek about 200 kilometres from Port Darwin in the early 1870s. The discoveries were not immediately followed up, but by 1873 the small public service in Darwin (then known as Palmerston) was in disarray as government officials were prospecting and pegging their own claims instead of attending to their duties.

John Lewis, a Territory pioneer whose son Essington would one day run Australia's biggest mining company, BHP, made a special trip to Adelaide to suggest the government import 'Chinese coolies' to develop the Top End. 'They should come simply to work for the Europeans, and be servants,' he said. 'They must not be allowed to enter into any trade or calling to oppose Europeans, but treated as a subject race.'[1] In fact, by then there were at least five Chinese in Darwin working at menial tasks in the hospital and the telegraph office.

Lewis was not alone in his advocacy. The prevailing view was that the white races were unsuited to work in the tropics; this was best left to the Orientals since the local Aboriginals were notoriously 'work shy' unless their duties involved riding a horse. The South Australian government sent the commissioner for crown lands, Thomas Reynolds, on a fact-finding tour to Java, Macassar and Singapore. He confirmed the view that 'the Territory 'ere long must necessarily embrace a large coloured population if the land and the mines are to be worked satisfactorily. Hence special legislation may soon be deemed necessary to meet the character of the people assembled there.'

Reynolds asked the government resident in Darwin, John Knight, to make inquiries in Hong Kong and further contacts were made in Mauritius, Ceylon (Sri Lanka) and the eastern states of Australia, before they finally settled on Singapore as the best source. After protracted negotiations, the *Vidar* arrived in Darwin on 5 August 1874 with 187 Chinese aboard.

The new arrivals were quick to acclimatise. Within a few days they had discarded their Chinese dress and startled the European shopkeepers by bargaining over each item of local clothing. The government selected 24 to work on the Overland Telegraph Line and despatched the rest to the various mining companies. They walked to the mines carrying their goods on bamboo poles and when they arrived built their own huts from paperbark and local bamboo. They did their own cooking from the rations supplied and within a few weeks had mastered the skills necessary to mine and crush the ore.

The mine owners' biggest problem was the mines themselves which were turning out to be much less lucrative than expected and some companies were facing liquidation. One company which was owned by John Lewis broke the conditions of contract and when the Chinese refused to work he took them to court. The magistrate found for Lewis and ordered the Chinese workers to be jailed, but in Adelaide the Mines Minister reversed the decision. 'I see no justification for this imprisonment,' he said.[2]

Indeed, the Chinese themselves began independent goldmining under the guidance of one of the early migrants, Ping Que, whose achievements in the Territory would become legendary. Ping Que had arrived in Victoria from Guangzhou where he had been a storekeeper. After tasting success in the southern goldfields, he spent almost a year in New Zealand adding to his fortune before reaching the Territory as a headman in 1874. He was 37 at the time and almost immediately invested in quartz mining with the British-born Lambert Smith. He engaged fourteen of his compatriots and according to John Knight, 'Ping Que is an intelligent Chinaman who speaks good English. He manages his countrymen very well and works them to make his mining pay, which is more than can be said of other employees of coolies.'

He also won the support of the *Northern Territory Times* which editorialised: 'Ping Que's party deserves great credit for energy and perseverance and it is time that fortune smiled more favourably upon them. If Ping Que could get any run of stone to turn out even a steady ounce, he would employ all the coolies in the Territory.'

In fact, his fortunes did improve. Yields from his five mines in 1877 increased markedly. On one of them he had fifteen compatriots working three shifts with a shaft 40 metres deep from which the stone was raised by a horse turning a drum attached to a rope and bucket. Each 200 tons produced 227 ounces of gold.

However, the most striking aspect of the Chinese experience in the Northern Territory was the comparative harmony between them and the British colonials. John Knight became particularly friendly with Ping Que and when the government resident learned that Lewis's mine had failed to supply Chinese workers with rice for a month, he rode there personally and ordered the company to meets its obligations. Indeed, when the government decided to import more Chinese labourers, Knight asked Ping Que to travel to Singapore and negotiate the deal. And when the Ping Que pointed out that 'experienced Chinese miners from Victoria would be three times more valuable than raw coolies from Singapore', the resident readily agreed.

By 1874 the Queensland government had joined the eastern colonies in seeking to restrict Chinese immigration with a poll tax and a limit governed by the size of the ship on which they travelled. In South Australia there was a growing use of the term 'white' racially and a widespread objection to intermarriage. The parliamentarian James Henderson Howe declared in 1881 that he would rather see his children dead than intermarried. Two years later an ex–cabinet minister in Victoria, Charles Henry Pearson, produced a book claiming the 'lower races' bred faster than the whites who were defending 'civilisation'. This, he said, would lead inevitably to a clash between the two worlds.

Nevertheless, when dealing with what was then its 'northern territory', South Australia stood out against the trend. By July 1877 the government was in the market for even more Chinese labourers and in October that year the first 250 arrived via the SS *Bertha* from Cooktown. Soon afterwards Ping Que added to his own workforce with a shipload of labourers from Singapore. A similar influx occurred the following year; and when a new alluvial discovery was registered at 'the 12-mile' (soon to be renamed Chinamen's Rush), at least 500 Chinese miners were soon working that field alone. Knight told his political masters in Adelaide that at this rate, 'the Northern Territory of South Australia will practically become an Asiatic settlement'.

Mining in the Territory was largely governed by the seasons with almost all rain falling during the 'wet' from November to March. The work was difficult enough during the rainy season with extensive bogs and flooded creeks. But as the country dried out, alluvial mining became practically impossible and miners had no option but to seek 'relief' from the government in Darwin itself. In April 1878 the new resident, Edward Price, circulated a notice printed in Chinese advising that, 'When the water fails at the alluvial goldfields where the Chinese are at work, anyone destitute may apply after the 15th May to the officer in charge, Yam Creek, where the applicant will receive sufficient rice to enable him to reach [Darwin] where permanent relief work will be given him.'[3]

In Darwin, the Chinese workers received a weekly ration of rice, salt fish, tea, sugar and vegetables from the government gardens. They congregated in a small suburb which soon became known as Chinatown. And when the wet season arrived, they returned to the goldfields.

The migration continued, and Ping Que put most of them to work in his various enterprises, from mining to stores, butcher shops, slaughter houses for cattle and sheep, and an active opium sideline which attracted a modest government import duty. On the goldfields, as one operation was worked out, another was opened and in 1879 most of the Chinese were concentrated on the Pine Creek alluvial gold.

Ping Que and his fellow merchants extended their influence into community facilities such as the miners' hospital which treated Europeans, Chinese and Aboriginals alike. Several extensive market gardens were established on Darwin's outskirts and in a report to government, John Knight wrote that, 'It seems to me that if we must have a Chinese population they would do less harm in cultivating Chinese [agricultural] products than in robbing the earth of its gold.' The government responded by surveying small blocks for cropping and abolishing survey fees for the Chinese buyers. By the end of 1879 Knight and Price estimated that the Chinese population had reached 3036, and they were joined towards the end of the wet season by three ships carrying a further 1240.

As the miners trekked to the goldfields, they faced the danger of losing their way in the seemingly endless scrub or being attacked by Aborigines. Even when they reached their camps, they were not altogether safe. Two Chinese were working their vegetable garden at Pine Creek when they were speared to death. Others succumbed to malaria and pneumonia.

In the other colonies, moves were afoot to restrict Chinese immigration. At a conference of colonial leaders in Melbourne and Sydney in 1880–81, they considered a resolution calling for concerted action to seek both British and local legislation to end the inflow. Again the South Australian government stood out. They agreed to a poll tax of £10 on every Chinese arrival, but it would not apply to the Northern Territory. However, they promised to crack down on the collecting of the annual 10 shilling miner's licence fee which had largely been ignored since it cost more to collect than it was worth. In fact, if a Chinese miner was arrested for non-payment, he had no objection to serving time in jail where he enjoyed better food and shelter than in his own camp. And as John Knight noted, 'The present lock-up would not hold a refractory tomcat.'[4]

In 1882 a South Australian parliamentary delegation toured the Territory accompanied by a journalist, W.J. (later Sir William) Sowden, who wrote of 'the celebrated Ping Que' who alone had 'sent home from the Union goldfield half a ton of gold'. Indeed, a few days before Sowden arrived at one of Ping Que's mines, his workers had acquired 500 ounces from a single bucket of stone.

Returning to Port Darwin, Sowden wrote that the Chinese supplied vegetables, fish and other seafood to the European population. One of the leading Chinese merchants told him they could grow rice and sugar and Chinese fruits in the area: 'We will send out thousands of Chinese workmen to make your railway, then China will do big trade with this place,' he said. 'Suppose railway made right to Adelaide, get all through country. Welly good.'[5]

The parliamentarians, it seems, were not enthused by the prospect. In 1882 they passed the *Constitution Amendment Act* that barred all unnaturalised Chinese from the vote. In the courts the newcomers were unable to engage a qualified lawyer to act on their behalf and only a single layman, Vaiben 'Black' Solomon, who had enjoyed a partnership with a Chinese mining entrepreneur, was permitted to assist. But in any case, the Chinese remained an increasingly influential and well-regarded part of the community. When the government resident Edward Price departed in 1883, they paid him the tribute of a formal procession through Darwin streets in sumptuous robes accompanied by a Chinese band of cymbals, gongs and trumpets, and further enlivened by exploding fireworks. Price responded in kind, praising them for building the Darwin Town Hall which had been designed by his predecessor John Knight.

By 1885 only 102 Northern Territory Chinese had been naturalised and thereafter no further naturalisations were forthcoming. And not even the naturalised Chinese had the full rights as citizens. They had no vote, no rights in any colony except the one that had issued the certificate, and laws could be specifically directed against them to the exclusion of their fellow colonists. Nevertheless, the Northern Territory stood out against the rest of the country in its comparatively benign attitude to the Chinese. The new resident, John Langdon

Parsons, believed that they were 'essential to the continued development of the Territory'. However, there soon came a subtle shift in the government's approach. Parsons' recommendation for 50,000 acres to be surveyed for Chinese cultivation was ignored. And in May 1886 the community lost its brightest star when Ping Que suffered a sudden heart attack and died. His application for naturalisation had been approved months earlier but he died before the formal certificate was issued.

The *Northern Territory Times* editorialised, 'Ping Que will be missed by many who have profited by his experience and advice. We can only express sorrow at the unexpected death of one of the pluckiest and straightest men it has been our lot to meet in the Northern Territory.'

On the goldfields the Chinese and European miners worked together peacefully. But opposition came from a small group of British businessmen in Darwin. They were dismayed when the contract to build the railway from the port to Pine Creek was won by a company – E. & C. Miller – that planned to use Chinese labour, and they redoubled their public agitation. While some 3000 Chinese were employed on the remarkably successful rail link, the British businessmen scored a legislative victory with the *Goldfields Amendment Act* of September 1886. It excluded all Asians from any new goldfields discovered in the Territory for the next two years.

Nevertheless, 1887 saw a continued inflow of more than 1000 Chinese migrants, bringing the total to more than 6000, at least three times the size of the European population. And by now Darwin was the only port in the country where the Chinese were free to land.

CHAPTER THIRTEEN
ANTI-CHINESE POLICIES

In May that year the Qing emperor dispatched two commissioners, General Wang Ronghe and E Tsing, to review the conditions of their countrymen in the Philippines, Malaya, Indonesia and Australia. General Wang had been schooled in Penang where he gained British citizenship. In 1860 he worked as an interpreter for Major General Charles 'Chinese' Gordon during his campaign against the Taiping. E Tsing was a respected Mandarin who would shortly take up the post of consul-general in San Francisco.

The Chinese business community in Sydney did its best to add to the status and impact of the first official Chinese delegation to visit Australia. A substantial residence was leased in Macquarie Street and refurnished in Chinese style to accommodate the commissioners and their servants. A busy schedule of meetings allowed the delegation to meet those politicians and businessmen who took enthusiastically to the prospect of developing trade with China.

But while their visit was conceived as a friendly diplomatic gesture between governments designed to overcome misapprehensions on both sides, it became a lightning rod for the racist anti-Chinese forces. The closure of Chinese migration to the United States in 1882 was recalled to whip up fear that the Chinese were about to turn their full and undivided attention to Australia. A letter in the *Daily Telegraph* from a cabinet-maker reflected the attitude of the opposition: 'It is amazing to me that a horde of Asiatics should be allowed to settle down and destroy the cabinet trade of this city. This Colony was never founded for their benefit surely . . . It is a nice thing that an Englishman should lose his time learning a trade to compete with a lot of slaves, for they are nothing better . . . What chance has a white man, who pays rates and taxes, and keeps a wife and family with them?' It was signed, 'Victim'.

In a sad irony, the visit had been organised in part by the man who by now had become the most prominent and admired of all the Chinese migrants: Mei Quong Tart.

In the years since his youthful adventures in Braidwood, Quong Tart had notched up one success after another. He'd opened several new mines in nearby Araluen and Major's Creek. He'd become a driving force in the cultural and sporting life of the district and organised a series of popular race meetings. He was an enthusiastic No. 10 batsman in the Braidwood cricket club where his real skills flourished as club treasurer. And he entered the inner sanctum of British fellowship when accepted into the local Masonic Lodge.

He frequently reunited in Sydney with his unofficial adoptive parents, Robert and Alice Simpson, and in 1881 made his first return visit to his Chinese family in their small town 100 kilometres from Guangzhou. He carried with him a letter of introduction from Sir John Robertson, the former premier of the colony, and testimonials from his Lodge brothers. According to his biographer, Quong Tart's first words to his father in the 22 years since they had seen each other were, 'I have kept the promise I made you, father. Since I left your care I have not tasted opium.'[1]

Indeed, Quong's distaste for the drug habit among his compatriots in Australia would propel him to wide public notice in his adopted country. He was aware that it was one of the barbs employed by the colonists to denigrate his compatriots. And no doubt he had witnessed the effects of addiction on the goldfields. He would become an outspoken leader of the anti-opium movement in the years ahead.

He remained in China for three months and successfully resisted his mother's plea that he take a local bride of her choosing. However, he did engage his family in a venture that would bring his activities to the attention of Sydney's business elite and the wider population. The thirst for Chinese tea had gained an enormous following in the colony and his father, who was well respected in Guangzhou, provided the essential personal contacts to start an export business with the Loong Shan Tea plantation. They agreed to send quantities of their leaf to Guangzhou each month where Quong Tart's brother would make a selection and supervise its transport to Sydney.

On his return to Sydney, Quong set up a distribution network to popular cafes and oriental restaurants. Soon afterwards he opened his own tearooms in the City Arcade where he also sold a selection of his father's ornamental wares and rolls of fine Chinese silk. He then brought a unique innovation to the trade by parcelling his tea for sale in small packets decorated with his 'double-heart' trademark.

He was a natural promoter and with his Scottish-Chinese accent, idiosyncratic sense of humour and open-hearted manner soon became a favourite of the metropolitan press. As his tea shops flourished he was able to indulge his sporting enthusiasms on the cricket field, even winning over the anti-Chinese *Bulletin* as an 'Anglo-Mongolian' whose oriental appearance was 'only skin deep'. In fact, they gushed, he was 'a man of the world, a true Briton, an expert at manly sports who at a recent cricket match between the two arcades . . . shone with refulgence'.[2]

In November 1883 he was commissioned by the inspector-general of police, Edmund Fosbery, to accompany an old acquaintance from his Braidwood days, Inspector Martin Brennan, on an investigation of the Chinese camps that remained in the Riverina towns in the wake of the goldrush. According to Sydney's puritans and chauvinists, the camps were the repositories of rampant oriental depravity.

Brennan had distinguished himself in the riots at Lambing Flat, having his mounts twice shot from under him while defending the Chinese against the European insurgents. Irish born, he had joined the police force on arrival but unlike most of his confederates had educated himself through correspondence courses. Indeed, he and his daughter Sarah had sat together for the matriculation exam at Sydney University. He had passed with flying colours but remained in the police force to provide for his other children. He and his Chinese companion made an unlikely but thoroughly congenial duo on the journey by train, cart, coach and on foot, enduring what the *Town and Country Journal* called 'summer blaze, heavy rain, hail, long frosts and, almost incredible sight of all, snow'.

Brennan and Quong visited all the major towns of the region and interviewed scores of men and women, including the British wives of Chinese shopkeepers and market gardeners, many of whom were reformed prostitutes. According to Brennan's report, 'The women scoffed at the idea of being in thrall to any foreigner and smile at the credulity of any person believing such.'

The final report came as a great disappointment to the agitators. Brennan took issue with the racist attitudes they found among officials. He was particularly critical of a schoolmaster in Albury who refused admittance to a seven-year-old Chinese boy whose hair was cut in the traditional pigtail style. Brennan wrote: 'The exclusion of this child, cleanly and intelligent in appearance, whose mother is a native born British subject, from a public school is no more valid than if applied to European children wearing their hair in any one of the extraordinary styles which European custom sanctions.'

The experience confirmed Quong's opposition to opium and he used a combination of government statistics and personal experience to provide a lively account of life in the camps and towns. And though they submitted the report in record time to Fosbery, he merely passed it on to the police superintendent at Wagga Wagga and thereafter it gathered dust in a station pigeonhole.

Back in the city Quong redoubled his business and charity activities, fending off the competition from Indian tea and opening new cafes at the zoo and in the suburbs, while at the same time hosting charitable events for the destitute and the mentally frail. Shortly afterwards on a trip back to Braidwood, he met the young woman who would become his bride. Margaret Scarlett, the attractive daughter of a Lancashire migrant, had secured a teaching position in a small private school there. She had not only heard of Quong long before she met him, she had collected news clippings and magazine references. She had even kept a journal of all his activities as they reached her. Unsurprisingly, Quong was overwhelmed by her ardour and they were soon engaged to be married.

Her parents, George and Ann, met with the hopeful bridegroom in Sydney where George was a station master and while he later claimed to like the Chinese 'well enough', he was implacably opposed to the marriage. However, once Margaret turned 21 he was unable to prevent the wedding which was solemnised with Presbyterian rites by the Rev. Dr Steel at Sydney's Macquarie Street Church one day after her birthday. And while her parents refused to attend, Margaret was given away by the colony's attorney-general, Jack Want, and Alice Simpson stood in her mother's place. That evening George Scarlett scratched his daughter's name from the family bible.

The newly married couple departed on their honeymoon to Ballarat, the scene of some fierce anti-Chinese demonstrations during the goldrush. On this occasion they were met at the station by the mayor, several MPs and a crowd of well-wishers. That evening the Jubilee Singers serenaded the couple at a public banquet where Margaret was presented with a bracelet made from local gold. Next night there was a Scottish sing-song at the Town Hall where Quong gave his hosts one of his unique renditions of several Caledonian ballads. Twelve of the new-fangled telephones had been linked to Government House in Melbourne where the Edinburgh-born Governor Henry Loch and his wife Elizabeth listened in to the concert. Even the *Bulletin* wished the couple well for the future 'with the fervent hope that the lovely bride, though Tart in name, will never become Tart in nature'.

On their return to Sydney, Margaret immediately settled in as the chatelaine of Huntingtower, Quong's mansion whence he conducted his campaign against the import and sale of opium. It was here that he met with the two commissioners from the Qing emperor in 1887. The following year Quong was informed that the emperor had conferred upon him the rank of Mandarin of the Crystal Button. But before he could travel to Beijing for the induction, Quong was enmeshed in the political manoeuvrings of Premier Henry Parkes, whose anti-Chinese prejudice was never far beneath the surface of his appeal to the voters of New South Wales.

By now agitators in the trade union movement, led by cabinet-maker turned politician Ninian Melville and the city-councillor-cum-newspaper proprietor John Norton, were conducting a virulent anti-Chinese campaign. When a violent demonstration erupted over the arrival of the ships *Afghan* and *Tsinan* containing Chinese immigrants, Parkes turned to Quong Tart to board them and decide who among the passengers carried genuine naturalisation certificates. After a hastily assembled court case, the *bona fide* citizens were permitted to disembark (at 3 a.m.) while the 93 undocumented passengers departed in steerage.

In December 1888 Quong finally headed to China for his Crystal Button induction. On the way he called at Port Darwin where he addressed a public meeting, warning that the recent demonstrations in Sydney signalled a new phase in the anti-Chinese movement as 'an outcry by the labouring classes' against Chinese competition. He hoped, he said, that it would be overcome by 'Europeans and Chinese pulling together, and burying all dissentions'.

Alas, his call was either naive or simply wishful thinking. At exactly the same time, the *Daily Telegraph* in Sydney was editorialising, 'The objection to Chinese immigration is not confined to what some superficial critics may describe as the fears and prejudices of the working classes. [They ignore] the fixed determination of Australians to preserve this country for men of their own race.'

By then Sydney had hosted the 1888 Intercolonial Conference of Premiers on the Chinese question that was to lay the foundation for a national White Australia policy. It received petitions from the Victorian Chinese Residents Committee, a group of Sydney's Chinese merchants, and a separate one from Quong Tart that was considerably more conciliatory in tone, perhaps reflecting his social acceptance within the wider community if not his own in-laws.

All were ignored. It concluded that 'the further restriction of Chinese immigration is essential to the welfare of the people of Australasia' and it would be secured by diplomatic pressure on the imperial government in Westminster and uniform legislation in the colonies. The laws would restrict the numbers any ship could carry to Australia depending on its tonnage at the rate of one Chinese for every 500 tons, and make it an offence for any Chinese to travel from one colony to another without express permission.

However, the colonies did little to harmonise their legislation. Tasmania, where from the 1870s some 1000 Chinese tin miners had worked in the northeast of the island, retained its 1887 Act imposing a £10 poll tax and one migrant to 100 tons, while New South Wales imposed a £100 poll tax and one to 300 tons. Western Australia had barred Chinese from working on its 1890s gold discoveries so was not greatly affected; while the other colonies had abandoned the poll tax but retained the tonnage restriction.

The Northern Territory remained the odd man out. The chief customs officer, Alfred Searcy, wrote, 'It is only those who have lived in the Territory who can realise what an important factor the Chinese are. Remove them tomorrow and the residents would be left without fish, vegetables or fruit, to a large extent without meat, without laundries for their washing, neither would there be any tailors, cooks or domestic servants.'[3]

By now John Langdon Parsons and Vaiben L. Solomon were members of the South Australian parliament and Solomon, in particular, had turned against his former Chinese associates. Both now campaigned against them, claiming that their associations were nefarious secret societies or triads. However, in his annual report for 1890, John Knight made no mention of the secret societies and no action was taken by the parliament. Nor did he consider there was any need for additional police supervision. On the contrary, he wrote, 'The love of the Chinese for the Northern Territory is just about equal to that of the white man' and 'notwithstanding all that has been spoken and written against the Chinese, there is not a single mine where Chinamen are not working'.[4]

During the early 1890s several Chinese merchants emerged as leading mining entrepreneurs. And in 1891 the South Australian governor, the Earl of Kintore, visited Darwin where they entertained him at a banquet. The earl opined that the 'cheap and efficient labour' they employed was 'a prime factor in the successful development of the northern portion of the Territory'. But lest he be thought as being 'soft' on the Chinese, he later added, 'I desire to say that I entirely appreciate and sympathise with the determination of the colonists of the temperate zone not to be overrun by an alien race.'

As new gold strikes in the Northern Territory became increasingly rare, some of the poorer Chinese decided to move to Queensland, travelling on foot and carrying their meagre possessions. The Queensland police arrested some and turned others back, but a fairly steady stream made it through and the total Chinese population in the Territory fell by 2400.

In his South Australian election campaign of 1893, Solomon argued against the Chinese retaining any permanent footing in the Territory including freehold land or mining leases. Their role, he said, was merely that of labourers or servants. He was returned with an increased majority and two years later introduced a bill to give effect to his anti-Chinese policies. It was amended slightly in committee but passed into law as the *Chinese Exclusion Act*. It was the beginning of a permanent decline in the Chinese population in the Territory and by 1898 only about 1300 remained on the goldfields. Nevertheless, the merchants and the tradesmen remained an intrinsic component of the Darwin community.

When the new century arrived, the *Northern Territory Times* reporter was thoroughly entranced by the 1900 Chinese New Year celebrations: 'For an hour or two the streets lost their usual dreary aspect and became filled with a barbaric conglomeration of sights and sounds strangely out of tune in an Australian town,' he wrote. 'Gay coloured costumes, enormous banners sporting strange devices, and palanquins (or whatever they may be called) covered with gilt scroll work and loaded with edibles – and occasionally dignitaries – made up a rather gay spectacle, whilst the explosion of guns and crackers, the shrieking of bagpipes and the crashing of the infernal gongs kept things lively, and informed all and sundry that the Chinese element in our midst is still very much alive.'

But not for much longer.

PART TWO
CHINESE HISTORY AND POLITICS

CHAPTER FOURTEEN
'CHINESE' MORRISON

While Quong Tart was being duchessed as the smiling face of China in his adopted land, a remarkable Australian was becoming one of the most influential figures in the Middle Kingdom. Improbably, Geelong-born George Ernest Morrison would soon play a crucial role in the downfall of the Qing dynasty and China's political transformation as a republic.

His father, also George, was the first headmaster of Geelong College, having taken up the post shortly after his arrival from Scotland with his young wife Rebecca in 1861, and he would eventually become the principal shareholder in the college. George Ernest was born the following year, the second child of the union. He would be joined by three brothers and two more sisters, growing up in a boisterous, sports-loving family on the school grounds. 'We may not have been hard students but we lived healthy, happy lives,' he wrote later. 'We probably gave more time to outdoor play than to study.'[1]

In his teenage years his passion for long, solo walks began to show itself. 'My tastes were those of the nomad,' he wrote in his unpublished autobiography, *Reminiscences*. 'During the Christmas holidays I followed my bent, each year travelling further afield.' By 1880, aged seventeen, he was 180 centimetres tall and well built at 78 kilograms with fair hair, strong, regular features, good manners and in his own words, 'a very bashful nature'. In January that year he walked the 1000 kilometres from his home to Adelaide, informing his parents by letter posted ten days into his journey. 'I do hope you are not anxious about me at all,' he said. 'I shall be home in about three weeks or a month.' He reached his destination on 14 February and returned to Melbourne by steamer.

Young Morrison had read the works of the famous journalist-explorer Henry Stanley who had found the 'lost' missionary Dr Livingstone in darkest Africa, and he decided upon a career in journalism. 'It is the noblest, in my opinion, of all the professions,' he told his mother, 'as energy, courage, temperance and truthfulness are necessary to its success.' But his father insisted he at least give medicine a try. So George dutifully enrolled at Melbourne University. But while he was a bright student, he spent more time planning his next adventure than in studying his medical tomes and at eighteen he set forth in a canoe to paddle the length of the Murray River, from Echuca more than 2500 kilometres to the sea. Along the way he kept a meticulous diary and sent regular accounts of his adventures to the Melbourne periodical *The Leader*, published by David Syme, owner of the daily newspaper *The Age*.

Syme took a special interest in the young adventurer and this was certainly a factor in Morrison's concentration on writing rather than his medical studies. When he failed his second-year subjects, his parents sought an interview with his examiner, who told them that to allow George Ernest to become a doctor was 'akin to letting a mad dog loose in Collins Street'.

At the time Morrison was outraged but later confessed that being sacked from the course 'was one of the fortunate episodes of my life'. He approached David Syme with a plan to travel to the Pacific Islands and write an expose of the Kanaka trade led by the chief 'blackbirder', Robert Towns. And since *The Age* was a vigorous campaigner against the trade, Syme commissioned the project. En route Morrison wrote, 'I go to Queensland to commence the apprenticeship of a profession in which I earnestly hope some day to make my mark.'

He was soon sending back scarifying first-hand accounts of the kidnapping and ill-treatment of the islanders. The series caused an outcry from the shipowners and the sugar farmers engaged in the trade, and Morrison joined the argument calling it 'an accursed thing'. However, once the series was complete he was anxious to move on and in December 1882 he began a lone expedition that would bring him to international attention.

As a boy, Morrison had been fascinated by the tragedy of the Burke and Wills expedition of 1860 that sought to span the continent from south to north but ended with only one man surviving. His next adventure was to retrace that journey, starting in the small town of Normanton near the Gulf of Carpentaria to 'stroll' the 3250 kilometres south through the Queensland outback, New South Wales and Victoria to Melbourne.

The Normanton locals had called it 'suicide' since Morrison was heading out in high summer heat through sparsely populated country with only the rations and equipment he could carry in a small knapsack. And as it happened, he would be confronted by heatwaves, floods and all manner of dangers from crocodiles to venomous snakes. He often stopped at station homesteads where he was warmly welcomed. But there were times when the journey seemed endless. In western New South Wales the landscape, he wrote, 'seemed the very incarnation of dreary desolation. The days were very, very lonely.'

However, he arrived in Melbourne on 21 April 1883, exactly four months after setting out from the northern rim of the continent. It was an extraordinary feat of endurance and letters to *The Age,* which had run his accounts sent from post offices along the way, praised his 'dauntless courage' and 'invincible determination'.

The London newspapers also followed his progress and *The Times* editorialised, 'Mr Morrison's feat commands the admiration of all interested in exploration and must be set down as one of the most remarkable of pedestrian achievements.'

Morrison himself said later, 'If nothing else, my walk proved how great had been the progress of colonisation in the interior during the 22 years that had elapsed since the Burke and Wills party met with their disasters.'

Buoyed by his protégé's success, Syme then entrusted the 21-year-old with the leadership of an expedition to cross the wilds of Papua

New Guinea from Port Moresby to the northern coastline. It appealed to Morrison's desire to emulate his hero Stanley and he leapt at the chance. It was an appalling misjudgement on both men's part. And though Syme invested heavily in the equipment and manpower, and Morrison devoted himself single-mindedly to the task, it ended quickly and disastrously. After an exhausting 38 days they had penetrated no more than 50 kilometres into the jungle when their bearers deserted them and they were attacked by a war party of tribesmen. Morrison was speared in the face and stomach: 'As soon as I fell, I pulled out the spear which had hung from the corner of my eye and a torrent of blood rushed from my nose.' His second in charge, John Lyons, broke off the second shaft but that left the spear tips in Morrison's face and abdomen.

He was carried into Port Moresby on a blanket and after several days caught a ship to Cooktown where a medico gave him sufficient treatment to permit a further voyage to Melbourne. The facial spear point was extracted, without chloroform, by the city's leading surgeon, Sir Thomas Fitzgerald. However, his abdominal wound eluded the doctor's best efforts and Fitzgerald then accompanied Morrison on a long and painful voyage to Edinburgh. There Professor John Chiene, assisted by the celebrated Joseph Bell (the model for Arthur Conan Doyle's Sherlock Holmes), finally extracted the last of the wooden slivers.

The experience, Morrison found, had sapped his enthusiasm for journalism and at the same time revived his interest in medicine to the point where he returned to his studies at Edinburgh University. He was a model student and graduated with distinction in 1887. 'His knowledge of Medicine and Surgery is extensive and accurate, his abilities are great,' his examiner wrote. 'He is a widely read and cultured man. I know few whose success in life I can look upon as more certain.'

He was only 25 years old.

Having suppressed his wanderlust for almost three years, Morrison immediately surrendered to its charms and took ship for Canada, beginning a globe-trotting odyssey that would take him to the United States, the West Indies, Wales, Spain, Morocco and France, before returning to his native land in 1891.

He took up an appointment at the Ballarat District Hospital where he remained for two years until a dispute with the recalcitrant administration. They parted with mutual recriminations and he would never return to his medical career.

The wanderer set off again. He sailed first to the Philippines and then to Shanghai and Beijing (then known as Peking). In the Chinese capital he was immediately entranced by the panoply of the Qing dynasty when the melancholic young Guangxu emperor and his cortege passed by on their regal procession to the Forbidden City. Morrison then returned to Shanghai where he pawned a pair of boots, hat and socks for his fare to Japan. But the images of China had captured his imagination and it was during his brief sojourn in Kobe that he conceived the idea of crossing southern China from Shanghai to Burma and writing about his adventures in a travel book.

Once decided he was impatient to begin, so he sold a treasured telescope for the return fare. When he reached China's bustling second city, he had only 15 shillings to his name. He telegraphed home with his plan and his mother wired him £40. 'I always pay my debts,' he told her in a thank you letter, 'and I will of course return every penny with 5% interest.' Then he took out a map and traced the route of a very long march across the country which, in 1893, was largely unknown to the rest of the outside world.

Unbeknown to the peripatetic Australian however, a small band of his compatriots were already sprinkled across southern China in the garb of Christian missionaries. And most had been recruited from Melbourne. They had been inspired by the British head of the China Inland Mission, the Rev. Hudson Taylor who had visited Australia in 1889. According to his son Howard who accompanied him, four Melbourne ministers of various Christian denominations became 'much exercised about China's spiritual needs and claims' during the visit. 'To each of them came the conviction that Australian Christians ought to be doing something toward the evangelisation of the greatest heathen country in the world, and the one nearest their own shores.' By the end of his visit to Australia more than sixty eager recruits had applied to join the Mission and during his final meetings 'Mr Taylor was surrounded by the bright young volunteers who were returning with him to China.'[2]

They would be joined there by newcomers from around the Christian world. From October to December 1890 at least 53 volunteers in nine parties reached Shanghai from Europe, Canada and Australia. A further 78 arrived in the following three months including a party of Americans. Once in China the new recruits took a six-month course in the Chinese language and customs as well as instruction on spreading the Word. They were then posted to an inland station under the supervision of a senior missionary. After two years, successful candidates became junior missionaries and after a further three years were regarded as fitted for developing their own stations.

According to Howard Taylor, while the Australians were most welcome, it was the 50-strong Scandinavian contingent that really set their pulses racing. 'To the accompaniment of their guitars and hearts overflowing with praise, they taught us many a sweet refrain from their Swedish hymns,' he wrote. 'Few of them could speak much English, but they prayed with perfect freedom in our meetings and though we could not understand [their language] the sense of fellowship in Christ was very real.' He was especially moved by 'the postscript to a letter of thanks they wrote on leaving Shanghai for their up-country destinations: "March along – we are going to conquer! We have victory through the Blood!"'[3]

CHAPTER FIFTEEN
AN AUSTRALIAN IN CHINA

Before setting out on his expedition, Morrison outfitted himself in Chinese winter clothing – a wide-sleeved tunic, flowing skirt, sandals and a somewhat incongruous umbrella. He also attached a pigtail to the inside of a silk skullcap, perhaps to denote some observable loyalty to the emperor and so fall within the responsibility of the imperial officials in the lands through which he passed. Certainly it was not part of a deliberate disguise. The tall, fair, blue-eyed stranger attracted widespread curiosity throughout the 4800-kilometre journey. In his own words it was being undertaken 'by one who spoke no Chinese, who had no interpreter or companion, who was unarmed, but who trusted implicitly in the good faith of the Chinese'.

His notions of 'faith' bore no resemblance to that of his evangelising compatriots. Indeed, he had a roving eye and a healthy appetite for the opposite sex, and his early journal entries record his appreciation of the Chinese woman. 'She is head and shoulders above the Japanese,' he wrote, 'prettier, sweeter, more trustworthy ... I have seen girls in China who would be considered beautiful in any capital in Europe.'

Morrison began his journey by catching a regular British steamer up the Yangtse to Hangzhou then another to Yichang before broaching the famous Three Gorges *en route* to Chongqing. Here the mighty stream was navigable only in junks and smaller craft hauled over the rapids by teams of 'trackers' who worked, often in their hundreds, to drag the boats against a rushing current and unpredictable wind shifts. It was a perilous life and the workers were frequently torn from the narrow tracks cut into the rocky banks and flung to their death in the flooding waters.

The Australian hired a crew of four in a small boat and soon they were in rough water between the soaring cliffs. Morrison recalled: 'The boat danced in the rapid. My men on board shrieked excitedly that the towrope was fouling – it had caught on a rock – but their voices could not be heard by the trackers who were brought to with a jerk . . . our captain frantically waved to let go, and the next moment we were tossed bodily into the cataract; a wave buried the boat nose under and scared out of my wits I began to strip off my sodden clothes; but before I had half done both my men had miraculously fended the boat from a rock and we had slipped from danger into smooth water. Then my men laughed heartily. How it was done I do not know but I felt a keen admiration for their dexterity.'

On arrival in Chongqing they berthed by the customs boat. The European officer looked at Morrison's papers. 'Where from?'

'Australia.'

'The devil, so am I. What part?'

'Victoria.'

'Town?'

'Last from Ballarat.'

'My native town, by Jove. Jump up.'

When he saw the traveller's name the officer said, 'When I was last in Victoria I used to follow with much interest a curious walk across Australia from the Gulf of Carpentaria to Melbourne done by a namesake. Any relation? . . . The same man! I'm delighted to meet you.'

From Chongqing Morrison began his land journey accompanied by two coolies to carry his modest luggage and to buy and cook his food. 'On the morning of 14 March, I set out to cross 1600 miles [2575 kilometres] over Western China to Burma,' he wrote. 'Men did not speak hopefully of my getting through. There were the rains of June and July to be feared apart from other obstacles.' These included mountainous pathways, rock slides, rushing waters, bandits, virulent diseases and the ever-present danger of physical accident or food poisoning.

He walked at a very brisk pace and regularly covered 48 kilometres a day. From time to time he would hire a sedan chair and bearers to ease the way. The price was trifling. Indeed, the entire journey from Shanghai to Mandalay cost him no more than £20. According to Morrison, 'At nightfall, we always reached some large village or town where my cook selected the best inn for my resting place, the best being the one that promised him the largest squeeze [kickback].' However, while the inns were often rough, the hospitality offered was invariably warm and friendly.

Morrison often came upon mission stations where the welcome from the isolated Christians was overwhelming. However, he found little evidence that their enthusiasm was securing the promised conversions of the 'heathens'. There were, however, groups of 'rice Christians' who attached themselves to the missions in the hope of securing earthly favours such as a ration of rice.

The Wanhsien Inland Mission, opened in 1887 and run by Australians, was typical, as Morrison observed: 'There are, unfortunately, no converts, but there are three hopeful "inquirers". One of the three was shown to me and I do not wish to write unkindly but I am compelled to say that [he] was a poor, wretched, ragged coolie who sells the commonest gritty cakes in a rickety stall round the corner from the mission and belongs to a very humble order of blunted intelligence. The poor fellow is the father of a little girl of three who is both deaf and dumb. And there is the fear that his fondness for the little one tempts him to hope that when the foreign teachers regard him as adequately converted, they may be willing to restore speech and hearing to his poor little offspring. It is a scant harvest.'

Morrison was also scathing about the opium trade which was now being cultivated across southern China: 'From the time I left Hupei till I reached the boundary of Burma, a distance of 1600 miles [2575 kilometres], I never remember to have been out of sight of the poppy.' One of his coolies smoked it regularly, but without noticeable effect. 'However', he wrote, 'Morphia pills are sold in Chongqing by the

Chinese chemists to cure the opium habit. This profitable remedy was introduced by the foreign chemists of the coastal ports and adopted by the Chinese. It converts a desire for opium into a taste for morphia, a mode of treatment analogous to changing one's stimulant from colonial beer to methylated spirit.'

The adventurer reached Mandalay in excellent health and with more than enough material to write what would become a classic travelogue, *An Australian in China,* and he was anxious to begin the book. But when he reached Calcutta by ship, he almost died from malarial fever. He was nursed back to health by Mary Joplin, a Eurasian girl, and when he was sufficiently recovered they went on a trip to the French settlement in the hills above the city where they became lovers.

By the time he returned to Australia, he was faced with the prospect of resuming his medical practice or heading for the UK with £30 in his pocket and the half-finished manuscript of his journey across China. For Morrison, 'There was never any doubt as to the decision. I never seriously contemplated the discomforts of a private medical practice.' He signed on to the SS *Warrego* as ship's surgeon and over the next two months of the voyage completed his book. And when he arrived in London the first publisher he showed it to – Horace Cox – offered him an immediate £75 advance. While awaiting publication, he wrote a thesis for his doctorate on the hereditary transmission of abnormalities. It was immediately accepted by his Scottish examiners and the Edinburgh University awarded him his MD in August 1885.

Morrison then experienced a life-changing coincidence. When the book was published and well-reviewed, a medical colleague to whom he'd confided his journalistic ambitions happened to share a club with George Buckle, the editor of *The Times.* They fell into conversation over brandies and on Tuesday 22 October, to his 'profound astonishment', Morrison received a letter from the paper's manager, the legendary Moberly Bell, asking him to call on him at Printing House Square.

When he arrived, Bell came straight to the point. 'I have read your book,' he said. 'Would you care to go to Peking as our correspondent?'

Morrison, with the directness of the Australian-born, responded that he would prefer Siam.

Bell pressed the point. 'Compared with China, Siam is of minor importance to us. Will you come and dine with us quietly one evening?'

Morrison agreed and, after dinner with the Bells, Buckle and most of the foreign department of *The Times,* the appointment was formalised. Moreover his journey would include an assignment on behalf of the British secret service to French Indo-China where Britain was negotiating a treaty with the French colonial administration. He was still in transit when the treaty was signed. Nevertheless, he said, 'I did the work I was asked to do, whether satisfactory or not remains to be seen.'

Arriving in Peking on 15 March 1897, he wrote, 'My new life was about to begin.' And while his journalism in China would be of intense interest to the British Foreign Office, they would never again seek to engage him in undercover operations. There was no need – Morrison's public disclosures would be far more extensive than any intelligence gathered through their diplomatic and clandestine sources.

CHAPTER SIXTEEN
AUSTRALIAN FEDERATION

In Australia, the 1888 Intercolonial Conference was only the first of a series that adopted and formalised the country's racist inheritance. According to White Australia historian, Myra Willard, thereafter 'the cry of "Australia for the Australians" completely drowned the feeble voice of . . . cosmopolitanism'. It was fuelled by wild rumours. 'Some thought that China had the ultimate design of forming a colony in some part of the north remote from the European settlements,' she says. 'The suspicion was groundless, but at the time it intensified public feeling [and] the idea obtained the greater credence because it was publicly expressed by Sir Henry Parkes.'[1]

As the panic spread, meetings were held in all the colonies' large centres. They demanded Britain act diplomatically to end Chinese migration. Premier Parkes telegraphed the British colonial secretary, Lord Knutsford, in the pompous circumlocution of the day: 'If protection cannot be afforded as now sought, the Australian Parliaments must act from force of public opinion in devising measures to defend the Colonies from consequences which they cannot relax in their effort to divert.'

The inference was that the public would take matters into their own hands. Indeed, according to Willard, 'The disorderly and cowardly elements of the populations of Brisbane and Sydney seized the opportunity to attack some of the Chinese and to damage their property.'

Parkes later complained that, 'Whatever we might do, we knew we should be blamed. If we did nothing it would be cowardly indifference to the danger; if we went half-way, it would be blundering incapacity to deal with it; if we went the whole way it would be high-mindedness and tyranny. We tried to see our simple duty.'[2]

His 'simple duty' became a draconian bill which the legislative council refused to pass. But its essential provisions in a Victorian equivalent were later approved by the privy council as providing for 'the exclusion of all aliens as a prerogative exercisable by the Crown'. Even that was insufficient to appease the mob. The blanket restriction of Asiatic immigration – including Indians and Japanese as well as Chinese – was continually raised in colonial parliaments in the early 1890s. And when Japan defeated China in the war of 1895 which gave them a foothold on the mainland and the transfer of Taiwan to their control, new fears were raised about Japanese expansionism.

These concerns were central to the Intercolonial Conference of 1896 when the premiers resolved to extend the 1888 Restriction Bill to include 'all coloured races', though the Queensland delegation made an exception for Pacific Islanders.

The British government, anxious about the reaction in its Asian and South Asian colonies, took a more conciliatory stand. The new colonial secretary, Joseph Chamberlain, told a meeting of the colonial leaders in London the following year that he 'sympathised' with the Australians' sentiments that 'there shall not be an influx of people alien in civilisation, alien in religion, alien in customs [who] would most seriously interfere with the legitimate rights of the existing labour population'. However, it would be 'most painful' for Her Majesty Queen Victoria, whose Diamond Jubilee they were celebrating, to be asked to sanction their exclusion by reason of their colour or race.

Chamberlain's solution was the 'Natal Method' first suggested by the South Africans, which involved a language test before admittance would be granted. He offered this compromise to the premiers: 'I hope that during your visit it may be possible for us to arrange a form of words which will avoid hurting the feelings of any of Her Majesty's subjects, while at the same time amply protect the Australian Colonies against any invasion of the class to which you would justly object.'

The premiers appreciated the subtleties involved and three of the colonies – New South Wales, Tasmania and Western Australia

– legislated to that effect, though the terms were slightly different in each case. South Australia and Victoria preferred to wait until a federal government, by then very much a live issue, could legislate for the Australian Commonwealth. Queensland, which had admitted more than 3000 Japanese indentured labourers to replace the Kanakas, was unwilling to place restrictions on this foreign workforce. For its part, the Japanese government was prepared to accept the status quo. Their only objection was to be treated as if they 'were on the same level as Chinese or other less advanced populations of Asia'.[3]

It was an attitude that would have the most profound effects on the future peace and security of East Asia and Australia in the years ahead. But at the end of the 19th century, Australia's stance on Asiatic immigration was piecemeal and unprincipled. All the colonies restricted Chinese immigration but the means would not be formalised until they united to become the Federation of the Commonwealth of Australia. Indeed, according to Alfred Deakin, one of the founding fathers and the second Australian prime minister: 'No motive power operated more universally or more powerfully in dissolving the . . . divisions which separated us than the desire that we should be one people, and remain one people, without the admixture of other races.'[4] Deakin himself was an unabashed racist, but with a twist: 'It is not the bad qualities but the good qualities of these alien races that make them so dangerous to us,' he said. 'It is their inexhaustible energy, their power of applying themselves to new tasks, their endurance and low standard of living that make them such competitors.'

The first Australian federal parliament was opened with due ceremony on 9 May 1901 by the Duke of York (later King George V) at Melbourne's Royal Exhibition Building, the only premises large enough in the Victorian capital to accommodate the 14,000 guests. Thereafter from 1901 to 1927, the federal members and senators met in the Victorian parliament (while the state representatives sat in the Royal Exhibition Building).

In the election of the first parliament 'White Australia' was the one issue that united all contenders. A census taken immediately after parliament assembled revealed a total population of 3,683,801 of whom the Chinese represented less than 1 per cent at 29,433 men and 474 women. In the Northern Territory they still outnumbered Europeans three to one, but overall in the ten years since the previous census Chinese numbers had decreased by 3500. Nevertheless, during the first year of the new parliament its members were in furious agreement in passing the Immigration Restriction Bill.

There were differing views on how the exclusion of aliens – particularly Chinese – might best be achieved. Many regarded the Natal Method as a back-door approach instead of the 'honest and straightforward' course of banning them outright. Indeed, were it not for the 'mother country's' plea to spare the feelings of the Queen and her colonial subjects, their exclusion would have been unvarnished and complete. Instead, the bill prohibited the entry to Australia 'of any person who, when asked to do so, fails to write out at dictation, and sign in the presence of an officer, a passage of 50 words in length in a European language'.

It also excluded 'criminals, persons diseased in body or mind, and those likely to become a charge on the public purse'. Moreover the rise of the union movement from the 1893 Depression and the newly realised clout of its political arm, the Australian Labor Party, added an economic element to the legislation. Also banned were 'any contractors prepared to work for wages which, in the Australian people's opinion, would react injuriously on Australian employment'.[5]

The Japanese lobbied hard to be excluded from the bill and to be treated the same as Europeans. The government of Edmund Barton, Australia's first prime minister, was unmoved so they appealed to Westminster which was equally obdurate. However, in 1905 Australia would make one cosmetic concession by changing the test from a 'European' to 'any prescribed language'. Five years later an amendment aimed directly at the Chinese dealt severely with the smuggling of immigrants in ships calling at Australian ports, particularly Darwin.

★ ★ ★

Meantime, events in China had taken a dramatic turn and – not for the last time – George Morrison found himself at the centre of the action. Almost from the moment he had arrived in Beijing, his meticulously researched and clearly written dispatches had marked him as an authoritative and uncompromising figure. He declined to live in the diplomatic quarter, preferring the Chinese section where he could receive visitors from all quarters in relative anonymity.

He would never become fluent in Chinese but he surrounded himself with local and expatriate assistants. And as well as the diplomatic corps, he was assiduous in making contacts with the Chinese political class and the *cognoscenti*. Moreover, at every opportunity he travelled to the areas where the news was taking place. It was this willingness to expend journalistic shoe leather that gave him his first major 'scoop': when he saw for himself that czarist Russia's gift of a rail link in northern China – partly funded by British bank loans – had changed course to give the Russians a direct line to China's most cherished defence project, the strategic warm-water anchorage of Port Arthur.

It caused a sensation in London and severely embarrassed the foreign secretary Lord Curzon who, after a diplomatic investigation, was forced to confirm the accuracy of the report in parliament. It also earned Morrison the enduring animosity of the Russian legation. In time they would be joined in their hostility towards the Australian by the Germans, the Italians and the Japanese.

However, it was the Boxer Rebellion of 1900 that propelled China – and Morrison himself – to the forefront of international attention. Its origins lay in a combination of the outrageous incursions of the Western powers on Chinese sovereignty, and a political convulsion in the Manchu court.

The Qing dynasty was in a parlous state, dominated by Cixi (pronounced Tse-Hsi), another of the remarkable women who had risen to the peak of imperial power. She had entered the Forbidden City as a teenage concubine to the Emperor Xianfeng and within a year gave birth to a son, Zaichun, in 1856. Five years later the boy was raised to the throne on the death of his father and Cixi became the dowager empress. A deft and merciless hand at court politics, she contrived the downfall of a group of regents who stood between her and the imperial prerogative; and when Zaichun died in 1875 she installed her nephew as the Guangxi emperor. (Coincidentally, it was this emperor's cortege that had so entranced Morrison during his first visit to Beijing.)

Cixi remained a power behind the throne, but in 1898 when Guangxi proposed a range of far-reaching reforms, she feared the loss of dynastic entitlement. The reformers plotted to assassinate her but she learned of their plans – probably through General Yuan Shikai, commander of the powerful 'Newly Created Army' – and placed the emperor under house arrest on an island in the lake of the Forbidden City. She then sent her guards to capture the plotters. Many were executed but the leader, Kang Youwei, escaped on board a British steamer and went into exile in Japan where, with Japanese encouragement, he organised attacks on the Qing government and particularly Cixi's military protector, Yuan Shikai.

Morrison first noted the presence of the Boxers – a European rendering of 'The Society of the Righteous and Harmonious Fists' – on 17 April 1900 on his return from a trip home to Australia. By then thousands of dispossessed and starving peasants, most of them patriotic young men, had flocked to their banner. 'The danger of the Boxers is increasing,' Morrison wrote in dispatch. He attributed the upsurge of unrest to a widespread drought for which the peasants blamed the evil influence of the foreigners. But while that undoubtedly sharpened their discontent, there was growing resentment among all classes towards the high-handed intruders. And the missionaries, with their patronising attitudes towards the 'heathens', were the most visible symbols of Western abuse and exploitation. They were the first to feel the Boxers' rage.

The Catholic Bishop of Beijing, Monsignor Favier, reported that 61 men, women and children in the hinterland had been killed, some of them burned alive. Soon reports were flooding in from around the country of fearful attacks on mission stations. Then, on 28 May, reports reached Morrison that Fengtai railway station, 24 kilometres from Beijing, was ablaze. He armed himself and rode to investigate: 'As we approached, black smoke was rising and the whole countryside was afoot, streaming towards the station. The sheds were on fire and the villagers from all around were looting. We could do nothing.'[6]

The Manchu leadership was divided. Grand Secretary Kangyi openly supported the Boxers and invited them into the city, while General Yuan Shikai, who had no patience with their claims to be immune to their enemies' firearms, proved his point by shooting some of the claimants in front of their compatriots. The dowager empress played an artful game between the two.

On 9 June the grandstand and stables of the Peking Race Course were burned down and word spread through the diplomatic community that the Boxers intended to kill every foreigner in the capital. The British minister Sir Claude MacDonald sent an urgent appeal for a relief column to Admiral Edward Seymour at the port of Tientsin 140 kilometres away. Seymour immediately dispatched 500 men on a train and arranged for more trains to follow, carrying a total of 1400 troops including members of the New South Wales Corps.

However, the Boxers attacked the leading train and halted it halfway between the two cities. Four days later the German minister Klemens von Ketteler reacted to a provocation in Legation Street by attacking a young Boxer with his walking stick. In response, according to Morrison, 'The Boxers came down in force from the north of the city, and the burning of foreign buildings began.' They swarmed into the area adjoining the diplomatic quarter that housed the Chinese converts and servants, as well as shopkeepers supplying goods to the foreigners. Chanting 'Kill! Kill!', they pursued wave after wave of terrified Chinese who swept down Legation Street to escape the massacre. Many were caught and butchered.

Other units burned Christian churches and mission stations and all the buildings in the eastern section occupied by foreign employees of the Maritime Customs. By 14 June, with the relief convoy still blockaded and under fire, the foreign legations deployed their defensive forces on the walls and in the alleys of the quarter and opened fire on their assailants. Their prospects trembled on the brink of catastrophe.

CHAPTER SEVENTEEN
THE BOXER REBELLION

Morrison joined the diplomatic community within the huge British compound. But he feared for the many hundreds of 'rice Christians' in the imperial city who had been abandoned to their fate by the Westerners. Travel writer Henry Savage Landor, who was also taking shelter in the legation, wrote on 15 June: 'Dr Morrison, who has a nobler heart than many of the selfish refugees, applied to Sir Claude for guards to rescue them. Twenty British were given to him and were joined by a force of Germans and Americans. Morrison guided them to the spot, and it will be ever after a bright spot in the record of the doctor's life that he was the means of saving from atrocious tortures and death over a hundred helpless Chinese.'[1]

Morrison himself wrote in his diary that on his mission he witnessed terrible scenes of devastation and butchery: 'Acres of buildings on fire. Slaughtered and burning people. Horrible sights. One young man and young woman lying hand in hand nearly dead, bleeding but rescued. Came back dead tired.' The next morning he was off again with his military escort and on this occasion he engaged in a fire fight with a band of Boxers. 'I myself killed six,' he wrote, 'we caught them while [they were] actually massacring five of their captives.'

The leading diplomats then called a meeting to discuss the crisis. They had been warned by the Chinese foreign office that unless all foreigners were evacuated from the city in 24 hours, their safety could not be guaranteed. The government offered a protective force of imperial troops to escort them to Tientsin. Sir Claude Macdonald dithered, unable to take a firm decision, but led by the American and Italian legates the ministers at the meeting decided to accept the ultimatum and leave Beijing, thus abandoning their faithful Chinese servants to the mercy of the Boxers.

When he heard of the decision, Morrison stormed into the British legation and confronted the minister then repeated his outrage to the American station head, Edwin Conger: 'I am ashamed to be a white man,' he snapped. 'Of all the inhuman, barbarous, pusillanimous decrees I have ever heard of, the decision of the eleven ministers yesterday is the worst.'[2]

His protests were in vain and later that morning Morrison saw ministers assembling at the French legation to plan the evacuation, while two colourfully decorated sedan chairs waited outside the German embassy for Baron von Ketteler. But when von Ketteler set off, a group of imperial troops loyal to the dowager empress surrounded his chair and a Manchu rifleman shot him through the head. All support for an evacuation instantly evaporated and that evening diplomats from less well defended legations, as well as missionaries based in the city, streamed into the British compound.

By the next day a total of 473 civilians, 409 troops and more than 3000 Chinese 'converts' and servants were besieged in an enclave comprising an open area known as the Fu, the Peking Hotel, several banks, shops and houses, and in an L-shaped wedge in the legations of Britain, Russia, America, Spain, Japan, Germany, France and Italy. To Morrison it was 'a seething polyglot mass' and he was in his element. He bunked with employees of the Hong Kong & Shanghai Bank and made daily rounds of the perimeter, helping out where he could. He often dined with his friends, the American first secretary Herbert Squires, his wife Harriet and their house guest Polly Condit Smith. Polly described him as 'the most attractive man at our impromptu mess. He works where a strong man is needed and he is as dirty, happy and healthy a hero as one could find anywhere.'

The relief column remained blockaded by the imperial forces and day and night the Boxers, together with military marksmen, hammered the legation defenders with incessant rifle fire. The death toll mounted and, by the beginning of July, 38 guards had been killed, with another 55 seriously wounded. When the hot winds blew in from the northwest, the Boxers tried to burn the foreigners out; and from time to time the legations mounted counter-attacks on their tormentors. But no attempt was made to overwhelm the legations with a massed assault by Yuan Shikai's Newly Created Army, and Morrison retained an abiding faith that the relief expedition would break through and rescue them.

News of the beginning of the siege had reached the outside world but then communications with Beijing were cut and rumours of their fate took the place of solid information. Morrison was deeply frustrated that he couldn't tell the story that was gripping the world and on 6 July he made a desperate attempt to smuggle a report to his newspaper. He wrote a dispatch in neat tiny writing on both sides of a thin, water-proofed paper measuring 8 centimetres by 4 centimetres. In 350 words he gave a graphic picture of a community 'in great anxiety at prolonged delay of troops' but 'in general good health'. He folded it in a small ball, placed it in a bowl of gruel and gave it to a young Chinese man who went over the southern wall with orders to make his way to Tientsin. However, the messenger was caught by imperial soldiers and sent back. A fretful Morrison pasted the dispatch into his diary.

He made several sorties across no-man's-land to visit the Fu and once among the Chinese he met a scene of terrible deprivation and danger. Many were diseased and dying. The Boxers took to shelling their compatriots and during one visit he counted 50 cannonades. He reverted from journalist to medico and did what he could to ease their suffering. But then, on 16 July, as he approached the Fu with a Japanese party led by the British Captain B.M. Strouts, the Boxers opened fire at short range.

'I heard some shots,' Morrison wrote later, 'how many I cannot tell, and felt a cut in my thigh. At the same moment, "My God" said Strouts and he fell over into the arms of Colonel Shiba. I jumped forward and with Shiba dragged Strouts out of fire though shots were still coming whizzing by us . . . I tried to slip my handkerchief round his thigh and stepped out to find a twig to use as a tourniquet. But the result was not good . . . the poor fellow was conscious and asked me where I was hit. I said mine was unimportant. Then I fainted.'

The Japanese troops carried both men back to a makeshift ward in Sir Claude's library where Strouts died. Morrison would recover in fairly short order, but on that day a bogus report appeared in his own newspaper stating that he and every other foreign defender in the diplomatic quarter had been massacred. It had been filed by an American fraudster in Shanghai and in the absence of the slightest indication from Beijing of any life remaining in the legation district, *The Times* joined every other newspaper in the rush to print.

In fact, the Manchu moderate Prince Qing had written to Macdonald that day suggesting a ceasefire. And the dowager empress herself had written a telegram to Queen Victoria attributing the attack on the legations to 'bandits' and 'as one woman to another', they should understand each other's difficulties and Britain should remain on friendly terms with China to protect her trade links. Victoria declined to reply but the dispatch of the telegram was evidence not only of the division within the Manchu court but of Cixi's realisation that the stalemate had to be broken.

Herbert Squires had attempted to smuggle another of Morrison's messages out to Tientsin and unbeknown to the Australian this one made it through. *The Times* gave it a major display when it finally arrived on 2 August. 'There has been a cessation of hostilities since July 18,' Morrison reported, 'but for fear of treachery there has been no relaxation of vigilance. The Chinese soldiers continue to strengthen the barricades around the besieged area and also the batteries on top of the Imperial City Wall, but in the meantime they have discontinued firing, probably because they are short of ammunition. The main bodies of the Imperial soldiers have left Peking in order to meet the relief forces.' He had little doubt that the international force, now expected to be 18,000-strong, would prevail. 'All the Ministers and the members of the Legation and their families are in good health . . . We are contentedly awaiting relief.'

When relief arrived on 10 August, the Boxers made a frantic, last-ditch assault. 'For the last two days we had to sustain a furious fusillade and bombardment and our casualties were many,' Morrison wrote. But then at 3 a.m. in the darkness of 14 August, he was awakened by 'the booming of guns to the east and the welcome sound of volley firing'. An hour later the first Indian troops under British command arrived in the Tartar City. 'They passed down Canal Street and amid a scene of indescribable emotion and marched to the British Legation. The siege had been raised.'

Four days later the whole of Beijing was under foreign control, including an Australian naval brigade of units gathered from New South Wales, Victoria and South Australia that had arrived just after the siege ended.

The Manchu court fled to the ancient capital of Xi'an while the foreign troops indulged in an orgy of looting and destruction. Morrison was scathing in his reports of their vandalism. The Australians were comparatively restrained, though their duties involved the official execution of scores of captured Boxers in the weeks and months that followed.

On New Year's Day 1901 Morrison attended a grand parade of the foreign forces before the Imperial Palace. It included the New South Wales Minister for Public Works, E.W. O'Sullivan, a dogged advocate of the White Australia policy. The parade was followed by a lunch in honour of the New Year and the founding of the Commonwealth of Australia. 'All the Australians were there,' Morrison wrote. 'Colonel O'Sullivan made a stupid speech at which all laughed.'[3]

The Bulletin's Andrew Barton 'Banjo' Paterson had arrived in September and written a profile of 'Chinese' Morrison whom he called 'a tall, ungainly man' who had become 'the uncrowned king of China'. Morrison told him, 'You can't conceive of the amount of trade there is here. And it's nothing to what it will be. There's gold mines and tin mines and quicksilver and all sorts of minerals in the interior. There's all this wonderful agricultural land on the coast and there are hills all over blue grass, splendid grazing land in the interior. But nobody's game to put any money into the trade because there's really no government in China.'4

CHAPTER EIGHTEEN
CHANGING CHINESE HISTORY

Two years later Morrison returned on holiday to Australia where he was given a rousing reception by leading members of the federal government, particularly Alfred Deakin who would become prime minister six months later. Indeed, Deakin would write of his pleasure at meeting 'the gifted Australian Dr Ernest Morrison who has attained a quasi-ambassadorial authority [in China], occasionally overshadowing representatives of the King'.[1]

Morrison was able to tell Deakin that little had occurred since his interview with Banjo Paterson to change his view of governance in Beijing. The Qing dynasty was in terminal decline. Since her return from Xi'an, a humiliated Cixi, resigned to the fact that her forces would never be able to resist the foreigners, sought desperately to regain 'face' with her people. The Manchu could no longer rule by *force majeure* so she proclaimed a widespread program of institutional reforms – the same reforms she had so bitterly opposed in 1898.

Under the new order, the sale of public offices was curtailed and in an overburdened bureaucracy useless officials were summarily dismissed. Traditional public examinations – both civil and military – were abolished. Yuan Shikai was given leave to create new regional armies (who answered to his personal command) and they would be headed by his own northern 'Peiyang' army. A new government school system based on the Japanese model was instituted. Proposals were discussed to develop a constitution. Bright students from Beijing and the provinces were selected to study abroad.

All were to no avail. Indeed, the exposure of the young scholars to alternative systems – particularly in Japan, Britain and the United States

– produced a group of activists determined to overthrow Manchu rule, preferably by persuasion but if necessary by force. Even as the proclamations issued from the Forbidden City, the gunsmoke of revolution was wafting on the political breeze.

While in Australia, Morrison had made contact with the leading Chinese merchants and encouraged them to develop shipping and trade links with their former homeland. He had found a congenial companion in Mei Quong Tart in earlier visits and they continued their friendship via correspondence. By now Quong Tart was regarded by political circles as the 'unofficial ambassador' of his country. On this occasion they met with a group of Chinese businessmen at Sydney's Elite Hall and Morrison noted in his diary that, 'The evening became rather merry. We drank much champagne.' The Chinese businessmen presented him with a petition to deliver to the emperor, requesting the appointment of a consul in Sydney and suggesting Quong Tart for the post. In the morning Morrison was farewelled at the wharf by colleagues in the Australian press 'and by Quong Tart and some of his henchmen who cheered me'.

It was the last occasion they would meet. In August the previous year Quong Tart had been viciously attacked by a deranged thief at his Sydney office. The intruder, Frederick Duggan, alias Flood, struck him several shocking blows on the head with an iron bar in broad daylight. Tributes poured in and the investigation engaged the entire New South Wales police force. Duggan stood trial twice because the first jury was unable to reach a verdict. On the second occasion, in December 1902, he was found guilty and sentenced to twelve years imprisonment.

Quong Tart appeared to be making a slow recovery but in the wake of Morrison's visit he aged rapidly and in July 1903 he became bedridden. Seven days later, at only 53, he died of heart failure. More than 1500 people – including an array of the state's political and business leaders – accompanied his coffin on its journey to Rookwood Cemetery where the service was conducted in both English and Chinese. An anonymous poet penned a verse which concluded with the appeal that 'God rest him and reward him with an everlasting name'.

By now the political affray in China had extended to the diaspora in South-East Asia and Australia. Formal associations arose in Sydney and Melbourne both for and against the imperial government. The debate found a public outlet in the *Tung Wah News* that championed the monarchy through the Empire Reform Association, and the *Chinese Times* published in Melbourne which would become the official organ of the revolutionary Kuomintang (the National People's Party). The *Chinese Australian Herald* remained neutral and would enjoy a 30-year lifespan with regular print runs of 6000 copies. The Chinese in Australia showed their support for reform in other ways – a queue-cutting society was organised in Melbourne to express their anti-Manchu sentiment. Its members defiantly removed their pigtails, the symbol of imperial China, and started dressing in Western style.

The revolutionaries' most prominent international face was that of Sun Yatsen, born in Guangdong in 1866 and raised for the most part in Hawaii by his elder brother, Sun Mei. There he quickly learned English and proved himself a bright student at the Iolani School where he was introduced to Christianity. He graduated to a local college but Sun Mei became concerned that his younger brother was embracing the Western religion and sent the seventeen-year-old back to China. But, the attraction of Christianity persisted and after matriculating from the Hong Kong Central School, Sun Yatsen studied medicine and earned his license to practise in 1892.

However the call to topple the Manchus outweighed his attachment to medicine and after his petitions for reform were ignored by the Qing viceroy, Sun Yatsen returned to Hawaii and embarked on a career as a revolutionary. His 'Revive China Society' attracted Chinese expatriates and with links to secret societies on the mainland, he staged several abortive uprisings in the south.

Despite their failures, Sun Yatsen embarked on a relentless fundraising campaign among overseas Chinese in America, Europe, Japan and

South-East Asia. He was detained at the Chinese legation in London where the imperial secret service attempted to kill him but he was spirited away – with the assistance of *The Times* – and operated from a Japanese headquarters.

By 1904 Sun Yatsen had developed his manifesto of a United League – *Tongmenghui* – to establish China as a republic with 'Three Principles of the People': nationalism, democracy and social welfare. But while his influence was spreading in the diaspora, each new uprising on the mainland met the same sad fate as its predecessor.

Morrison regarded him as an ineffectual 'crackpot'. However, by 1904 he had been joined in China by a fellow Australian newspaperman, William Donald, whose influence with Sun Yatsen, and through him the conduct of China's affairs, would rival and even surpass that of his senior colleague. In fact, Donald would change the course of China's history.

★ ★ ★

Born in Lithgow, New South Wales, in 1875, Bill Donald was raised in the sober Presbyterian home of his father George, a stonemason turned building contractor, and mother Marion Wiles, the daughter of a railway foreman. George insisted that his son learn a trade and found him an apprenticeship as a printer at the *Lithgow Mercury*. It was a small, 'hands on' workplace and the paper's veteran editor, James Ryan, taught young Bill the skills and pitfalls of early 20th century journalism. Ryan cultivated the social conscience the young man had absorbed at the parental dinner table and encouraged the self-confidence needed to interact with people of all race and station in the cut and thrust of his profession.

By 1898, the 23-year-old Donald had moved further west to Bathurst where he edited *The National Advocate* and two years later graduated to the metropolis at Sydney's *Daily Telegraph* as police roundsman. He was soon upgraded to the sub-editor's table and late one night had a fateful meeting with a visiting 'Asia hand', Petrie Watson, who was passing through and in need of a loan until the banks opened. They dined together and Donald gave him all the money in his pockets – 17 shillings – and thought no more of it. Clearly, he'd made a strong impression because a year later, after he'd moved to the Melbourne *Argus* as a political writer, he received a letter from Watson's employer, Thomas Reid in Hong Kong, offering him a job on his *China Mail*. He would start as a sub-editor but was promised the editorship once he settled in. Donald tossed it across the desk to a fellow reporter who read it quickly. 'Adventure,' he said. 'Take it.'[2]

Donald sailed from Melbourne in May 1903. At the time, according to his biographer, he was 'powerfully built with a bold, purposeful stride which might have seemed like a swagger in a lesser man. He dressed in tweed jacket or navy blue blazer, grey flannel pants, white shirt, tie often askew. He was five feet nine [177 centimetres] with a high forehead, blue eyes, a drooping left eyelid, straight nose and large mouth. His hair was brown, complexion fair. With his rugged Caledonian looks, he and George Morrison could have passed for brothers.'[3]

The *China Mail* had been founded in 1845 as a weekly and was one of three newspapers currently in circulation in the colony. Much of its news came from England and its China coverage consisted mainly of shrill editorials demanding reform of the Manchu government and greater British access to mainland trade. On Donald's arrival, the big issue of the day was the growing international anger towards an aggressive Russia which had annexed three Manchurian provinces from China in a secret treaty forced upon the weakened Manchu. Morrison had exposed the treaty in another of his remarkable scoops.

At the same time Britain had signed a defence alliance with Japan. The British government urged the Japanese, who had long had imperial designs on Manchuria, to solve the matter by diplomatic means. However, as negotiations dragged on, Morrison took the lead in one article after another, pressing them to take direct action. So blatant did his advocacy become that when hostilities finally broke out between the two powers in 1904, it was frequently referred to as 'Morrison's war'.

At 12.20 a.m. on 8 February, and without courtesy of a declaration, the Japanese launched a surprise attack on the Russian fleet at anchor in Port Arthur. Blacked-out destroyers fired torpedoes with deadly effect on the Russians' new battleships *Retvisan* and *Tsarevitch* and crippled the cruiser *Pallada*.

Bill Donald had just arrived in Japan on assignment to cover the war, while a deeply frustrated Morrison remained in Beijing since Moberly Bell had appointed Major-General Sir Alexander Tulloch, former military adviser to the Australian colonies, as the *Times'* military expert for the duration. Bell had also arranged the charter of a ship to carry another correspondent as close as possible to the fighting. The correspondent would radio his reports to a rewrite man at a receiving station on the China coast for relay to London.

While Morrison fumed in Beijing, Donald found himself stuck in Tokyo for several weeks until he was able to board ship for Tientsin *en route* – he hoped – for the fighting in Manchuria; but in the event no reporters were able to approach closer than 20 kilometres from the action.

Finally he abandoned the battlefront altogether and returned to Hong Kong where on 17 September 1904 he married Mary Wall, a blue-eyed blonde known as 'Polly' whom he had met back in Australia some years previously. According to his biographer, 'The newlyweds didn't really know each other: they had conducted most of their courtship by mail and neither realised that the other had a fiery temper. They had little in common . . . and were incapable of building a happily married life together.'[4]

Meanwhile, Morrison, courtesy of the Japanese, finally reached the captured Port Arthur but rather than applauding his host's fighting prowess, he was contemptuous of the Russian commander, General Anatoly Stoessel. 'No foreign officer can explain the reason for the [Russian] capitulation,' he wrote. 'All accounts praise the courage of the Russian rank and file . . . all accounts agree that no man who ever held a responsible command less deserved the title of hero than General Stoessel.'[5]

But the Russians were not done yet. The czar ordered the Baltic Fleet into the battle and when Britain denied them use of the Suez Canal, they sailed around the Cape of Good Hope and across the Indian Ocean, before finding a port in French Indo-China to bunker and resupply.

When news of their arrival at Cam Ranh Bay reached Hong Kong, Bill Donald decided to report the coming sea battle from the Russian side. He and a correspondent from *Le Matin* found the fleet at anchor; but coming aboard he quickly realised that 'the officers were drunkards and the crews were untrained, undisciplined and unpatriotic men who had no shred of interest in their work and no concern as to the outcome of the battle'. He immediately revised his intention to accompany them in action.

It was a wise decision. The Japanese Admiral Togo was waiting for them with his imperial fleet bristling with the latest long-range gunnery. By now Donald was back in his *China Mail* office in Hong Kong, but as reports came in from Tokyo and St Petersburg he compiled a stirring (and remarkably accurate) account of the encounter on the high seas: 'The mists now lifted and disclosed to the Russians the terrible trap into which they had run. On their port they saw the first and second detachments of the Japanese fleet while swinging round to starboard were the third and fourth. The fleets steamed alongside each other for a short time and when off Okinashima the Russians opened fire. Soon an incessant and thunderous cannonade was proceeding . . . the Japanese gunners found their marks and wrought havoc on the opposing ships, smashing the iron and woodwork and converting the decks into veritable shambles.'

Donald sent his story to the Australian press and it was widely reprinted in the major cities. The Brisbane *Courier* also recorded the bestowal on W.H. Donald of the Order of the Rising Sun by the Meiji emperor.

In China, there was an immediate clamour from the young and disaffected demanding to know why a relatively small Asiatic country like Japan could defeat one of the great powers, while their own Middle Kingdom, with its almost unlimited resources, remained in thrall to the Westerners.

Meanwhile, the Donald marriage had struck a reef. Mary wanted children while Bill regarded them as an impediment to his roving life as a journalist. And he revelled in the company of his hard-drinking compatriots. Moreover, his career was on the rise. He had received an offer from the *New York Herald's* publisher, James Gordon Bennett, who was looking for a correspondent to match the celebrated and influential Dr Morrison.

Bennett himself was something of a journalistic legend, having engaged Morrison's hero Stanley to 'find' Dr Livingstone who had been happily pursuing his missionary calling among the heathens of the Dark Continent. Donald accepted the offer on condition that he retain the editorship of the *China Mail* and Bennett agreed.

On his first assignment a week later, a further string was added to his bow. During an interview with the viceroy of Guangzhou, Chang Jenchun, he so impressed the Chinese official that he offered the Australian a role as 'adviser on all matters that pertain to government in South China'. Donald took it in his stride with the proviso that he would not accept any payment for his services.

It was a clever ploy as it secured Donald a high-ranking journalistic source without compromising his ethical independence. His point of contact was a young English-speaking staff member, Wen Zhang Yao, who had been educated at Sun Yatsen's alma mater in Hong Kong, the Central School, and in the United States. Donald was anxious to make contact with the revolutionary leader and he followed the trail through members of the movement until he reached the leading local apparatchik, Dr Hu Hanmin. Hu had been educated in Japan and was now editing the movement's propaganda sheet *Minbao* (*The People's Journal*). He and Donald struck up an immediate friendship and at the end of their initial meeting he stepped forward and shook the Australian's hand. According to Donald's biographer, 'From that time on he was solidly a part of the Revolutionary Movement. He met with them secretly and . . . they found themselves turning to him for explanations and advice.'[6]

CHAPTER NINETEEN
WINDS OF CHANGE

The death of Mei Quong Tart had removed the one acceptable Chinese face from the Australian scene and no one from the community was able or willing to take his place. As the federal administrators of the White Australia Policy turned the screws ever tighter on the Chinese migrants, their cause lacked a champion to expose its stony inhumanity.

Until 1903 those who had lived in Australia for five years could apply for a certificate of exemption from the dictation test in seeking naturalisation. Thereafter the *Nationality Act* prohibited any non-European from becoming a citizen. This gave rise to a complicated and confused system of exemptions and the *Northern Territory Times* wondered 'whether it be the embodiment of a great ideal or one of the most narrow, selfish and crazy pieces of legislation ever placed upon the Commonwealth Statue Book'.[1]

The law had allowed 'highly respected' Chinese to bring out their wives and families provided they travelled with them, but the provision was suspended in 1903 and repealed two years later. Thereafter wives could only visit on temporary entry permits. Even Chinese ships' stewards and cooks were closely watched when coming ashore to buy supplies.

In Queensland, the *Aboriginal Protection and Sale of Opium Act* had made it illegal for Chinese to live with Aboriginal females. And since the two oppressed groups were frequently in each other's company, the power of propinquity had forged many happy relationships that were now wrenched apart. Moreover, the Act also prevented Chinese from employing Aborigines which threw many of the indigenous Australians out of work.

In the Northern Territory, the Aboriginal Protector, Baldwin Spencer, an anthropologist, conceived a particular hatred for the Chinese. 'There are a few decent ones,' he said, 'but 98 per cent are low, depraved beasts who want deporting.'[2] He was not alone in his racist views. Many Chinese were totally opposed to 'mixed marriages' with Aboriginal women and the children of these unions were not given a Chinese clan name as it would bring 'shame' to the extended family.

Quong Tart's petition for a Chinese consul, duly delivered by Morrison to the Chinese foreign office in 1903, finally secured an appointment five years later. The imperial court nominated Liang Lan-hsun as consul-general but first it had to receive the approval of the British government which still had charge of Australia's foreign affairs. The *Sydney Morning Herald* was unfazed: 'It shows for one thing that the name of Australia is being recognised in China as standing for great potentialities,' it editorialised.

The Mandarin in traditional garb finally arrived the following year and took up residence in Melbourne. There were high hopes among the Chinese that forceful representation would bring a relaxation of the oppressive migration laws, as well as their high-handed treatment in business and within the community. They were disappointed on all counts.

Liang was much more concerned with trade than human rights, an attitude that would pervade the Australia–China relationship from both sides of the divide. Over the next four years, one consul-general after another investigated the problems of Chinese in Australia and gently urged the Australian government to remove the restriction on immigration. They might as well have saved their breath.

The consul-general gave a typically diplomatic view of the state of play in his country when he claimed, straight-faced, 'With our new Emperor and our new government, China is forging ahead steadily . . . We are building railways and opening up large districts. We are, in fact, rejuvenating the nation.'

However, while the climate slowly worsened for the Chinese in Australia, the winds of change in their homeland were blowing up a storm.

★ ★ ★

Consul Liang's Panglossian vision could hardly have been further from the truth. On 14 November 1908 the Emperor Guangxu, whom Cixi had confined to his island prison, had died suddenly, perhaps at the hands of the dowager's eunuchs. Then she herself succumbed less than 24 hours later and many were quick to blame Yuan Shikai who they believed was slated for assassination himself by her bodyguards. The truth will forever be hidden beneath clouds of rumour and conspiracy, but the effect was to elevate the three-year-old Pu Yi to the Dragon Throne. Pu Yi's father, Prince Chun, would rule as regent until his son turned eighteen and Guangxu's widow would be the new empress dowager.

One of the court's first actions was to remove Yuan Shikai from all power; but they did so in a peculiarly oriental manner, blaming their actions on 'an affliction [which they wrongly spelled 'affection'] of his foot' making it 'hardly possible for him to discharge his duties'. He would now 'return to his private place to treat and to convalesce from the ailment'. The 52-year-old general accordingly retired to Tientsin and his Garden for Cultivating Longevity where he would continue his plotting. Morrison had formed a good working relationship with him and the Australian sent a telegram expressing his best wishes. Yuan Shikai replied that he was 'much moved' to receive it.[3]

Soon afterwards Morrison set off on one of his extraordinary journeys, this time overland from Beijing to Moscow – first by train to Xi'an then mounted on a pony accompanied by two horse-drawn carts loaded with provisions and books. It would take him almost six months to reach the Russian capital, after which he continued to London.

Meanwhile, his equally energetic compatriot, Bill Donald, had risen to become managing director of the *China Mail*, founded *Who's Who in the Far East* and assisted in the establishment of a university in Hong Kong. The two Australian journalists had met again when Morrison passed through the British colony. The older China hand was aware of Donald's ties to the revolutionaries, though not the degree of intimacy between them. Indeed, Donald's contacts among the rebels had passed him the news that Sun Yatsen had slipped into Macao in the vanguard of yet another attempted uprising. He set out immediately for nearby Guangzhou where it was planned to take place.

On this occasion Sun Yatsen was smuggling a shipload of arms and ammunition into that boiling pot of insurrection to be used in an attack on the imperial barracks. They arrived on a Japanese vessel but Chinese customs officers intercepted the ship and arrested the officers and crew. When Donald arrived, confusion reigned. His friend Chang Jenchun, the Guangdong viceroy, was torn between his officials' actions and a newly arrived order from the Manchu court, fearful of offending Japan, that demanded he release the ship, pay an indemnity of US$15,000 and kowtow to the Japanese flag.

Donald wrote his story then assisted in creating an even bigger one by helping persuade the Chinese business and trading guilds of the city to retaliate by boycotting all Japanese goods. In less than 48 hours, the boycott secured the support of 157 merchants who agreed to keep it in place until the Japanese had suffered losses of ten times the indemnity – US$150 million! Faced with a massive popular protest, the Manchu court backed down and paid the indemnity from the Beijing treasury.

Donald had, by now, become totally committed to his adopted country. According to historian Peter Thompson, 'Donald worked tirelessly to place positive stories about China on international news schedules. One of his brainwaves was to suggest to Gordon Bennett an alliance between China and the United States, "linking the oldest country in the eastern world with the youngest and most vigorous in the West." Bennett liked the idea so much he ordered the *Herald* to run stories supporting it day after day at the expense of coverage for that year's presidential election.'

Soon afterward the Australian stepped down from his post at the *China Mail* and opened his own office in Hong Kong, sandwiched between two department stores, the Sincere and the Wing On. He was in congenial company. Both had their genesis in Australia.

The Sincere was part-owned by Ma Yingbiao whose father had joined the Victorian goldrush in the 1850s. Twenty years later the nineteen-year-old Yingbiao followed in his father's footsteps. He worked among his Chinese compatriots at Sydney's Haymarket where he converted to Christianity and proved an astute businessman. On his return to his homeland after a period with his wife 'witnessing for Christ' in southern China, he and his partners opened their department store in July 1900 as an exact duplicate of Anthony Hordern's Sydney store. It was a first for Hong Kong and customers flocked to its colourful displays.

The Wing On store was founded seven years later by two brothers who had also made their fortunes at the Haymarket in Sydney. Kwok Lok and Kwok Chuen copied Ma Yingbiao's business template to the last detail and later added the Wing On bank.

The Sincere and the Wing On, with two other stores – the Sun Sun and Sun Company – would be known collectively as 'The Four Great Companies'. 'It was an astonishing feat,' says Thompson. 'A group of Australian Chinese entrepreneurs had used their experience of Sydney retailing methods to revolutionise China's commercial life.'[4]

Freed from the weekly demands of the *China Mail* and peeved at Mary's announcement that she'd fallen pregnant, Bill Donald headed to Shanghai on the way to the opening of a new port at Hangzhou on the north bank of the Yangtse. His revolutionary party friends had given him a contact in Shanghai, an American-educated Christian named Charlie Soong. Donald visited him at his print shop where he combined the printing of bibles and religious tracts with an undercover line in revolutionary pamphlets.

Soong and his attractive wife had six children and their three daughters – Ayling, Chingling and Mayling – would grow to be vivacious beauties with sharp political minds. All would play leading roles in the revolution to come. Ayling would marry the banker H.H. Kung, the richest man in China; Chingling would work for and eventually wed Sun Yatsen; while Mayling would marry and share power with Generalissimo Chiang Kai-shek. Donald would become close to all three but particularly Mayling. Their three brothers would also hold high posts in the Chinese government.

Donald told Soong of the latest failure of Sun Yatsen's attempt to trigger a mass insurrection in Guangzhou, blaming the revolutionaries' appalling mismanagement. They needed men trained and capable to bring down the Qing and prepare for government themselves, he said. But while Donald's advice was well received, Sun Yatsen's leadership remained more inspirational than practical and the revolutionaries blundered from one failed uprising to another.

However, the Manchu were even more maladroit than their opponents and when they announced on 11 May 1911 that they had taken over two provincial railway lines from Szechuan and Guangzhou to Hangzhou – to be used as collateral for loans from a foreign consortium – there was a mass protest in Szechuan and the gulf between Beijing and the people widened perceptibly.

Five months later, in one of the more farcical opening stanzas to a full-scale revolution, a team of bomb makers in the Russian concession of Hangzhou blew themselves and their headquarters up when a bomb detonated prematurely. As the imperial authorities searched the wreckage they found a list of conspirators, including officers of the New Army, who were planning an uprising the following week. In another part of the city that night, police raided a meeting of radicals and shot three of them at dawn the following day.

This raised the tension to breaking point and later that morning elements of the New Army in the residential district of Wuchang attacked the offices of the provincial governor, who escaped down the Yangtse in a Japanese gunboat. By mid-afternoon the revolutionaries had taken control of the whole city and were locked in combat with the Qing garrison of about 3000 soldiers. By nightfall the imperial forces were overwhelmed, with a reported 800 dead in the city streets. Other

New Army units joined the fray and captured the biggest southern arsenal and the government mint with its treasure of two million taels in silver.

Morrison had returned from his latest travels and as news filtered into Beijing he did the rounds of the embassies where the ministers chose unanimously to do nothing to support the Chinese government and let the chips fall where they may. 'The rebellion gains increasing force and its well-organised appearances indicate that the government is confronted with the most formidable danger since the Taiping rebellion,' he wrote. 'At any moment a message may arrive announcing a sympathetic outbreak at [Guangzhou] where revolutionary agitation has been simmering for a long time.'[5]

In fact, appearances were deceptive. The rebellion was far from 'well-organised' as his compatriot Bill Donald in Shanghai attested. There, Donald visited Dr Wu Tingfang, the former minister in Washington who had returned and joined the revolutionaries. 'He was striding up and down his living room, hands behind his back, muttering,' he said. 'Other than the general idea that the Manchu must be ousted, there were no workable plans. The revolution had been born in a dream. Until now it had remained beautiful and visionary, undisturbed by practical matters. Worst of all, no one had heard from Dr Sun Yatsen.'

In fact, China's leading revolutionary was on a fundraising trip in the United States and to his eternal distress Sun Yatsen missed the beginning of one of the most momentous events in his country's history.[6]

CHAPTER TWENTY

THE CHINESE REVOLUTION

By now the rebels had appointed the former Qing commander in Wuchang, Lieutenant-Colonel Li Yuanhong, as military governor in charge of the provisional government at Hangzhou. He was a reluctant starter, having been found hiding under his wife's bed and forced at gunpoint to have greatness thrust upon him. However, once he had promoted himself to general he brought a measure of order to the rebellion and his associates sent telegrams to other provinces urging them to cut their ties with the Manchu.

In Shanghai, Donald arranged a meeting between Dr Wu Tingfang and other leaders of the revolutionary party with the British consul, Everard Fraser, and the Australian briefed him on developments in the struggle that was spreading like a grass fire across the south. Fraser duly passed the intelligence on to the new British minister in Beijing, Sir John Jordan, with whom Morrison had developed a good working relationship. The Australian doyen was able to assure the diplomat that 'Donald knows more about the inside of the revolutionary movement than any other foreigner'. In fact, his Shanghai compatriot had by then enlisted Fraser as the revolutionaries' 'chief advocate and protector' within the British diplomatic establishment.[1]

The Manchu were becoming desperate as all attempts to quell the fires were overwhelmed by revolutionary fervour. They turned to the only man with the military power of command to defend the house of Qing – Yuan Shikai, who was dutifully tending his afflicted foot in his Garden for Cultivating Longevity. Prince Chun sent him an urgent summons to the Forbidden City to receive a new posting as viceroy of Hunan and Hubei, with orders to suppress the Wuchang rebellion. But before he could respond, Yuan Shikai received a second proposal, this time from the rebels, offering him the presidency of the republic should the revolution succeed. He thanked the rebels for their offer and returned to his wives and concubines among the pleasures of his garden.

Morrison stalked the capital as panic seized the government. On 17 October he wrote, 'I cannot meet anyone, Chinese or foreign associates of the Chinese, who will not tell me the same thing privately – that they wish for the success of the revolution.' The following week he reported, 'Manchus are leaving because they fear the future. Treasure of all kinds is being sent out of [Beijing] to places of safety.'[2]

Prince Chun raised his offer to Yuan Shikai. Now he would be 'imperial commissioner in charge of the entire army and navy'. Again the general declined the honour in favour of remaining in his garden; but then he suddenly raised the stakes with a demonstration of his military command. He ordered General Duan Qirui, his former chief of staff, to retake Hangzhou but to leave the foreign concessions untouched. General Duan responded with an artillery attack that devastated the city and the rebels retreated across the river to their Wuchang stronghold. Yuan Shikai's hand could also be seen in a public demand from the 20th Division in North China that a constitutional monarchy be established within a year.

The forces were closing in on the Manchu. Prince Chun responded on 31 October by offering Yuan Shikai the prime ministership in place of his Manchu relative, Prince Qing. And finally, Yuan Shikai agreed.

In Shanghai on that 1 November the revolutionaries proclaimed the Military Government of the Chinese people. The police force immediately joined the mutiny and bands of revolutionaries, wearing white badges that celebrated 'the restoration of the Han people'. To demonstrate the new order, the rebel government decreed that men must cut off their queues and police units armed with scissors helped any recalcitrant passers-by to remove their pigtails.

In Nanjing a former groom to Dowager Empress Cixi, General Zhang Xun, and his soldiers attacked the rebels spreading terror through the surrounding area, butchering on sight anyone wearing the white badge of the revolution. Everard Fraser helped to organise a force of revolutionary soldiers to set out by rail from Shanghai in a counter-attack. By now the reluctant General Li was beginning to relish his newfound authority and sent a notice to the foreign consuls in Hangzhou that he had been appointed the military governor of all China. Moreover, he assured them that 'all treaties and loan agreements concluded by the Qing Government will be honoured'. In Shanghai, Donald's friends, Dr Wu and Wen Zongyao, another experienced diplomat, were appointed to run the regime's foreign affairs. And all agreed that the first President of the Republic – once they were able to contact him – would be Sun Yatsen.

On 14 November, Yuan Shikai finally left his garden and boarded a train for the capital, arriving with a bodyguard comprising, in Morrison's words, 'wild-looking halberdiers carry long two-handled swords'. Sworn in as prime minister, he named a central government of ten Han and a single Manchu in the first step towards the creation of a constitutional monarchy. It was the instinctive response of a student of his nation's long history wherein authority had always flowed down from above, and a military man committed to the chain of command. The revolutionaries' rough-hewn concept of people-power providing legitimacy to the ruler was foreign to all his native and learned precepts, the more so given its provenance from a group of unruly southerners.

Morrison's conduit to Yuan Shikai was his representative in negotiations with the revolutionaries, Rear Admiral Cai Tinggan. A tall, dapper sophisticate with a neat moustache, Cai had studied in America and had perfect command of the English language. He had known General Li earlier in his career when Li was a lowly third engineer in a torpedo boat he had commanded. He and Morrison became close and the Australian suspected Cai was more inclined toward the revolutionaries than his prime minister. 'While defending the constitutional monarchy in theory,' a sarcastic Morrison told his diary, 'he is as strongly Manchu as the men with whom he was sent to parley.'³

It was a measure of Morrison's influence that Cai conveyed Yuan Shikai's invitation to a meeting soon after the new prime minister took up residence in the capital. The Australian travelled in his own carriage to Yuan's private home where he found the 52-year-old schemer in poor physical condition but with his powers of political manipulation undiminished. It was a long and productive meeting for the journalist. Yuan was 'cordial and complimentary' and when Morrison left he had little doubt that the prime minister wanted him to help pressure the Qing court to abandon Beijing for a retreat to their summer residence in Chengde. That would signal the total collapse of the imperial government and clear the way for Yuan to create a new order with himself at its summit. But for the moment, the ragged Qing regime held on.

Meantime, in Shanghai on 21 November, delegates from half of China's 22 provinces assembled for the first national convention of the revolutionary movement. Their first order of business was the drafting of a new constitution, but Donald was more interested in the battle for Nanjing. And while the combat would certainly provide great copy for his readers, it was now quite clear that he had exchanged his journalist's hat for a participant's battledress.

The revolutionary units gathered in Zhenjiang just to the west of Nanjing where the Australian discovered their ally, the military governor General Ling, half-paralysed by his opium habit. Donald told him he was speaking on behalf of the National Assembly and ordered him to transfer command to his rival, General Zhu Koqing. Ling complied and Zhu reluctantly accepted the responsibility, but then delayed his advance for fear of enemy artillery on the nearby Purple Mountain. Donald had to climb the mountain himself where he had tea with a group of monks in a monastery before he could persuade Zhu his fears were unfounded. Indeed, he suggested Zhu place his own artillery on the strategic heights.

Finally, on 30 November the combined revolutionary forces mounted their attack in three columns and rushed the strongly fortified positions in the face of blistering fire. And when the artillery opened up from Purple Mountain and the surrounding hills, the imperial defenders ran for their lives. The republican armies swarmed into the city, sacked its buildings and burned many to the ground. Donald duly filed his reports which were reprinted back in Australia as a triumph for the republicans over the decaying Qing dynasty. And four days later in Beijing, Prince Chun abdicated as regent and the new dowager empress asked Yuan Shikai to negotiate a peace settlement with the revolutionaries.

One of the prime minister's first moves was to invite Morrison to travel to the southern battlefields in a private railway carriage in which he was 'fed and wined with sybaritic luxury'. After touring Hangzhou and talking to the locals he wrote that, 'China is indifferent whether Yuan Shikai makes himself President or Emperor; the Manchus must go. There seems absolute unanimity about this.' He was half right. The Manchus had certainly surrendered the Mandate of Heaven, but the revolutionaries would never permit the exchange of one dynastic line for another. It was a misapprehension that would return to haunt both Morrison and Yuan Shikai in the months and years ahead.

On 18 December, Dr Wu presented the negotiating demands of the republicans: abdication of the Manchus, with generous pensions for the emperor and the ruling family; and an immediate proclamation of a republic. Yuan's negotiating team – with Admiral Cai supporting Tang Shaoyi, a native of Guangdong who had also been educated in America – was perfectly prepared to abandon the Qing. Indeed, Tang had ostentatiously cut off his own queue before attending the talks. But as ever the devil was in the details, not least the personnel who would assume the mantle of republican power.

By now Donald had been installed as Dr Wu's confidential secretary and Morrison had arrived to report the conference first-hand. The two Australians swapped information and views as each then filed their reports to the English-speaking press. It was a partnership like none other in the annals of international journalism; and it was the practical beginning of an association that would endure for a decade that encompassed some of the most dramatic developments in China's long history.

The negotiations were suddenly interrupted on Christmas Day by the arrival of Sun Yatsen from the United States. General Li discovered the fleeting nature of political glory when the delegates welcomed the prodigal home. 'The revolution was finished when he reached China,' the general complained. And even his colleagues were stunned when Sun Yatsen introduced his travelling companion, a diminutive American fantasist named Homer Lea who falsely claimed Confederate General Robert E. Lee as a relative. On their journey across the Pacific, Sun Yatsen had promised him command of the entire Chinese Republican Army.

Sun Yatsen's claims to the presidency found little support from the Australians. After meeting with the new arrival, Donald confided to Morrison that he doubted the man's sanity. Morrison told the republicans that neither Sun Yatsen nor General Li 'could ever persuade the foreign powers to recognise the Republic'; the only figure who could achieve that was Yuan Shikai. And while the leaders were suspicious of the military manipulator, they recognised the value of the Australians' advice. So on 29 December, delegates from sixteen of the seventeen provinces elected Sun Yatsen '*provisional* president of the Chinese Republic'. Sun Yatsen acknowledged Yuan Shikai's primacy and notified him that he could take over the presidency if he declared allegiance to the republic.

Morrison then sought out Admiral Cai. He had conceived a plan that he confided in a cable to a colleague at the *Times*: 'The question is, will Yuan Shikai accept this appointment.' The general had told Sir John Jordan that he and his ancestors had served the Manchu faithfully and he could not go down in history as a usurper. 'So,' Morrison wrote, 'suppose the Manchus themselves should desire his appointment. Their interests would be better safeguarded with him in the presidency than with any [other] Chinese in the empire . . . I do not see why it cannot be arranged that the Manchus themselves support his appointment should it be offered to him by the National Convention. This seems to me to be the best possible solution. It is my own idea. I have not yet had time to develop it.'

When he spoke to Cai two days later, the plan was fully formed and the admiral recognised its value. He eagerly passed it on to Yuan Shikai and reported back that the prime minister was 'tickled to death' with the idea.[4] No doubt the wily political tactician had conceived something similar himself, but Morrison regarded his brainwave as one of the more decisive elements in the transfer of dynastic power to the novel republican form of Chinese governance. Admiral Cai agreed. He said Morrison should thereafter be styled, 'The Australian Hero of the Chinese Reform Movement'.

Sun Yatsen took the formal oath as provisional president in Nanjing at 11 p.m. on 1 January 1912, promising to 'faithfully obey the wishes of the citizens, be loyal to the nation and perform my duties until the downfall of the despotic government . . . then I shall relinquish the office of provisional president. I hereby swear this before the citizens.'

Donald was on hand for the occasion and filed his story for the *New York Herald* before returning to Shanghai. According to his biographer Thompson, 'Twenty-four hours later he received an urgent plea from Sun Yatsen himself. He was being pressured to publish a manifesto. Would Donald write it? Despite his reservations about Sun, the Australian needed no persuading. The republicans needed to explain their aims to the Chinese people and the wider world. Sitting down at his battered typewriter, he started to type.'

The result was a clear and unadorned program of political reform. 'We will remodel our laws,' Donald wrote, 'revise our civil, criminal, commercial and mining codes; reform our finances; abolish restrictions to trade and commerce; and ensure religious toleration . . .' He worked through the night, drafting and revising, with the help of a bottle of Kentucky mountain dew, until it met his demanding standards. Next morning, he cabled it to Sun Yatsen in Nanjing and that afternoon it was released unchanged under the name of Provisional President Sun Yatsen.

In Beijing, Morrison was gratified to watch his plan being translated into action and on 10 January Yuan Shikai gave him a copy of the official edict, signed but not released by the dowager empress, ending the Qing dynasty. Morrison used it in one of his many 'scoops' to make a firm prediction of the abdication to come. However, nothing was completely certain in the febrile atmosphere of the day and Yuan himself almost came to grief when a band of revolutionaries attempted to assassinate him as he travelled to the palace to make the final arrangements for the transfer of power.

By chance his carriage was just rounding the corner towards Morrison's home when 'there was a loud explosion and a burst of smoke', the journalist wrote. 'At once I knew a bomb had been thrown.' Standing at the gate with his young New Zealand–born secretary Jennie Robin, he watched as a riderless horse dashed past, other men riding after it, and after a moment of suspense the carriage came round the corner. 'It raced quickly past giving us a glimpse of Yuan seated,' he said. 'Nothing had happened to him, thank God.'[5]

CHAPTER TWENTY-ONE
CHINA'S SECOND REVOLUTION

On 12 February 1912, Yuan Shikai led his cabinet into the great Yanxin Hall of the Imperial palace where they were joined by the imperial kinsmen and court officials come to pay their tribute at the closing act of a dynasty that had ruled for 267 years. The Empress Dowager Longyu and the six-year-old Emperor Pu Yi entered and ascended their thrones. A eunuch presented her with the Abdication Edict and with tears streaming down her face she read the document amid the wailing and sobbing of her courtiers:

'Yuan Shikai, having been elected Prime Minister some time ago by the Political Consultative Council, is able at this time of change to unite the north and south. Let him then, with the full power so to do, organise a provisional republican government . . . that peace may be assured to the people and that the complete integrity of the territories of the five races – Han, Manchu, Mongol, Muslim, and Tibetan – is at the same time maintained in a great state under the title of the Republic of China.'

Provision was made for generous pensions to ease the royal family's painful transition to obscurity and Pu Yi himself was held in virtual imprisonment by the Department of the Imperial Household to forestall any possibility of a counter-revolution. In the event, their lives of indolence went on very much as before.

In Australia the Chinese community celebrated. On the former goldfields of Atherton in North Queensland, now a thriving agricultural district, they ceremoniously burned the imperial flag and 'dozens of lopped pigtails were thrown into the flames'.[1] At the Chinese consulate in Melbourne they hauled down the Dragon flag and replaced it with the triangular Republican ensign. They gave the task to their popular sixteen-year-old clerk and translator, William Liu. The son of Lum Liu who had migrated from Guangdong to Sydney where he worked as a barber, William would become one of the most influential Chinese-Australians of the 20th century.

One month later, Sun Yatsen kept his bargain and handed his 'provisional' reins of power over to Yuan Shikai, a man utterly without republican instincts and to whom 'Chinese democracy' was an oxymoron. But for the moment at least Yuan Shikai persisted with the charade, even though he now headed a bankrupt government utterly dependent on gimlet-eyed foreign bankers and government treasurers to finance its operations. 'The Chinese Republic is a very young baby,' he said. 'It must be nursed and kept from taking strong meat or potent medicines like those prescribed by foreign doctors.'

There was, however, one foreign doctor he wanted at his side to navigate the financial shoals in prospect: the Australian, George Ernest Morrison. And coincidentally Morrison at 50 was ready for a total change to his *modus vivendi*.

After living a bachelor's existence during which Morrison enjoyed the charms of 'hundreds' of women of every nationality and rank, to his great surprise he found himself 'totally in love' with his accomplished 23-year-old secretary. And Jennie Robin, who had been private secretary to Lord Balfour, the Scottish Secretary in the Arthur Balfour government, was equally entranced with the 'great man' for whom she had journeyed across half the world.[2]

Admiral Cai put the proposition to Morrison on Yuan's behalf: a five-year contract at an annual salary of £3500 (almost triple his pay at *The Times*), a £250 housing allowance, and all travelling expenses, the last a particular attraction to a man of Morrison's peripatetic tastes. He would now be able to offer his young wife-to-be a comfortable life in the great capital and all the prestige of an honoured adviser to the Chinese government.

When Bill Donald came to Beijing to cover the momentous fall of the last emperor, Morrison offered him the job as his successor at *The Times*. Clearly taken aback, Donald asked for time to consider. And on his return to Shanghai he wrote that, 'When you were flattering enough to mention this to me I didn't say much. You know that I would but indifferently follow in your footsteps. However, I appreciate to the bottom of my heart the kindly feeling embodied in your suggestion and I will not forget it.'

For the moment at least, Donald was totally engrossed in the political manoeuvrings of the southerners and in a subsequent letter to Morrison he complained that Sun Yatsen's supporters 'are in as great a muddle as they could possibly get this side of open anarchy'. They still addressed their champion as 'President' and played to his ego by 'virtually prostrating themselves in the despised kowtow'.

As to Sun himself, 'I am convinced he has come to imagine himself to be the Moses of China destined to lead the hordes to the promised land.' He had taken Donald into his office where he laid out a map of the empire and proceeded, with brush and a stick of ink, to draw plans for a new Chinese rail network that filled every province 'with as many lines as he could cram in'. In no time, the reporter said, 'the map was nothing by a grotesque Chinese puzzle. Sun sat down on the floor to explain things to me, and as he sat there I thought that never could such a scene be drawn to depict the ineptitude of this, the first President of the Chinese Republic. He is mad!'

Donald's one consolation was that Sun's American 'general' Homer Lea amid all the excitement had suffered a fatal stroke and expired. Donald then added a postscript by hand. 'I shall now go and get drunk ... for this is the 4th [of July] and I'll jubilate because the Lord so worked it that we are not responsible for Americans!'[3]

Morrison's appointment as political advisor to Yuan Shikai and his government, while a dismal blow to his editors, was widely applauded in the West. The *New York Times* carried a prominent op-ed report praising him as 'a unique man in a unique job, and his success or failure may affect the whole future of the Far East and, incidentally, of the other nations of the world'. In Britain, where he and Jennie were married in August 1912, he was interviewed at length and his opinions respectfully dissected. Australia applauded its native son as a man of 'immense influence' and 'solid good sense' who would be of 'incalculable value to the untested Chinese republican government'.[4]

In Morrison's absence, Yuan Shikai invited Sun Yatsen to Beijing where the wily politician offered him the role of 'Director for the Construction of all Railways in China'. Sun was overjoyed and prepared to set forth in Yuan's gift – the personal rail carriage of the old Empress Dowager Cixi – to tour the entire system. And he selected Bill Donald as his personal advisor for the journey. Prominently displayed in his luxurious quarters was 'The Map', a tarted-up version of the conglomeration he had created for Donald during their interview. It would be shown to foreign correspondents at the start of the tour, he said, to convince them of his commitment to his portfolio. The Australian was appalled at the prospect and when the international press filed aboard, Donald contrived to 'disappear it', much to Sun's consternation. (It would magically reappear once the correspondents had departed.)

When one reporter asked Sun, 'Are you a socialist?' he turned to Donald. 'Am I?' he asked his adviser.

At a time when 'socialist' had radical anti-Confucian overtones of heresy verging on sedition, the Australian turned diplomat: 'You are everything required as a Nationalist,' he said. Then, to a prearranged signal, an officer of the Chinese bodyguard declared a security alert and the pressmen were bundled off the train. Only then did the harassed adviser relax.

But not for long. As the official party, which now included Sun's political confederates and Ayling Soong as his personal secretary, headed out on their railway odyssey, Donald became acutely aware that Sun intended to oppose Yuan's presidency. He wrote to Morrison, 'While he [tells] the world he is devoting his energies to the development of China's natural resources, he is conspiring here with his bottle-washer coterie to become the President.' Nevertheless, for all his doubts about the man's stability, he could not help liking him. 'I must hasten to add, we are good friends,' he said, 'despite his being a willing instrument in a crowd of wire-pullers.'

He also suggested that Morrison advise Yuan to 'take a big stick' to the agitators among the revolutionaries who were intent on destabilising the new government. It was well-meant advice. Sun's people were even then combining with other progressive factions to form the Kuomintang, with the declared intent of 'preparing the way for the introduction of socialism to facilitate and better the standard of living . . . and evenly develop the resources of our country'.

Yuan responded by dismissing his old friend and Prime Minister Tang Shaoyi, who had negotiated with the republicans and whom he suspected of sympathising with them. Tang departed the scene with a warning: 'Yuan Shikai is the only man who can unify the country, provided he cooperates sincerely with the Revolutionary Party. But judging from what has happened in the past three months, I fear that disillusionment may come in the end.'[5]

On his return from the marathon train journey, Bill Donald received yet another influential journalistic appointment, the joint editorship of the *Far Eastern Review* with the American right-winger George Bronson Rea. But unlike Rea, he was determined to promote a positive Chinese–American editorial direction. The new job required him to relocate to the political hotbed of Beijing and a reluctant Mary made the move with their daughter Muriel, to whom Donald was utterly devoted despite his initial objections to fatherhood. They lived comfortably with five Chinese servants, including an *amah* (nanny) for Muriel and a groom for Donald's two horses that conveyed him daily to his offices in a former Russian bank building.

On Morrison's return from his British honeymoon, the two Australians saw a great deal of each other. The Donalds attended the christening party of the Morrisons' first child, Ian, early in 1913, and by then both men had great concern for the stability of the new government. The Kuomintang had won handily in the initial elections for the American-style senate and house of representatives as proscribed in the new constitution. But then on 20 March the Majority Leader of the House, Song Jiaoren, was shot twice at close range on the platform of the Shanghai station and he died two days later. The trail of evidence led to the secretary of Yuan's cabinet but the investigation of the conspiracy ran foul of government interference and further assassinations. While no charges were ever laid, Yuan himself was widely believed to have ordered the shooting.

As he lay dying in hospital, Song asked for pen and paper and wrote, 'I hope the President will rule our country with sincerity and justice and strive to protect the rights of the people. In so doing, he will help the assembly make a permanent constitution. If that can be done, my death will not have been in vain.'

Morrison was asked to serve on a board of inquiry into the killing but declined. 'As an official employed by the government it would not be appropriate,' he said.

However, all thoughts of legal recrimination were overwhelmed by the outbreak in July of the 'Second Revolution' when northern and southern troops clashed in Jiangxi province. Yuan responded with a statement accusing Sun and Kuomintang leader Huang Xing of 'making a nuisance' of themselves. 'If they dare to organise another government, I swear I shall use force to smash them!'

The president tried to involve Morrison in the propaganda war. He sent the Australian a translation of a Chinese newspaper article that he wanted published in the foreign press. It said the Kuomintang leaders were 'inhumanely and mercilessly persecuting the people'.

Morrison replied, 'I'd never be party to the publication of such a foolish, undignified diatribe.' However, he excused Yuan himself. 'That it should emanate from the President's office is evidence itself of the evil influences with which [he] is surrounded.'[6]

Yet another Australian journalist, Lionel Pratt, joined the little cabal as a reporter for Donald's *Far Eastern Review*. He declared himself a

Yuan supporter and suspected that Sun Yatsen was being manipulated by the Japanese ex-army officers who had infiltrated his group. Donald did nothing to dissuade him from his story but events in the National Assembly were overtaking him. The Chinese newspapers carried daily lists of Kuomintang members resigning to join other groupings. Donald told Morrison that Yuan's men were openly offering bribes to secure their defections.

A loan from the five major powers to Yuan's government which Morrison had helped to negotiate was about to be signed. Donald believed it was unconstitutional and Sun wrote publicly to protest and threatened, 'If you reject my sound advice I shall adopt the same measures against you as those used against the absolute monarchy. I have made my mind up now. This is my last advice and I hope you consider it well.'

Yuan spurned the advice, dismissed Sun from his railway post and signed the loan documents. The funds, he believed, would at least give him the means to put down any insurrection.

Donald was downcast. 'Bloodshed cannot now be avoided,' he said.

Sun fled to Japan where he was joined by a rising star of the revolution, Chiang Kai-shek, who had studied at the Japanese military academy. Donald's old friend, the influential Charlie Soong, also arrived with most of his family, although youngest daughter Mayling was still at college in America. Indeed, she had graduated from the relatively obscure Wesley school in the Deep South to the highly prestigious Ivy League Wellesley College in Massachusetts.

Kuomintang leader Huang Xing hurried from Shanghai to Nanjing where he persuaded the military governor to declare independence from Yuan and tried unsuccessfully to take charge of the rebel forces in the field. But the battle was soon lost and he, too, retreated to Japan as Yuan's troops re-established control of the south. Then in Beijing on 6 October, Yuan's men, acting in the name of a 'Citizen's Association', surrounded the parliament building and refused to leave until the two chambers had elected a permanent president and vice-president.

Yuan Shikai and Li Yuanhong were duly chosen and four days later Morrison – recently decorated with the Order of the Excellent Crop (Second Class) – joined Admiral Cai in his carriage for the ceremonial swearing-in at the Hall of Great Harmony. There, in delicious counterpoint, Yuan outlawed the Kuomintang.

Morrison retained his belief that only Yuan and his army had the power to prevent total anarchy across the empire, yet he was deeply troubled. At times he would rail against Yuan and his 'cohort of unscrupulous Chinese jealous of the foreigner' and his moods were affecting his life with Jennie. He confided to his journal: 'She fears that I will lose all energy and ambition and think only of my salary. But if this [situation] continues I am bound to deteriorate, bound to find my energy and ambition sapping away.'[7]

At this time an item attributed to Donald appeared in *The Bulletin* in Sydney: 'I see Mr Morrison daily and he does not know whether to be tired of his job or not. He has a hard time of it. Advice is easy to give: the Chinaman listens to advice, but will do what he thinks he wants to do. Morrison feels that, frequently.

'During the Revolution he asked me, in Shanghai, why I did not enter the service of the Government. They were then offering me £250 a month. My reply was that once a man entered the paid service of a Chinese his influence was gone. Morrison scoffed – now he admits it. Bitter proof. As *Times* correspondent he had twice the prestige and three times the influence.'

Donald was mortified when the item, taken from a personal letter, was published, though neither he nor Morrison could dispute its accuracy. Morrison was concerned at the effect it would have on his reputation in his home country. But the two men knew the world of journalism too well to allow it to impede their friendship.

In June 1914 Morrison set out for London with Jennie and baby Ian to promote the 'New China' in a series of lectures and interviews. *The Times* devoted a column to his assertion that in the aftermath of the rebellion, 'There is peace and quiet in every important city throughout all China.' He refuted suggestions that Yuan Shikai had cut himself off from New China or that he aimed to establish his own family dynasty. Instead, he claimed, the president 'has drawn his advisers from every party in the state'.[8]

However, the following week Bill Donald, who was standing in for Morrison's eventual successor at *The Times,* David Fraser, contradicted his compatriot. Yuan, he said, was in the process of becoming a 'dictator' and having dispensed with the Kuomintang had stacked the senate with his own people. 'There are 70 of them,' Donald wrote, 'their names all savouring of the past, a regular mobilisation of the old brigade.'

Morrison's reaction to his friend's report is lost to history, but in any case China was about to become little more than a sidebar in the news of the world. On 28 June Archduke Franz Ferdinand of Austria and his wife Sophie were shot dead in Sarajevo by members of the Serbian Black Hand secret society. Europe was about to be convulsed by the Great War. Indeed, by the time Morrison returned to Beijing, the Japanese army had drafted a secret campaign to occupy Germany's colonies in the Far East, including half of China's Shandong province. It was the first step in their master plan to turn their great progenitor into a vassal state by any means they could contrive.

CHAPTER TWENTY-TWO

A WORLD AT WAR

By 1915 a weakened President Yuan Shikai was struggling against forces both within and without the borders of his embattled country. The Kuomintang was running an underground campaign against his presidency, while the perfidious British were conspiring with their alliance partners the Japanese to cripple the sovereignty of China itself. The British minister Sir John Jordan had secretly agreed with the Japanese government that after the war they should retain the German concessions in Shandong in return for Japan's support for the Allies in the East.

Sun Yatsen in Tokyo gave comfort to his host's ambitions declaring, 'Without Japan there is no China; without China there is no Japan.' When 50,000 Japanese troops landed on Shandong Peninsula on 26 September 1914 and a naval force blockaded the port of Tsingtao, it was with Sun Yatsen's tacit support. And when Yuan Shikai appealed to Sir John Jordan for a joint action to secure the colony for China, the British minister was obdurate: the Anglo–Japanese alliance had precedence. The Kaiser ordered the 5000 German defenders to fight to the death but after Japanese planes bombed Tsingtao in one of the first aerial warfare actions in the East, and a British force of 1500 joined with the Japanese for a final assault, the German governor surrendered.

Then in January 1915 came an outrageous confrontation from the Japanese minister, Eki Hioki, when he delivered to Yuan a document that became known as the '21 Demands'. It was shamelessly designed to turn China into a Japanese dependency. The most egregious claims would give the off-shore islanders control over China's finances, its military and police forces, as well as a massive intrusion into its railway and mining industries.

Morrison had seen it coming. Even as the war beckoned he warned the London *Daily Telegraph*, 'Japanese activities are directed principally to the Yangtse valley where, during the rebellion [they] secured important contracts and concessions from the rebel leaders.' And this was the area where British interests were most concentrated. 'Japan is now increasing her troops at various points in China, particularly at Hangzhou and her general policy bears out the Anglo-Chinese apprehensions.'

Now he was returning from a survey of the situation in Manchuria where the Japanese were gaining control of the southern part of the province. When he reached Beijing, rumours of the 21 Demands were rife. There was even a well-attested story that when Hioki delivered them, the Japanese minister had banged his walking stick on Yuan's dining table. 'If he did not accept immediately,' the envoy had cried, 'this meant war! Britain must not be told. Secrecy was vital. Yuan Shikai must obey!'

Yuan asked Morrison to attend him at his office in the second week of March where he showed him the 21 Demands. The Australian was appalled. 'They are worse than many presented by a victor to his vanquished enemy,' he said. Moreover, they were similar to the claims Sun Yatsen had been making from his Tokyo redoubt where he had surrounded himself with a coterie of yes men, hangers-on and Japanese 'advisers'. Clearly, the Japanese had the revolutionary leader totally in their control and they could play him as a trump card should they march on Beijing and depose Yuan.

The Chinese president was unnerved and terrified of the Japanese response if he broke his silence. He was also outraged at Sun's apparent complicity and was coming to the view that only by asserting dictatorial control could he hope to defend the country from the conspirators. Indeed, Morrison believed that Yuan was under the foolish misapprehension that if he acceded to their demands the Japanese might support a return to the monarchical system with himself as emperor.

The Australian decided to act. 'Disclosure was China's one safeguard,' he wrote, 'and yet it was with the greatest difficulty that I could induce Yuan to reveal the text of the document.' In fact, presidential permission was never given so Morrison turned to Bill Donald in one of the classic cases of a journalistic 'leak' from 'informed sources'.

Donald was at last writing for *The Times* as a Special Correspondent and they were known to be close, so Morrison had to be able to deny that he had handed the document to his compatriot. He invited Donald to his home office where the reporter had no sooner completed the polite amenities than Morrison straightened some papers on his desk and excused himself to go to his library next door. Donald rose and examined the papers. He instantly recognised the 21 Demands and understood the adviser's ruse. He quickly scanned the contents then stuffed the papers into an inside coat pocket.

Morrison re-entered. 'Sorry old boy,' he said, 'that I kept you waiting so long.'

'That's all right, George,' Donald replied, 'I'll be running along anyway.'[1]

The Times had its scoop and Morrison had his way. Other Beijing correspondents quickly followed and it made headlines around the world. The Japanese remained silent for a month, then claimed that there were only eleven demands and falsified those. However, Yuan refused to take advantage of the exposure and declined to reject the demands publicly. The two Australians were thoroughly frustrated with the vacillating Chinese. Morrison told his diary, 'China is getting just the treatment she deserves. Nothing is ever achieved and all the government's energies are put into regulations and reports that never lead to anything.'

In the two years since Morrison had come aboard as an adviser, China had lost control over Manchuria, Shandong and the Yangtse, while she had effectively surrendered her authority in the distant provinces of Outer Mongolia and Outer Tibet. 'Soon there will be nothing left,' he wrote. 'And since my joining she has accomplished *not one single solitary thing.*'[2]

However, in May the exposure of the Japanese demands finally forced Britain to intervene and require the Japanese to withdraw their more aggressive elements. Minister Jordan then told Yuan that acceptance of the remainder was 'the best thing to do'. Yuan called a meeting of the Board of Political Affairs and reported that since Britain would not support their resistance they had no option but to accept. 'This is both sad and humiliating,' he said, 'but let us all remember it and do our best to wipe out this disgrace.'

Morrison wrote, 'Donald thinks there will be another Revolution. People getting to the limit of their patience. I am disposed to agree with him. We are back to the old Manchu regime.'

Both were more prescient than they knew. On 23 December 1915, Yuan Shikai abolished the military governors in all China's provinces, dissolved parliament and proclaimed himself emperor at the Temple of Heaven. Riots broke out across the country.

★ ★ ★

In Australia, the war had roused the nation to patriotic euphoria. Volunteers flocked to enlist in response to the federal government's pledge of a 20,000-strong expeditionary force to defend the British empire 'to the last shilling'. By the end of 1914, an astonishing 50,000 had signed up and were trained – many with broomsticks due to a shortage of rifles – for a conflict that would eventually rob the country of a generation of its best and brightest.

Among them were several hundred Chinese, many of whom had been born in Australia. They did so despite the 1909 and 1910 *Defence Act* in which individuals who were 'not of substantial European origin or descent' could be declared 'exempt' from combat duties. The military had added its own proviso that, 'Only British subjects substantially of European origin should be recruited.'

Prospective enlistees underwent a medical examination and also signed an 'Attestation Paper' which asked if they were natural-born or naturalised British subjects. But there was no specific question on the applicant's 'European origin or descent'. So officers probably made their decisions based on the applicant's name, appearance and fluency in English; and in many cases the enlistment officers would have known the Chinese-Australians personally. But while the military could be rigorously selective during the initial rush, as casualties mounted and a dwindling supply of reinforcements brought demands for conscription, it became much more flexible in applying the racial exclusion policy.

In the event, more than 200 young Chinese-Australian men would serve overseas in the AIF and in one of the ironies of international diplomacy, their troopships were escorted across the Indian Ocean by Japanese warships. This latter was kept strictly secret by the Australian government, much to the disgust of the Japanese press who took the country to task for its 'ingratitude'.

Once on the imperial battlefields, the Chinese-Australians distinguished themselves in combat. Indeed, nineteen were awarded at least 23 medals for gallantry. Caleb Shang, from Cairns, was the most highly decorated Chinese-Australian of the war, earning a Distinguished Conduct Medal and bar as well as the Military Medal. His numerous acts of bravery included stalking German snipers in no-man's-land in broad daylight, and manning a forward post until it was destroyed in a German advance. According to his DCM citation, 'His conduct showed a never-failing example of fearlessness, resource and initiative.'

The six Langtip brothers, whose father ran a successful market garden at Tarraville in country Victoria, travelled to Melbourne together in 1916 to enlist. But when the army medico learned they were all from the same family, he turned three away. The others – Henry, Leslie and Bertie – all became reinforcements for the Light Horse Brigade. Leslie rode in the famous charge at Beersheba and, according to family history, soon afterwards outside Damascus he came upon a lanky English officer berating his local troops. He gave the Englishman a piece of his mind and when he ignored the Australian, Leslie stepped forward and 'punched him on the nose'. The officer, later known as 'Lawrence of Arabia', was not best pleased.

But easily the most famous Chinese-Australian soldier was William Edward 'Billy' Sing who became the most feared and celebrated sniper in the whole AIF. Born in central Queensland cattle country in 1886, his feats in the Gallipoli campaign were the stuff of legend and Sing was credited with at least 150 confirmed enemy 'kills' during the Anzacs' eight months on the peninsula. Some put the figure twice as high.

Billy's father, John, had migrated from Shanghai in the 1870s and after the gold petered out he became a drover. He married an English girl, Mary Ann Pugh, and Billy and his two sisters grew up on a farm outside Claremont. All proved to be good pupils at the local school and Billy gained a reputation in his teens as a crack shot in competitive target shooting and as a kangaroo shooter. He was also handy with his fists when, according to his biographer John Hamilton, 'he was the subject of racial prejudice due to his ancestry'.

Sing worked as a cane cutter and in the haulage business. When war broke out, he hurried to his nearest recruitment post where the local enlistment officer decided his shooting skills outweighed his oriental looks. At the time, Sing was a neat 165 centimetres and 64 kilograms with a jet black moustache and a goatee beard.

According to Hamilton, Gallipoli was 'a country made for snipers. Each side sent out marksmen to hunt and stalk and snipe, to wait and shoot and kill, creeping with stealth through the green and brown shrubbery.'[3] Usually they were given a 'spotter' who would look out for marks on the other side and Sing's first off-sider was Ion Idriess, a country boy like himself who would later become a prolific and popular author. They operated first at Chatham's Post overlooking Shell Green and the Valley of Despair. Sing used his Lee-Enfield .303 to great effect and his fellow snipers left three particular enemy positions for his exclusive attention – a trench at 320 metres, a communications sap at 457 and a track in a gully at 914. Every day his casualty list mounted. According to a mate at the front, Private Frank Reed, 'Every time Billy Sing felt sorry for the poor Turks, he remembered how their snipers picked off the Australian officers in the early days of the landing and he hardened his heart.'

Indeed, the Turks had cut down the Australian General William Bridges on 15 May with a shot that sliced the femoral artery in his right leg and he died in the days afterward. Reed also claimed that, 'Billy never fired at a stretcher bearer or any of the soldiers who were trying to rescue wounded Turks.'[4] However, Hamilton refuted this: 'We have an anecdote where, after spotting an injured Turk, he said, "I'll put that poor cuss out of his agony" and just shot him. He was a very tough man.'

As it became obvious to the Turks that one man was taking a toll of their troops, they assigned their own top sniper, known to the Australians as 'Abdul the Terrible', to take him out. The Turkish sniper tracked the shots to Chatham's Post. According to Sing's new spotter, Tom Sheehan, when he alerted his man to a new target, the Queenslander was in the process of taking aim when he realised he was looking at Abdul himself. The Turk immediately went into his firing sequence but too late – Sing fired first and dispatched Abdul with a single shot. The response was a Turkish artillery barrage on Chatham's Post. The Australians ran for their lives.

In October, General William Birdwood, commander of the ANZAC forces, joined Billy Sing as a spotter on one occasion and later issued an order complimenting him on his 201 unconfirmed kills. According to historian Bob Courtney, Birdwood told Lord Kitchener, 'If his troops could match the capacity of the Queensland sniper the allied forces would soon be in Constantinople.'

Sing was hospitalised for myalgia – a painful muscle condition – at the end of November and would not rejoin his unit until March 1916 when he was awarded the Distinguished Conduct Medal. The unit returned to action on the Western Front in January 1917 where Sing received several commendations by his superior officers. However, he was seriously wounded in the left leg in March and evacuated to Scotland where, after a brief romance, he married a waitress, Elizabeth Stewart.

A month later he was back in action in France and in September he led a unit in the Battle of Polygon Wood where he was recommended for the Military Medal. Soon after he was a victim of a German gas attack and this brought his military career – and his marriage – to an end.

On his return Sing was feted as a hero but he withdrew from the public scene to the Queensland bush, where he worked on sheep stations and gold prospecting but without success. He died in poverty and obscurity in Brisbane during World War II. The war service of his fellow Chinese-Australians would not be acknowledged until family historians in the 21st century honoured them in websites and the Australian War Memorial collected their stories.

CHAPTER TWENTY-THREE
END OF AN ERA

In Beijing, Yuan Shikai's vainglorious attempt to occupy the imperial throne as the Son of Heaven would not be allowed to stand, and both Morrison and Donald were intimately involved in the imbroglio. Morrison had objected the moment he learned of the scheme and delivered the note personally. 'It is most injurious to your honour,' he wrote, 'for have you not affirmed in the eyes of the world most solemnly that you would uphold the republic and would be forever bound by the oath you swore in accepting the office of President.' Yuan's response was to refuse to meet with his adviser until the deed was done.

Three months later, with the country in turmoil, Donald confronted Yuan even more directly. He and his American associate and translator Roy Anderson were granted an audience. Yuan had met the Australian several times previously and referred to him laughingly as 'Old Southern Republican'. He was taken aback when Donald spelled out the dire state of the empire. The provinces were now in open revolt, Donald said, and China was in danger of disintegrating into another period of warring states.

According to Peter Thompson, 'Yuan Shikai stroked his walrus moustache. Only seven provinces were dissatisfied, he said. "Seventeen," Donald countered. "You must abdicate," he told him. "You must stop this make-believe." Yuan could have had Donald's head chopped off for such insolence but instead he murmured, "Old Southern Republican, I am tired," and shuffled out of the room.'[1]

Three days later Yuan Shikai issued a proclamation ending his three-month reign and restoring the republic. He declared his intention to resign and return to his now famous Garden for Cultivating

Longevity, in Tientsin. He then asked Donald to talk to the revolutionaries in Shanghai to see if they would grant him safe conduct for the journey from the capital. Donald made the trip to the Kuomintang's southern headquarters where he was surprised to find Sun Yatsen, who had left his Japanese redoubt to prepare himself for the Chinese leadership if the opportunity arose. The Kuomintang leaders readily agreed to Yuan's request for safe passage but before he could undertake it his health collapsed and in the morning of 16 June 1916 the 57-year-old soldier was found dead in his bed.

In the power struggle to succeed him, the Kuomintang leaders were effectively sidelined. Morrison and Donald took the opportunity to join with the new American minister, Paul Reinsch, in an effort to persuade the acting president, Li Yuanhong, to commit China to the Allied cause in the war. Otherwise, they said, his country would have no voice at the peace talks to demand the return of Shandong from the Japanese. Li vacillated. He had been trained by the Prussians as a military engineer and believed that Germany might well win the war. In any case his government was dominated by mercurial prime minister Duan Qirui, who ruled as the effective dictator of northern China, while in the rest of the country warlords arose to fulfil Donald's pessimistic prediction.

Morrison remained as an adviser to the central government and was unrelenting in his efforts to secure a declaration of war against the Germans. In February 1917 Germany announced that her submarines would sink on sight all ships in the vicinity of the British Isles irrespective of the flag at the masthead. Duan could see the value in lining up with the victors and soon afterward committed a force of more than 150,000 'coolies' to dig trenches and carry out other vital, non-combatant duties for the British army on the Western Front.

America broke off diplomatic relations and urged other neutral countries to do the same. Donald sent a message across the city to Morrison: 'China should follow suit within 48 hours. I am doing my best with the Chinese I know to stir the government up . . . Could you not get to the President tonight?'[2]

Morrison saw Li Yuanhong but returned to his home enraged by his 'weak, vacillating and tremulous' attitude. Moreover, the acting president had just dismissed Duan for his attempts to negotiate a secret loan with the Japanese, thereby alienating Sun and his pro-Japanese Kuomintang in Shanghai. However, when the French ship *Athos* was torpedoed in the Mediterranean with the loss of 543 Chinese labourers aboard, China broke off diplomatic relations with Germany and would formally declare war on 14 August 1917. Shortly afterwards, Morrison left for six months leave in Australia with Jennie and their family, now expanded to three sturdy and spirited young boys.

★ ★ ★

Throughout the war, the Chinese population in Australia had continued to decline as the White Australia policy took its toll. Their status within the national polity remained that of the unwelcome intruder. Across the country Chinese were progressively dismissed from commonwealth positions. They were gradually phased out of mining. In the Northern Territory they had numbered 575 to 101 Europeans at the outbreak of war but, according to historian Eric Rolls, 'Many were ageing and living rather hopelessly on less than one shilling a day . . . the atmosphere was one of general discouragement. The fields of work that the Chinese had established were now being progressively closed to them.'[3]

Generally, aliens could not vote, join the public service, carry mail or pilot aircraft. They could not form a company or even change its name without reference to the federal treasurer. In Queensland, no alien could buy or lease more than two hectares of land unless he could read and write English. In New South Wales, the alien could forfeit any purchase of crown land unless he became naturalised within five years, and this in spite of the commonwealth law that debarred aliens from naturalisation.

However, despite the tough conditions Chinese enterprise and energy provided the springboard for new ventures. Bananas had attracted Chinese merchants since the 1890s and in the early years of the new century they expanded their operations from Queensland to Fiji. One Sydney firm, Yock Sui, pioneered banana farming at Mullumbimby on the north coast of New South Wales; but they struggled with an infestation of black aphids. In the Northern Territory the Chinese started pineapple farms and secured yields of up to twenty fruit per plant. They planted peanuts in Queensland's Kingaroy area, an industry that still thrives a century later. The Chinese Chambers of Commerce in Sydney and Melbourne also arose in the war years to support their members wherever possible.

While on home ground, Morrison gave a series of public speeches in support of China as being critically important to Australia's security, particularly with the rise of an aggressive, expansionist Japan. He met with Prime Minister Billy Hughes and other leading ministers and intelligence figures, urging them to appoint diplomatic and trade consulates in China. He also met with leaders of the Chinese community and encouraged them to pursue two-way trade with their motherland.

Among them was William Liu, the young man who had raised the republican flag at the Melbourne consulate in 1912. Liu had been born in Sydney but, when he was seven years old, his English-born mother Florence became seriously ill and he was sent to live with relatives in Guangdong. He remained there for eight years and on his return to Melbourne completed his education at a variety of Christian schools and colleges. Now barely into his twenties, Liu was engaged in a daring venture to establish a shipping line between the two countries. The war had produced a virtual monopoly of Japanese lines for Australia–China freight as German vessels were withdrawn from the area and British ships were requisitioned for war service. The Japanese then took advantage of the lack of competition to raise freight charges by up to 1000 per cent.

The Chinese community was divided between the conservatives who retained their faith in the struggling central government and the progressive businessmen who supported Sun Yatsen and his Kuomintang. But the Japanese actions united them in outrage and in 1916 at Liu's initiative – supported by his father-in-law Gilbert Quoy – they had combined to raise £108,000 from investors in Sydney, Melbourne, Hong Kong, New Zealand and Fiji to buy two freighters, the SS *Gabo* and the SS *Victoria*.

The ships were registered in Liu's name as he was a native-born Australian and he took the role of general manager. But almost immediately, the Australian government requisitioned both vessels for war service. There was no appeal and the poor compensation offered meant that the company lost £20,000 in addition to the revenues foregone. Then, as the war ended, British ships returned to the trade and Liu's China-Australia Mail Steamship Line found itself in a price war with competitors who could call upon historic links with pro-British companies.

When the shipping line reported a loss of more than £60,000 in 1921, the old political and social divisions re-emerged and William Liu was replaced by Kuomintang leader Peter Yee Wing. This precipitated a revolt of the conservatives led by Gilbert Quoy and they withheld further financial support for the company, bringing about its total collapse in 1924. However, while William Liu paid due deference to his father-in-law, he was by no means a conservative himself. And at the risk of family harmony he joined the Kuomintang and became secretary of the Australian chapter. He also developed close links with the Commonwealth Department of External Affairs. The consequences would be far-reaching for Liu and Australia.

★ ★ ★

Meantime, China had secured its seat at the Peace Conference in Versailles. Indeed, after the Armistice was declared on 11 November 1918, 60,000 people turned out for the Victory Parade in Beijing.

Hopes were high that the peace talks would accept US President Woodrow Wilson's Fourteen Points which they believed would end extra-territoriality and, most importantly, the agreements imposed by Japan in the wake of the 21 Demands. Unfortunately, China's government was in disarray. In October, Xu Shichang, a close friend of the late Yuan Shikai, had been chosen as president in a compromise between the forces of Duan Qirui in the north and Sun Yatsen in the south. Morrison met with President Xu who asked him to attend the peace talks and assist the delegation to present their case. Though he was beginning to struggle with a disease of the pancreas that would end his life in less than two years, the Australian willingly agreed.

His compatriot Bill Donald remained in Beijing where his marriage was breaking up. He was frustrated about missing the 'big palaver' but was deeply concerned that he would lose contact with Muriel, the daughter he had come to love. Morrison travelled overland to Shanghai to judge the southerners' mood and was appalled at conditions in the interior: 'anarchy, no government, chaos, brigandage, piracy, highway robbery'. But he did have a useful meeting with Sun Yatsen. 'I was impressed by his sincerity and by a certain magnetism which I previously did not notice,' he wrote. The two men apparently resolved some of their long-standing differences.

President Xu had appointed the experienced diplomat and former foreign minister Lou Tseng-Tsiang to lead the delegation; but at the same time the young Chinese ambassador to Washington, the flamboyant Wellington Koo, travelled with his American hosts aboard the ship taking Wilson to the talks and they promoted him as the 'spokesman' for his delegation. When Morrison arrived in Paris at the end of January 1919, he found the Chinese 'at sixes and sevens'. At the Hotel Lutetia where most of the Chinese delegates were headquartered, he was dismayed to discover, 'it is like being with a circus'.

They had accepted their mission to abrogate the agreements with Japan entered into by Yuan Shikai and Duan Qirui and they demanded the return of Shandong. However, the dominant powers of the West, with their own 'concessions' on the mainland, had a vested interest in keeping Chinese claims at bay. According to historian John Fulton Lewis, 'The Allied powers realised the Chinese could do little harm to them, while the growing naval and military strength of Japan someday very well might.' Moreover, they looked to Japan to help prevent the Bolsheviks from effectively regaining control of those parts of Mongolia and Manchuria historically claimed by the Russians.

Wellington Koo gave an impassioned speech about the importance of Shandong province to China, describing the birthplace of Confucius and Mencius as 'the cradle of Chinese civilization'. If Japan were allowed to continue its lease of the Shandong territory, he said, it would provide Tokyo with a strategic gateway to all of north China. The Japanese not only demanded that the Shandong agreements be honoured, they volubly insisted on an end to 'international racial discrimination' by which they meant that they (though not necessarily the Chinese) must be accorded the same status as the Western powers in Wilson's plan for a League of Nations. The American president wanted to deal first with his vision for the league which he fondly believed would end the scourge of international warfare forever. And he was prepared to compromise to bring Japan into the fold.

Wilson was immediately confronted by Australia's 'Little Digger', Billy Hughes. The antipathy between the two men was immediate, vicious and deep. Hughes, whose selective hearing aid was legendary, violently rejected any agreement that tampered with the principles of his beloved White Australia policy. 'Sooner than agree to it,' he scribbled in a note, 'I would walk into the Seine – or the Folies Bergère – with my clothes off!' Wilson shook his head. 'What can you do with a man who won't read and can't hear?'[4]

Nevertheless, the American president tried to persuade the Japanese to 'demonstrate the spirit' of the peace negotiations and voluntarily withdraw from China. The Japanese remained intransigent. According to Lewis, 'Wilson decided that with the Italians already threatening to pull out, a similar exit by the Japanese would jeopardise the entire process . . . with some slight modifications the Allies accepted the Japanese terms. Many in the U.S. delegation warned that this was a shameful sellout of China.'

On 4 May 1919, as word flashed around the world, scores of Chinese students in Paris, and thousands of their angry compatriots in Beijing, took to the streets to protest against the American 'betrayal'. One of them, a young library assistant at Peking University, was so outraged he handed out leaflets and beset passers-by to the point of exhaustion. His name was Mao Zedong.

The Peace Conference, in Donald's words, 'knocked the stuffing' out of his friend and mentor. And in its wake a tired and sick Morrison retired to England where he engaged in an increasingly desperate struggle to counter the effects of his pancreas condition. But in vain. He simply wasted away at a rented cottage in Devon. And with Jennie at his side, he died on 30 May 1920, aged only 58. A wreath of orchids was placed on his coffin. It bore the inscription, 'In sorrow and gratitude, from the President of the Republic of China.'

CHAPTER TWENTY-FOUR
CHANGING THE CHINESE GUARD

Australia's Chinese population was dismayed, but perhaps less surprised than most, at the outcome of the Peace Conference since they had been the victims of discrimination for more than 40 years. But from time to time individuals had at least lifted the edge of the White Australia curtain.

Thomas J. Bakhap, for example, claimed the Chinese heritage of his adopted father as 'an Australian of mixed blood, a combination of Irish and Asiatic'.[1] He grew up in Tasmania and spoke Cantonese fluently. He was elected to the Australian senate in 1913 and at the outbreak of war he condemned the 'insulting' discriminations of the *Defence Act*. He remained in the senate until 1922 and often spoke for his Chinese-Australian compatriots.

Gordon Lum was born in Melbourne in 1903. His parents had migrated from Guangdong before Federation to work on the pro-revolutionary *China Times*. Young Gordon was a natural sportsman. He played a first-rate game of tennis and in both 1924 and 1925 partnered Gerald Patterson to become Australian doubles champions. The following year he met a touring Chinese soccer player, Lee Wei Tong, who encouraged him to move to China where he not only became national champion in tennis from 1927 to 1929, but also played with the former emperor Pu Yi on his red clay court within the Forbidden City.

William Ah Ket, whose father had come to Victoria during the 1855 goldrush, grew up in Wangaratta where in his spare time he acted as a court interpreter. Encouraged by his mother to study law, he graduated from Melbourne University and completed his articles in 1903. As a successful barrister Ah Ket became a leading activist for the Chinese community as the Victorian government set about driving the Chinese out of any occupations where they competed with Europeans. In 1913 he travelled to Beijing as the delegate of the Victorian Chinese Chamber of Commerce to take part in the election of overseas Chinese to the new republican parliament. And from time to time he acted as consul-general for China. Ah Ket became a friend and mentor to William Liu and supported his and Morrison's call for Australian diplomatic representation in China.

The Chinese activists were briefly successful in 1920 when Prime Minister Hughes, in an impulsive gesture over lunch, offered the role of trade commissioner to a visiting English businessman, Edward S. Little.

Under questioning in Parliament, Hughes recited a refrain that would echo down the years like some magic incantation to open the door to riches beyond dreams of avarice. 'Australia's geographical situation places her within reach of the vast markets of the East [which] are changing before our eyes,' he said. 'Their taste for Western dress and foodstuffs daily expands. China, with its teeming millions, has awakened from its age-long slumbers. It moves; it is on the eve of great developments, calling for a supply of huge quantities of material. No country is so advantageously situated, and none better able to supply China's wants, than Australia.'

But when Little put aside his plans to migrate to New Zealand and accepted the £2000 annual salary, the business community was outraged. So was Australia's federal bureaucracy to whom 'the appointment of an Englishman with no first-hand knowledge of Australia was a slap in the face'.[2]

Undeterred, the former missionary who had been tempted from his cause by the siren call of mammon and had spent several years operating out of Shanghai, signed a one-year Government contract with an option for a four-year extension. He returned to the bustling southern metropolis the following year with an array of samples and proposals for the Australian export-import trade. However, he was not only in bad odour with Australian officialdom, his British compatriots were equally miffed that their former penal colony was intruding on their imperial conduct of Australia's international affairs.

In Shanghai Little found himself under fire from all sides. According to Peter Thompson, 'For the next two years he fought valiantly to do his job while the city's expatriate Australian businessmen subjected him to what he described as "malicious and groundless agitation".'[3] The British consulate simply refused to recognise him.

Even his staff turned on him. He had employed two Australian expatriates, Luke Crommelin as his assistant and a Miss McKinney as stenographer/typist. But within weeks they began to compile evidence of mismanagement that would be used against him in two government inquiries. The second was conducted by Senator Bakrap who was scathing in his treatment of the 'betrayer' Crommelin, but by then the die was cast. Little returned to Shanghai where he ruefully closed the office and prepared to put his case to the Australian government for compensation, a vain endeavour that occupied him for the next sixteen years until his death in 1939.

Also in Shanghai at the time was Mary Donald, who had returned there from Beijing with daughter Muriel following the vitriolic marital collapse. At 44, Bill Donald had quickly recovered his *joie de vivre* and his splendid home near the capital's legation quarter was the scene of many a rollicking party replete with French wines and classical music played on the latest American gramophone. He resigned the editorship of the *Far Eastern Review* in 1922 when the major shareholder, George Rea, insisted on publishing pro-Japanese articles. He continued to write for *The Times* but once again Japanese militancy became an issue when he received a telegram from the editor in response to a critical article asking bluntly, 'Why attack an ally?' Donald immediately switched allegiance to the *Manchester Guardian* where his views found a more congenial outlet.

But without the companionship of Morrison, Donald found that Beijing had lost much of its professional stimulus and he decided to move back to Shanghai. He was about to put his house on the market when the Chinese government made him an offer he couldn't refuse – the opportunity to develop a Bureau of Economic Information that would at last provide reliable data on Chinese industry and demographics. Over the next few years Donald and his team published the *Chinese Economic Monthly* and issued a stream of soundly researched statistics.

When *The Times* proprietor Lord Northcliffe visited Beijing, he sought out Donald to effect a reconciliation. The Australian returned as an occasional Special Correspondent, free to warn his readers of Japanese territorial and military ambitions.

However, the political climate in Beijing was verging on chaos as the northern warlords ran rampant in the provinces and raised insurrections in the capital. In the south, Sun Yatsen and his regenerated Kuomintang (KMT) had become convinced that the only hope for a unified China lay in his own military conquest from his base in Guangzhou. But Sun could not succeed without assistance from abroad and he used his contacts in the United States and Europe to plead with Western governments for support. When it was not forthcoming, he first approached the budding Communist Party of China then took his cause to Moscow in 1923.

He found Lenin in decline and Stalin locked in a struggle with Trotsky for the succession. But Lenin approved his manifesto and he was able to meet with leaders of the Comintern. He developed an immediate relationship with Mikhail Gruzenberg, who had taken the *nom de guerre* 'Borodin' after his favourite composer and was given the task of bringing China into the Soviet orbit.

Sun arrived in Guangzhou later that year and set about hammering the Kuomintang into a political and military fighting force, while at the same time converting its members to Soviet-style communism. He established the Whampoa Military Academy just outside the city with a suspicious Chiang Kai-shek as the commandant of the National Revolutionary Army.

In 1924 Sun made a visit to Beijing where to his delight he was met by a 10,000-strong cheering crowd; but almost immediately he was struck down by a debilitating illness which was diagnosed as cancer of the liver. Bill Donald visited him in hospital and found 'a gaunt little man with very large, brilliant eyes'.[4] Sun was later moved to the home of Wellington Koo where on his death bed he urged his wife Chingling and commander Chiang Kai-shek to take counsel from Borodin. Chiang Kai-shek agreed, but only to assuage the feelings of his dying leader who finally passed away on 12 March 1925.

In an editorial marking Sun Yatsen's departure, *The Times* reflected Donald's view that the Kuomintang had become divided between its moderate and its Bolshevik arms and 'it remains to be seen whether the extremist or the moderate group will control the party in the future'. In fact, the entire country would soon split into two contending forces, neither of which could be called moderate. They would be led by the two men who would dominate Chinese history for the next 60 years: Chiang Kai-shek and Mao Zedong.

★ ★ ★

Chiang Kai-shek had been born in 1887 to a family of salt merchants in Jiangsu province. His father died when he was eight and he was raised by his mother whom he later called 'the embodiment of Confucian virtues'. He was drawn to the military and attended the Japanese Military Academy in Tokyo where in 1907 he and his fellow Chinese students became zealous republicans determined to bring down the Manchu dynasty. When his classmates returned to China, Chiang remained to serve two years in the Imperial Japanese Army from 1909.

After the revolution he joined the Kuomintang and, when Sun Yatsen fled to Japan to escape the wrath of Yuan Shikai, Chiang joined him in exile. He returned to Shanghai from time to time where he gained a reputation as an associate of the murderous Green Gang of criminals and stand-over merchants. This collusion with the Triads reflected a mercilessly violent strand in his personality, one that would burst forth many times in his military and political careers.

Sun Yatsen sent him to Moscow early in 1924 to study the Soviet political and military system prior to his own visit and Chiang met with Leon Trotsky and other Soviet leaders. But unlike Sun he quickly decided that their methods were totally unsuitable to China. Nevertheless, he remained in contact with them by sending his eldest son, Ching-kuo, to study in Moscow. The boy was the product of an early arranged marriage with a fellow villager, Mao Fumei, who was five years his senior. Chiang would also take two official concubines before his most famous marriage in 1927 with Mayling Soong.

After the death of Sun Yatsen, Chiang operated from the rightwing faction of the KMT and used his military backing to outmanoeuvre his rivals, rising to become Commander-in-Chief of the National Revolutionary Army. He then launched a military campaign in July 1925 to defeat the northern warlords and unify the country.

In May of that year, yet another Australian journalist arrived in China to make his mark in the Chinese chronicle. Basil Riley was the son of the Anglican Archbishop of Perth and a Rhodes Scholar from the Hale School who read history at New College Oxford. At 30 years of age, he arrived in Shanghai as a Special Correspondent for *The Times*. Unlike his older compatriots, he observed a strict neutrality in his reporting and threw himself into the dangerous task of covering Chiang's civil war from its elastic front lines.

Riley took a special interest in General Feng Yuxiang, a Christian who reportedly enjoyed baptising his troops *en masse* with water from a fire hose. Feng had also spent time in Moscow but returned in 1926 and weighed in on the side of Chiang Kai-shek in a battle the following year that would pave the way for the conquest of Beijing. However, as Riley travelled north from Hangzhou to Zhengzhou, he broke away from the safety of staff headquarters and set off along a railway line to talk to some villagers. A small crowd gathered and this attracted a group of Feng's soldiers who took affront at the 'interference' of a foreigner. They attacked him with swords and cut him down before dragging his body into a nearby field and burying it. It has never been found.

Chiang Kai-shek led his troops into Beijing in June 1928 and declared himself head of the Nationalist government, with Feng Yuxiang as his vice president. At the same time in the south, Mao Zedong had fallen foul of his own communist compatriots and was being fiercely criticised for his 'military opportunism' and for his leniency with 'bad gentry' – communist jargon for the wealthy peasantry from whom Mao had sprung.

Six years younger than Chiang, Mao Zedong was born in Hunan province to an abusive father and a devoutly Buddhist mother. At school he much preferred the inspiring and engrossing tales within *Romance of the Three Kingdoms* to the formal texts promoting Confucian fealty to the old ways. At thirteen he reluctantly bowed to his father's insistence that he marry the seventeen-year-old daughter of a neighbouring landowner but immediately after the ceremony he renounced the relationship. At sixteen he moved away to continue his education and in 1911 he began middle school in Changsha, a hotbed of revolutionary fervour. He became a devoted reader of Sun Yatsen's newspaper, *Minli Bao* (*The People's Independence*), and cut off his queue in a symbolic rejection of the Manchu. The following year he joined the rebel army as a private soldier and once the emperor abdicated he put aside his weapons and expanded his reading to the world of socialism.

Over the next few years Mao tried many occupations while continuing his self-education at the Changsha library and gradually moved into the more radical left-wing groups. He fell under the influence of Professor Yang Changji and in 1919 followed him to Peking University where he was working as a library assistant when China was 'betrayed' at the Paris Peace Talks. Soon afterwards he moved to Shanghai where he flirted with the Kuomintang before taking the fateful step of joining the nascent Communist Party of China (CPC) in 1921.

From there Mao moved back to Hunan province where he organised communist branches and mass industrial actions. In June 1923 at the third congress of the Communist Party, Mao was elected to the leadership committee and sent to Shanghai. The party continued its cooperation with the KMT and the following year he became an alternate member of the KMT Central Executive. Soon the communists took control of the left wing of the KMT and when Chiang Kai-shek assumed the leadership after Sun Yatsen's death, Mao continued to assist the Nationalists in the revolutionary struggle, thereby earning the enmity of his party's leaders for his 'military opportunism' and other political felonies.

His response was to ignore them and in a mountainous area of Hunan he developed his own fighting force of 1800 peasant soldiers. In the political chaos that followed, Mao found himself attacked by the KMT and supported by Communist Party regiments as the fighting swept northward. He was then challenged by the pro-Russian wing of the Communist Party. Like Chiang Kai-shek, he believed that they had little grasp of the real China and he soon emerged as their most potent rival. But by the time Chiang had secured the presidency, the political gulf between them had become a chasm. In the years ahead China herself would be dragged into the abyss.

CHAPTER TWENTY-FIVE
CHINA IN THE 1920s

Australia's involvement in the political tumult of China in the 1920s was marginal at best. In 1925 the Communists had fomented a series of industrial strikes in Shanghai that degenerated into open conflict and a boycott of British goods. In the streets Westerners were spat upon as 'foreign pigs'. Strikes and protests spread to neighbouring provinces. Bill Donald, who was in the city at the time, wrote, 'War is wanted with Great Britain. The curious thing is that the Chinese believe they could fight anyone and defeat them – the valour of ignorance, of course.'

By chance the Australian light cruiser HMAS *Brisbane* was in Shanghai at the time as part of the British China Squadron. There was a sudden fear that Australia would be dragged into the fray. In parliament, a senior Labor figure, Frank Brennan, protested, 'God forbid that [members of] this House should lend themselves to the movement to crush the proletariat of the Chinese Empire who are emerging with difficulty from centuries of tyranny. I cannot imagine any action which would more gravely shock the Australian conscience than that we should so employ our navy.'[1]

Publicly, the government sought to make light of the affair but behind the scenes it cabled the British, demanding details of *Brisbane's* position and insisting that the ship should not be employed in any action 'unless absolutely necessary in order to protect lives and property of British subjects'. When an ambiguous reply was received from London, the Australian government responded immediately: 'As this is a matter of paramount importance it is imperative that it should be placed beyond any possibility of misunderstanding.' This triggered a quick response from the China Squadron commander: the Australian ship was returned to Hong Kong and its seamen put to work running tugs and harbour craft for the duration of the emergency.[2]

The Australian authorities were generally more concerned with the rise of Japanese militarism. In 1923 the new prime minister, Stanley Melbourne Bruce, secured an agreement from Britain to build an 'impregnable' base in Singapore to protect Australia from a southern Japanese thrust and thus save his government from heavy expenditure on its own defences. But China was drawn into sharper focus as the Communist Party gained a greater prominence and Chiang Kai-shek's government carried out a series of vicious purges of communist activists.

The most blood-curdling of these attacks began just before dawn on 12 April 1927 when 2000 hired gangsters, posing as members of the 'China Mutual Progress Association', moved through the deserted streets of Shanghai. During the night Nationalist soldiers had been posted in key positions in Nantao, Chapei and Hongkou, the western suburb of Jessfield and across the river in Pudong. At a given signal, the heavily armed thugs launched raids on dozens of union branches and Chiang's troops shot anyone who tried to escape. 'Members of the General Labour Union barricaded themselves in the Huchow Guild house,' *The Times* reported, 'while 300 communists with machine-guns stood at bay in the Commercial Press building.'

The workers resisted heroically but were overwhelmed when Nationalist artillery pieces were brought into play. Those who surrendered were mostly shot or beheaded. 'It is too much perhaps to say that the Communist power is broken,' *The Times* concluded, 'but certainly the communists have had a heavy setback.'[3]

The following day a huge procession of Chinese citizens marched down Paoshan Road with the intention of presenting a petition protesting the slaughter of their husbands, fathers, sons and brothers to the Nationalist military commander, General Pai Chung-hsi. Sentries and nests of hidden machine-gunners opened fire, killing 66 people and wounding 316. While soldiers with fixed bayonets murdered civilians who had been chased into alleys, the bodies of the dead and wounded were thrown into trucks and driven away.

Over the next few weeks, the Nationalists' military camp at Lunghwa on the outskirts of the city became a death camp where hundreds were executed. Among those who escaped the carnage was Zhou Enlai, who moved into room 311 at the Astor House Hotel with his wife. To avoid detection, he reverted to his thoroughly middle-class upbringing, donned a three-piece suit and passed himself off as a successful businessman.[4]

Australia's Christian missionaries in China became the target of an anti-foreign movement in 1927 when that year alone saw 98 evangelists withdrawing from their posts and returning to their home country. They brought accounts of 'Godless Bolshevism' in their emotional baggage. But there was so little interest in China from the general public that when the Anglican Missionary Society compiled and published a Christian textbook entitled *China: Ancient and Modern,* only six schools in the entire country acquired it for their classrooms.

Australia's Chinese population had fallen from about 33,000 in 1901 to only half that number (including those the statistician termed 'half-castes') twenty years later and was still declining. Indeed, when Bill Donald at the end of 1928 wrote to the government asking for the number who had immigrated to Australia that year, 'the Department of Home and Territories suggested it was a loaded question and refused to provide figures'.[5]

It was one of Donald's last projects for China's Bureau of Economic Information. He had not been paid the promised 2000 Mexican silver dollars a month for some time and he objected to the government's attempts to turn the operation into a propaganda vehicle. He was not short of alternative employment and had now become so engaged with China's political future that, like Morrison, he was prepared to surrender journalism for a direct involvement among the country's movers and shakers. He chose the rising military leader, 27-year-old Zhang Xueliang – known as 'The Young Marshal' – who succeeded his father as the military ruler of much of northeast China after the Japanese assassinated him in June 1928.

Donald had met the young man in Beijing where he was known as 'a dashing Romeo and a fine sportsman'. Zhang's headquarters were now in Mukden and Donald caught a train north to the old walled city where he discovered the Young Marshal had developed an opium habit. However, he was sufficiently in command to raise the Nationalist flag over Manchuria and he made it plain that he would resist the persistent Japanese incursions that had led to his father's murder. Chiang Kai-shek recognised his usefulness in maintaining control of the north and appointed him deputy commander-in-chief of the Chinese army and governor of North China. As his only foreign adviser, Donald would exercise an increasingly powerful influence over the young man.

Chiang Kai-shek had left his government in Nanjing and married the slim, elegant Mayling Soong in a civil ceremony at Shanghai's Majestic Hotel in Bubbling Well Road. He would subsequently convert to Christianity and declare Jesus, 'the first champion of national revolution'. However, while he had achieved a re-unification of his country on paper, China remained wracked with internal divisions north and south while the Japanese refined plans for complete conquest of the mainland from its island fortress.

By 1930 Mao Zedong was armed with a fighting force of 40,000 communist troops and citizen soldiers in Shanghai's hinterland and on 30 December they ambushed a unit of 9000 Nationalists, most of whom surrendered without a fight. Mao addressed the delirious victors and to the roars of the crowd, the Nationalist general was decapitated. The soldiers placed his head on a wooden door and launched it down the Yangtse as a 'present' for Chiang Kai-shek. It was a dramatic declaration of war.

In the north, Donald persuaded the Young Marshal to fight his opium addiction and early in 1931 he booked at entire wing of the Rockefeller Hospital in Beijing to undergo treatment. Donald accompanied him together with the Australian's latest girlfriend, a beautiful young Russian named Irina.

In Manchuria, Chinese engineers were building a rail line parallel to the Japanese South Manchurian Railway which was guarded by their Kwantung Army in total contravention of Japan's treaties with China. In the Young Marshal's absence, the Japanese set off a small explosive charge beside their own line and manufactured evidence that it was the work of Chinese saboteurs. The following day Japanese planes from Korean bases bombed Mukden and their troops invaded the Manchurian capital.

That evening Donald and the Young Marshal dined at the British legation and, to the Australian's dismay, his Chinese principal showed every sign that the hospital treatment had been ineffective. The next day Donald flew to Nanjing where Chiang Kai-shek had established his southern headquarters to discuss the crisis while the Young Marshal organised a rear-guard action in Manchuria.

Chiang decided to appeal to the League of Nations to intervene and ordered the Young Marshal to open a second front against the Communists. Both responses were ineffective; the Japanese poured in reinforcements and overwhelmed the Young Marshal's defences. They captured all three provinces of Manchuria – with its 30 million population – and declared 'Manchukuo' a Japanese suzerainty. They then installed the former boy emperor, Pu Yi – now a dissipated 25-year-old – as president and two years later would elevate him to emperor. The Young Marshal's troops were forced to withdraw south of the Great Wall.

At the same time the Japanese pursued their undeclared war in the south where in Shanghai their consul demanded the immediate banning of all anti-Japanese organisations and compensation for 'insulting offences'. Donald was in Chiang Kai-shek's headquarters in Nanjing, preparing to return to the Young Marshal in Beijing, when his old Shanghai friend Dr Wu Tingfang, now the city mayor, telephoned seeking his assistance. He caught an early morning train and arrived to discover the city in chaos.

The Japanese had established a 2000-strong garrison in Shanghai's Hongkou district and stationed a flotilla of warships in the port with 1200 imperial marines ready for action. 'I was at the mayor's house until 10.30 that night,' Donald wrote. 'I got to the Astor Hotel where I was staying at about 11 o'clock. As I reached Soochow Creek, I could hear rifle fire and machine-gun fire.'

It was the beginning of a fierce attack on the southern city with Chiang's 19th Route Army battling 4000 Japanese troops and marines in Shanghai's Zhabei district. The invaders' victory in the north freed 20,000 soldiers for service in the south and they established a firm beachhead from which later advances could be made as the strategic climate permitted.

Meanwhile, the Japanese government joined the diplomatic battle at the League of Nations over their northern acquisition. The league sent a five-man team under Britain's Earl of Lytton on a fact-finding mission to Manchuria, and Bill Donald joined it as an adviser to Wellington Koo who had been engaged as an 'assessor'. Donald wrote to his sister: 'We had a hectic time of it, being shadowed by [Japanese] detectives and harassed by police. Any Chinese who came near me was arrested. One fellow merely asked if I stayed in the Yamato Hotel at Mukden and for his pains was arrested and held by the Japanese incommunicado for six weeks – until the Commission left Manchuria.'

Donald kept the Young Marshal and Chiang Kai-shek informed throughout and when the league found against the Japanese – due mainly to American influence – the aggressors staged a dramatic walk-out from the assembly and on 27 March 1933 gave formal notice of Japan's withdrawal from the League of Nations. By then Pu Yi was totally controlled by his Japanese minders and his wife Wanrong had sunk into the opium addition that would lead to her ignominious death as a figure of fun to her Japanese jailors in 1946.

Chiang Kai-shek's internal struggle with the Communists was also intensifying. In Jiangxi, Mao was conducting guerrilla incursions while Zhou Enlai fought pitched battles against Nationalists.

Zhou, who would become one of the most revered of Chinese leaders, had been thrust into the role of military commander. Born into a family of civil servants in 1898, he had become a student leader in Tianjin. Like Mao, he devoured the chivalrous epics *Romance of the Three Kingdoms* and *Dream of the Red Mansion* and quickly gained a reputation as an outstanding scholar. In 1920 he travelled to Europe and in Paris joined with other radical students in the communist cause. On his return he joined the Kuomintang but broke with it as Chiang Kai-shek turned on its communist wing.

The Generalissimo – as Chiang now styled himself – had adopted the policy of 'encirclement and annihilation' against the communist strongholds and Zhou Enlai soundly defeated their first and second attempts. Chiang Kai-shek then arrived personally to command the operation but after another reverse he broke off to counter further Japanese incursions. However, when he returned in 1933 with the fifth encirclement campaign, he abandoned all restraint and with a massive construction of concrete and barbed wire he built a 'wall of fire' around the province and unleashed an aerial bombardment on the communist positions. The Red Army leaders were soon left with no choice but to evacuate and in 1934 began the legendary Long March, perhaps the most protracted, savage and ultimately the most successful rear-guard action in military history.

Meanwhile in the north, in early 1933 the Japanese had claimed the rich Jehol (later Rehe) province just north of Beijing as part of 'Manchukuo' and Donald accompanied the Young Marshal as they drove through a blizzard to the capital Chengdu. They found the city virtually abandoned by Chinese troops and the Young Marshal accepted his inevitable dismissal by Chiang Kai-shek. 'After my departure,' he told his troops, 'you must obey Generalissimo Chiang's orders and support the government unanimously.' Donald then convinced him to try once again to defeat his opium addiction and Zhang, together with his two wives who were equally addicted, put themselves under the care of an American Seventh Day Adventist doctor, Harry W. Miller Jr, who applied a radical deep sleep treatment.

The treatment was a remarkable success, so much so that the 32-year-old Chinese warlord would live to become a centenarian. Meantime, he and his party – including the Australian and his 'secretary' Irina – set forth on a European tour that included meetings with Italy's Benito Mussolini and several high-ranking British politicians. When urgent telegrams arrived with stories of mutiny against Chiang and with pleas for the Young Marshal's return, Donald persuaded him to continue his rehabilitation while he himself took a ship for Shanghai.

He arrived in December to discover the Nationalists totally divided between those who believed all their energies should be devoted to resisting the Japanese and others led by Chiang whose first priority was the destruction of the communists. Here was an opportunity, Donald believed, for the Young Marshal to mend his relationship with Chiang and further his own cause in the country's leadership. He arranged to meet Zhang's ship in Manila and brief him on tactics during the short voyage across the South China Sea.

He had prepared the ground for Zhang's arrival at a lunch with Mayling where no doubt he reported his complete cure. When she asked, 'What does the Young Marshal really want?' Donald was at his diplomatic best: 'Madame, as strange as it may seem to you, the Young Marshal only wants to serve China in the best way he can.'

As anticipated, Mayling reported the conversation to her husband and a meeting was arranged on neutral ground at the beautiful West Lake near Hangzhou, the setting for some of the most exquisite imperial poetry. Donald attended and fifteen years later recalled the meeting to his American biographer, Earl Albert Selle. A reinvigorated Zhang, he said, opened the conversation with a personal attack on the Generalissimo: 'Europeans don't think much of you or of China.'

Donald himself then followed the opening salvo with one of his own. With Mayling translating he said: 'You are ignorant because no one dares to correct you ... the country is riddled with graft and corruption while millions of ordinary Chinese people die of flood and famine. Where is the decency and nobility for the common man? Goddam it, sir, you've all become insufferably stupid.'

Chiang sat stony-faced as Mayling repeated the diatribe. 'China should be ashamed,' Donald continued. 'There is the obesity of wealth on the one hand, the hog wallow of poverty on the other. The rickshaw man and the wharf coolie are worse off than the horse and camel in many other lands.'[6]

Whether Donald was quite as roughly spoken at the time as his memory served cannot be known, but according to Selle the Young Marshal confirmed that Mayling 'even put in our Goddamns'. And it is not in doubt that following the meeting Chiang not only restored Zhang to his role as deputy commander-in-chief of the Nationalist forces, but gave him the task of defeating the remaining communists in three central provinces.

Mayling then asked Donald to take a formal advisory role in Chiang's inner circle. He declined, but in language that kept the door ajar. Meantime, the Young Marshal appointed him director of the Central China Economic Investigation Bureau, charged with developing trade and natural resources in Zhang's region of responsibility. Donald saw it as an opportunity to oppose the flood of cheap Japanese products, but he quickly realised that his plans were hamstrung by 'Chinese officials who care not one iota for the country or its well-being; who regard it as being a bonanza for their exploitation; who bleed it white'.

He reported his frustrations to Mayling and sought urgent action to stamp out the opium menace. Chiang introduced draconian measures to break up the trade with more than 100 public executions of dealers in Shanghai alone. Donald protested that only the small fry were being punished and asked Chiang to raise the stakes with the controllers at the top of the chain. Instead the Generalissimo, whose connection with the trade dated back many years, launched a 'New Life Movement' seeking a return to the Confucian values of old.

Donald's response may be imagined. But when the Young Marshal took up his new post in the ancient capital of Xi'an, Donald finally accepted Mayling's offer and transferred his allegiance to Chiang (who he called 'The Gissimo') and Mayling ('The Missimo'). He also farewelled Irina when she fell for an Englishman who offered her the security of marriage. Thereafter Donald and Mayling would become very close but there is no evidence from either party that the relationship was ever sexual. However, as reported in the *Herald Tribune* by a journalist who knew him, the 'increasingly well-polished rough diamond perhaps killed more ladies (in the complimentary Edwardian sense of "lady killer") than any other man in China's . . . Shanghai-Peking set'.[7]

Soon Chiang heard well-attested rumours from Xi'an that the Young Marshal was disobeying his orders to wipe out the Communists and instead was fraternising with the enemy. And it is true that Zhang had conducted an all-night discussion with Zhou Enlai, who had now become Mao's chief lieutenant in the Long March. The two sides had agreed 'in principle' to a united front against the Japanese since, in Zhang's words, 'they were Chinese so why fight each other?'.[8] The meeting would precipitate one of the most dramatic and far-reaching events of Donald's life. Indeed, without the Australian's involvement, China's history would have taken a very different turn.

CHAPTER TWENTY-SIX
CHINA IN THE 1930s

Early in December 1936 Chiang Kai-shek flew to Xi'an to personally take over from the Young Marshal and exterminate the Communist forces. In a fiery meeting Zhang protested that a political settlement was within reach that would permit a united front against the Japanese aggressors. And if Chiang persisted he would withdraw his loyal Manchurian soldiers to Fujian. The argument became extremely heated and at mid-afternoon Chiang broke off the talks and retired with his entourage to a hot spring pavilion on the outskirts of the city.

The Young Marshal then held an urgent meeting with his top commanders – including General Yang Hucheng – and decided on direct action. They sent a raiding party to capture the Generalissimo and force his hand. But when at midnight shooting broke out at the pavilion, Chiang leapt from his bed and with difficulty climbed a wall of his quarters, injuring his back in the process. Zhang's men found him shivering in a nearby 'cave', barefoot and without his dentures. They returned him to General Yang's headquarters where Chiang, having recovered his clothing (though not his teeth), dared them to shoot him.

Bill Donald in Shanghai heard of the kidnap from Mayling next morning and set out in Chiang's private plane, having cabled the Young Marshal to do nothing until he arrived. Before leaving he had armed himself with Chiang's diary – courtesy of Mayling – that proclaimed his hatred for the Japanese and pledged that once he had defeated the Communists he would spare no effort to expel the intruders.

When he arrived in Xi'an, Donald showed the extracts to the Young Marshal. He then asked permission to see the Generalissimo. According to biographer Peter Thompson, 'Donald found Chiang lying in bed with a blanket pulled over his head. It was bitterly cold and the room was unheated. He was also in great pain from his injured back. Chiang himself wrote an account of the kidnap in which he said, "At 5pm Donald came to see me. I was very much moved by his loyal friendship, especially as he is a foreigner (an Australian) and yet is willing to come so far on such a dangerous mission".'

Donald gave Chiang a letter from Mayling pleading with him to open negotiations with his captors. He then prevailed on the Young Marshal to make his prisoner more comfortable in his own quarters – albeit under tight guard – and promised to take his former employer's demands to the government in Nanjing. This he did and the following day set out with Mayling herself (and a spare set of dentures) to negotiate Chiang's release. They flew through a storm-wracked interior but made good time. On arrival Donald sought out Zhou Enlai and persuaded him to participate; and once all the parties had gathered, Mayling and Chiang hammered out a four-point deal with Zhang and the Communists.

Under the agreement, the Communists would confine their recruiting to their current area of influence and they would accept Chiang as the head of China's armed forces. In return, the Nationalist government would supply them with a large sum in silver every month; and Chiang himself would oversee the delivery of arms and ammunition to their soldiers. After the obligatory toasts to seal the bargain, Donald walked out of the Young Marshal's compound with the dishevelled and exhausted (but dentally restored) Generalissimo on his arm.

Whatever the bona fides of either side at the time, it was an agreement written on water. None of the undertakings were complied with, even though the Young Marshal performed his part in the shadow play. He accompanied Chiang's party on their flight back to Nanjing, declaring his involvement in the kidnap 'a criminal act' for which 'I shall accept even death if beneficial to my country'.

But he had no sooner left than his followers in Xi'an rose up against Chiang's forces and when the Nationalists put them to flight they eventually joined up with the Red Army. Chiang was displeased. He would keep the Young Marshal under 'house arrest' in various parts of China – and later Taiwan – for the next 55 years. Zhang would spend his days in peaceful pursuits, studying Ming dynasty literature.

The Generalissimo later denied that Donald was a paid adviser. In words very reminiscent of Donald's own style, he wrote, 'The fact is that he is a private friend and a frequent guest at my house. I might also add that, although drawn into my circle, he has sternly refused any honours.' In fact, in the wake of the kidnap he was prevailed upon – perhaps by Mayling – to accept the Order of the Brilliant Jade with Blue Cravat.

Donald's part in the drama was broadcast throughout the international press, and not least in Australia. He told his sister in a letter that, 'Somehow, without any effort I have managed to hold the confidences of all political factions in China.' The reason, he said, was that 'I have none of the European superiority complex. I tell them exactly what I think of them when they are wrong, which is much of the time, and I never humbug them.'

★ ★ ★

In Australia at the time humbug enjoyed free rein. As Japanese military ambition spread its poisonous tentacles on the Chinese mainland, the federal governments of the day knew little and cared less about the political machinations within its massive northern neighbour. The remnants of its Chinese community, with rare exceptions, stayed out of public sight. In 1936, a fortnightly magazine, *The New China,* published a poem that captured the sense of alienation felt by so many in the community:

> *Sink into the vastness of distant Australia*
> *The land is desolate, perpetual Autumn meets the eye*
> *Beat my chest and regret that I moved my feet so carelessly*
> *I wander in poverty. Among barbarians I do not feel free.*
> *My pockets are empty, I know no one who can help.*

There is a road to return home
But I would have to turn an ashamed head to take it.
An alien land is not dear.
Do not rashly throw yourself into such a place.

One of the more notable exceptions was the indefatigable William Liu who in 1932, as the Great Depression ravaged the Australian economy, succeeded in developing the first wool shipments to China. However, since Japan at the time took almost a quarter of the entire clip, the Chinese initiative provided very little commercial or political leverage.

Liu had been one of the founders of a lecture series honouring G.E. Morrison the year before. But the real instigator, he claimed, was Sir Colin McKenzie, the first director of Canberra's Institute of Anatomy. Canberra was still in its infancy with a population of less than 10,000 and the institute housed the city's only tertiary institution, the Canberra University College, which held its classes among the rooms devoted to anatomical specimens ranging from Ned Kelly's skull to Phar Lap's heart.

Liu visited the national capital in September 1931 and when he met Sir Colin, the director confided it had long been his dream to honour Morrison with a lectureship memorialising his remarkable role in China's recent history. He followed this with a letter to Liu suggesting that, 'If it were founded by Chinese citizens it would be a remarkable gesture of scientific friendship from China to Australia, especially if the first lecture were delivered by the Chinese Consul-General.'

William Liu took the idea immediately to William Ah Ket and by mid-January 1932 the Chinese community had raised £402 ($34,000 in today's money) to establish the series. The consul, W.P. Chen, had in fact known Morrison personally and he was more than happy to deliver the first lecture that year on the understanding that 'it would always be free of politics'. It was a stricture that subsequently would be honoured more in the breach than the observance.

The Australian government had declined to recognise Japanese sovereignty over 'Manchukuo' but otherwise had shown no particular interest in China's territorial struggle. Indeed, it formally asserted its 'neutrality' in the conflict. In 1932 the defence department received a request for small arms from the Nationalist government and the minister of the day, Senator Pearce, saw an opportunity to re-open the Lithgow Small Arms factory in Bill Donald's hometown. But when Britain placed an embargo on all arms to China in 1933, the former colony broke off negotiations.

The following year the Lyons government showed a glimpse of independence when it mounted the Australian Eastern Mission led by (Sir) John Latham, as attorney-general and minister for external affairs in the conservative government of the day. He had been the head of naval intelligence in the Great War and he was later Australia's naval attaché in London. Latham's favoured pastimes included fly-fishing in the Snowy Mountains with a group that included Colonel James Macarthur-Onslow, a descendant of John Macarthur.

The mission's itinerary included 'the Netherlands East Indies, Malaya, French Indo-China, Hong Kong, China, Japan and the Philippines', with the declared object of 'promoting friendly relations' all round. Latham spent twelve days each in China and Japan and declared that, 'The Chinese appear to have a great instinct for politics but little instinct for government. They can write wise books and enunciate fine principles, but they do not appear to be expert in the actual tasks of governing the country.'

According to historian E.M. Andrews, 'This superior attitude towards China was revealed in more embarrassing speeches he made in Canton (Guangzhou). In one he roundly upbraided the Chairman of the Provincial Government for the treatment of the British there, and in another he condescendingly praised the Chinese for improved buildings and roads.'[1]

On his return Latham wrote, in icy condescension, 'It appears to be universally admitted even by the most enthusiastic supporters of what is described as the Chinese Republic that the conditions of the people are more wretched and hopeless than they were in the last days of the Empire ... China is in pieces today, and may be in fragments tomorrow. It is, I suggest, desirable to frame a policy covering this contingency.' Accordingly, he urged a 'firm policy towards China', while on the other hand Japan was 'an example of a nation that has modernised and accepted Western ways under a strong government'.

Consul-General W.P. Chen took issue with the tone and content of Latham's remarks and wrote directly to the envoy: 'You spent your time in China mostly with Britishers or Europeans. When you were with Chinese you lectured and they listened. In Japan, however, the order was reversed.' Mr Chen protested formally to the government, but attempted to remain on good terms while doing so.

Latham was unmoved. He told parliament that China had been the 'aggressor' by using boycotts against Japanese goods and Japan had good reason to respond. Moreover, Manchuria had 'never been subject to Chinese authority'. His one concession to the importance of China to Australia's fortunes was in the geographical conundrum contained in his parliamentary address. It might be the 'Far East to Europe,' he said, 'but it was the *Near East* to Australia.'

Other Australian instrumentalities, both intellectual and commercial, explored the prospect of greatly increased trade with the region's most populous polity. The University of Queensland dispatched an academic to survey its possibilities on the ground; the chambers of commerce and manufacturers established advisory committees in each state as a precursor to a national trade delegation to explore China as a market for Australian primary production.

In 1935 the government decided to appoint a second trade commissioner to China even as the first, the increasingly desperate E.S. Little, mounted yet another futile offensive in his compensation campaign. Alas, on this occasion their choice of personnel – I.V.G. Bowden – was also unfortunate. Bowden had been born in Sydney in 1884 but his English family owned businesses in Japan where he was working when World War I broke out. He hastened to Britain and served in the Royal Engineers, marrying an English girl, Dorothy Dennis, while on leave. He returned with her to Japan and later to Shanghai where his trading house had opened an office. He was fluent in Japanese and several other languages but not Chinese. When his name was announced, the Chinese responded in bewilderment and refused for some weeks to accept the appointment. Finally, in September, he and an Australian assistant opened their office on the Bund.

There is very little evidence to suggest that Bowden's mission expanded Australian trade with China. In fact, in the absence of diplomatic representation he and his single staffer spent much of their time dealing with visitors passing through and complaining about the absence of recognisable Western food. The one occasion when his activities rated a mention in the Australian press occurred in 1936 when he responded to two English visitors who firmly believed the Chinese should be encouraged to eat more butter. Bowden set them straight in a press release which revealed a certain impatience. 'The only way the Chinese would be likely to eat butter is with bread,' he said, 'and bread and butter cannot easily be introduced into a Chinese meal.' Moreover, oils and fats were available to them at a few cents a pound whereas Australian butter cost more than £2. Besides which, 'rice took the place of bread' and to convert even the wealthier class of Chinese to a Western-style cuisine 'would be a disheartening task'.

Nevertheless, he came into his own in 1937 as Japanese aggression burst forth in August with their bombers attacking Hangzhou, Suzhou, Nanjing, Zhenjiang and the Shanghai–Nanjing railway. On Friday 13 August, the Japanese Third Fleet steamed up the Whangpoo River. The next night Bill Donald was at a council-of-war with Chiang Kai-shek and his commanders at the Nanjing Military Academy when a message was handed to the Generalissimo. He passed it to Mayling. 'They're shelling the Shanghai Civic Centre,' she wept, 'they're killing our people.'

More than 1200 Chinese and 26 foreigners lost their lives on Shanghai's 'bloody Sunday'. And that was just the beginning.

CHAPTER TWENTY-SEVEN

DIPLOMATIC CHANGES

In September 1937, Robert Menzies, who had replaced John Latham as attorney-general (and as the member for Kooyong), made a statement to the House of Representatives which showed very little appreciation of China's plight. Despite the detailed reports from Trade Commissioner Bowden of the ruthless Japanese aggressors who had 'slaughtered hundreds, if not thousands, of innocent civilians', Menzies' 'great regret' was that the conflict had led to the postponement of meetings to improve Anglo-Japanese relations.

In August 1938 Menzies travelled to Nazi Germany where he spent several weeks touring the country and emerged as a strong supporter of the appeasement policies of Britain's Chamberlain government. On his return to Australia he confronted waterside workers at Port Kembla who were refusing to load scrap iron for shipment to Japan. Menzies forced the issue to allow strike-breakers on the wharves. And when they displaced the union wharfies, Chinese market gardeners drove into the town with van loads of fresh vegetables for the strikers and their families. Menzies won the battle but thereafter was tagged 'Pig Iron Bob', a slighting sobriquet that would remain with him throughout his long political career.

One of his close associates, Essington Lewis, the chairman and managing director of Australia's biggest company, BHP, had visited Japan during one of his regular international fact-finding missions and been shocked to find a nation in ferment. On his return he told his board that, 'Japan may be described as a big gunpowder magazine and the people as fanatics; and any day the two might connect and there will be an explosion.'[1] He immediately set to and sketched out plans to fight back against a possible invasion of Australia.

When Menzies became prime minister in 1939 following the death of Joseph Lyons, Lewis warned the new Australian leader that in his view the 'impregnable fortress' of Singapore was nothing of the kind. However, Menzies was, in his own words, 'British to the bootstraps' and his faith in Britain's mastery of the seas was almost unbounded.

When Britain declared war on Germany in September and Menzies intoned his 'melancholy duty' to inform Australians by radio that 'as a consequence' they, too, were at war, his government reassessed its attitude to its Pacific neighbours. In a public address he corrected Latham's geography and declared, 'What Great Britain calls the Far East is for us the *Near North*' and gave notice that Australia would henceforth develop its own diplomatic relations with the United States, Japan and China.

The British government was not pleased at this show of colonial independence and in the case of China suggested that Australia might simply attach a liaison officer to the British legation. However, the new Chinese consul-general in Sydney, Dr C.J. Pao, sought to stiffen Australia's backbone and was widely reported when he called the move 'a new force in efforts to maintain tranquillity' among the nations bordering the Pacific. 'The present world situation and the Sino Japanese war,' he said, 'have made the promotion of closer Sino-Australian relations more urgent than ever before.'[2]

He then cabled Menzies and with breath-taking diplomatic insouciance recalled that, 'The peoples of your great country and of China have enjoyed a cordial relationship for more than a century ... In pioneer days, my people who were here helped in your struggle to conquer nature to build a solid foundation suitable for settlement. Twenty-five years ago when 150,000 industrious and hard-working sons of China met the gallant soldiers of Australia in the battle-fields of Europe jointly defending the liberties of mankind, the vital importance and great future of this country was fully recognised by China ... and when Australia appointed a trade commissioner to China, trade relations between our two countries were brought to the highway of development.'

Pao followed this with a letter to the minister for external affairs, John McEwen, then deputy leader of the Country Party in coalition with Menzies' United Australia Party, seeking 'an early exchange of diplomatic representatives between our two countries' and pointing out that 'it would hardly be in accord with . . . policies of justice and goodwill should Australia exchange diplomatic representatives with Japan without simultaneously adopting a similar step with China'.[3]

Meanwhile, in a burst of *realpolitik* Menzies cabled the British foreign secretary, Anthony Eden, that 'If Japan actively joins Germany it would seem obvious strategy to associate ourselves as strongly as possible with Chiang Kai-shek in supplies or even with reinforcements . . . and so limit [Japan's] striking powers against any part of the British or French empires.'

By now the Japanese forces had taken control of Shanghai and advanced up the Yangtse to Chiang Kai-shek's capital, Nanjing, where they would commit one of the more barbaric acts of the 20th century in the rape and slaughter of up to 300,000 Chinese. While Japan would challenge the extent and depravity of the atrocity – then and now – the evidence is against them and Chinese outrage has never been fully assuaged.

Bill Donald had been in the city as the Japanese bombers unleashed their deadly loads before he retreated with the government to Hangzhou. He had then joined Chiang and Mayling in a further withdrawal to Chongqing where he wrote speeches for Chiang for several months before he drafted an anti-Nazi passage which Chiang returned with a curt comment: 'I am not at war with Germany.'

Donald responded: 'I am.'

That was the moment when the Australian, at 64, decided his time in China was coming to a close. He said his goodbyes to Mayling and took a flight to Hong Kong where he loaded his yacht *Mei Hwa* on to the deck of a freighter bound for the South Seas. As the ship left the dock, he made his way to his stateroom where Ansie Lee, the eighteen-year-old daughter of a merchant banker friend, was acting as his 'secretary'. And there he began pounding out his memoirs on his trusty portable typewriter.

In July 1940 the Japanese prime minister, Prince Konoye, demanded that Britain withdraw her garrison from Shanghai and close the Burma Road, a move that would prevent munitions and supplies reaching the Chinese resistance forces. In Canberra, Menzies urged London to agree (though the New Zealand government took the opposite view on 'moral and political' grounds) and Australia refused to accept Chinese refugees from Hong Kong. But at the same time Menzies privately condemned Japanese aggression.

Stanley Melbourne Bruce, now Australia's minister in the United Kingdom, urged Menzies to back either one side or the other, while John McEwen argued that the Burma Road should be kept open. Menzies stubbornly pursued his 'middle road' of delaying tactics in the belief that 'time is on our side'. However, time ran out in September when Japan signed the Tripartite Pact with Germany and Italy. Their Imperial General Headquarters then set out to destroy Chinese resistance with massive air raids on Chongqing and other major cities in unoccupied China, leaving millions dead, injured and homeless.

Suddenly Australian public expressions of sympathy for China became the order of the day.[4] Even Sir John Latham, whom Menzies appointed as Australia's minister to Japan, criticised his hosts to their face. And while Dr Pao did not get his wish for the simultaneous appointment of a minister to China, the wheels were turning. Early in 1941 when Menzies was in London, the acting Australian PM, Arthur Fadden, leader of the Country Party, cabled him that conciliation with Japan now seemed 'out of the question' and the China appointment would be in line with United States policy. Moreover, there had been 'a substantial development of local opinion in favour of closer relations with China'.

Menzies discussed the issue with Eden and cabled his agreement that cabinet should make the appointment. They did so, in principle, the following day, 2 May 1941. However, it would be a further two months before they agreed on the identity of the man who would occupy the post. Menzies offered it to a former Labor prime minister, Joseph Scullin, who declined on grounds of ill health. The cabinet then turned to a civil service mandarin, a figure who might well have been drawn from the pages of C.P. Snow, Sir Frederic William Eggleston.

Born in 1875 to a legal family of Methodist faith, the young Frederic attended Melbourne's Wesley College which his grandfather had helped to found and at sixteen, during a family sojourn in Britain, he spent two terms at the Leys School, Cambridge. However, the temporary collapse of family finances prevented him from entering Melbourne University and he was forced to pursue his legal career by taking articles at his father's firm. Undaunted, in 1897 he won the Supreme Court prize for the best results in the final examinations and was admitted to the Victorian bar. He then began a lifelong association with Melbourne University and gave vent to his literary ambitions with essays on the interplay of literature and the law.

In his twenties, Eggleston overcame the intellectual restrictions of his Methodist upbringing and began a long courtship of 'Lulu' Henriques, the daughter of a Jamaican Jewish family with strong ties to Melbourne's artistic circles. They would marry six years later in 1904 when he started his own firm of solicitors. He entered public life as a municipal councillor and during World War I served as a lawyer in the court martial section of the AIF in Britain. He was transferred to the staff of Billy Hughes at the Paris Peace Talks, where he conceived a loathing for the 'Little Digger' that would add a full measure of cynicism to his political outlook. However, he became close friends with two other conscripts to Hughes's delegation, Robert Garran and John Latham. In time, they would together form the nucleus of a movement dedicated to the understanding and promotion of Australia's place in the Asia–Pacific region.

On his return to Australia Eggleston stood for the Victorian parliament and in the 1920s gained ministerial rank. However, he retained a fascination with regional affairs which would gradually evolve from the rather superficial view in 1930 that 'the Pacific is a good place for a holiday . . . and our economic future is bound up with it', to a much deeper understanding of the forces at play.[5] It was largely a process of self-education. In 1927 on his departure from elected office he joined the Institute of Pacific Relations (IPR), a quasi-political group of policy-makers and intellectuals from the US, Canada, Japan and China, and two years later he led the small Australian delegation to the IPR conference in Japan. He was 'awestruck' by Japan's 'organisation, efficiency and sense of civic consciousness' compared with his own country, which was 'putting herself to sleep . . . behind restrictions and tariffs'.

By contrast, like his friend Latham, Eggleston found China 'weak and unstable' and regarded Sun Yatsen's policies as 'a farrago of half-baked political radicalism'. But he broke with his colleague to show great sympathy for China's outrage at the system of 'extra-territoriality' imposed upon them by the colonial powers, Britain chief among them. In 1933 he joined with Garran and Latham to found the Australian Institute of International Affairs (AIIA) and though he would become the first chairman of the Commonwealth Grants Commission that year, his involvement in regional affairs continued unabated. He remained the commission's chairman throughout the decade and by then had become, in his biographer's words, 'a trusted servant of the commonwealth'.[6]

Sir John Latham's hand could easily be detected in his friend's appointment as minister to China while another Melbournian, Richard Casey, had already taken up his ministerial post in Washington. Unlike his compatriots, however, Eggleston – widowed at 60 and knighted at 66 – had allowed himself to become fat to the point of obesity. He suffered from arthritis and gout and walked with a cane. He would conduct his Chongqing office largely from the comfort of his favourite chesterfield. When he ventured out, his sedan chair had to be carried by four coolies instead of the usual two. Nevertheless, he made a strong, favourable impression on his hosts to whom his ample proportions and magisterial demeanour were in the honoured tradition of the Confucian sage.

According to historian E.M. Andrews, the legation became 'one of the bright spots in Chongqing's rather dull intellectual life', a haven where scholars, journalists, merchants and travellers met and discussed China and the world. It supported a staff of two (later three) of which only Australian-born Charles Lee, a Queensland University graduate, actually spoke Chinese.

Lee was a rare bird in the Australian diplomatic aviary. He was born at Pine Creek in 1913, the grandson of a Chinese miner whose son had established a store there and married within the Chinese community. But when he won the Northern Territory scholarship to the Southport School on the Gold Coast, the family moved to Brisbane while he boarded at the school. In his senior year he won a Commonwealth Scholarship to Queensland University where he completed a bachelor of arts degree in Latin, English, philosophy, history, politics and law. He assimilated so successfully that he was selected in the Queensland rugby union team and proved a brilliant scrum half.

Lee joined the Commonwealth Department of Trade and Customs in 1936. But he was clearly more suited to the diplomatic arena. He had learned Cantonese from his parents and in the next two years he studied Japanese at Sydney University. He transferred to the Department of External Affairs in 1941 and within six months was assigned to Chongqing.

The Chinese legation in Canberra from 1941 had a staff of 24 headed by Dr Hsu Mo, an American-trained international lawyer and experienced diplomat. On his arrival in Sydney, Dr Hsu had been welcomed by a crowd of Chinese waving Nationalist flags. He was widely reported when he told journalists that the two countries 'shared the same perils'. However, once settled in Canberra, he and his colleagues' exposure to Australian political and intellectual life was restricted to the offices, reception rooms and very occasionally the bungalows of the bush capital.

Eggleston's reports to Canberra were invariably lengthy and often bewilderingly discursive. Indeed, they were said to cause hilarity in London when read by Minister Stanley Bruce and the British panjandrums in the Dominions office.[7] But they included insightful reports of his meetings with everyone from Zhou Enlai, who ran the Communist office in Chongqing, to Chiang Kai-shek himself. In a note to Menzies he said, 'The China I do see is interesting but not inspiring. One or two heroic figures like Chiang, a few very fine minds, a lot of intriguing politicians and a mass downtrodden by landlords, moneylenders and profiteers, tolerating with smiling faces and full but undernourished bellies what could not stand for a moment with us.'

Eggleston is said to have had at least one meeting with Bill Donald before his departure from Chiang's entourage. But by now Donald had conceived a well-rooted contempt for Australia's attitudes to China so it was unlikely to have been productive. Indeed, when Donald and Ansie reached Auckland on his yacht – en route to Tahiti – William Liu heard of it and tried to persuade Donald to give that year's Morrison Lecture but without success; he would never set foot on his native land again.

By the time they reached Tahiti, Donald had abandoned his memoir on grounds that he 'would have hurt too many people'. But life on the fabled isle, punctuated only by the lapping of gentle wavelets on the *Mei Hwa's* hull, went from blissful peace to boring irrelevance. So when a series of cables and letters arrived from Mayling pleading for his help during her proposed tour of America, he found the siren call irresistible. 'I am returning,' he cabled. However, it was no easy task to travel from the middle of the Pacific to the Chinese mainland at war; and though he stayed in touch with Mayling and Chiang by cable, he and Ansie would only reach Manila before Japan's all-out attack on America and its Pacific neighbours on the fateful night of 7–8 December 1941.

By then the conservative Australian government had fallen and been replaced by the Labor Party headed by the former journalist John Curtin. Trade Commissioner Bowden had been transferred to the

Department of External Affairs and relocated to Singapore where he became Australia's representative on the Far East War Council. And in the wake of Pearl Harbor, Australia – in lockstep with America – entered the war in the Pacific.

China lost no time in joining the Allies and formally declared war against Japan the following day. Within three weeks Chiang's Nationalist troops had joined battle with Japanese ground forces in Mao Zedong's old stamping grounds of Changsha. They scored a decisive victory. However, British vacillation meant that the Burma Road would be denied to the Allies as a supply route to the Chinese defenders for much-needed materiel. Instead, after Japan occupied Burma, the Americans would be forced to fly 'over the Hump' to carry arms and ammunition to the Chinese fighters.

Elsewhere, the Japanese seemed unstoppable. As their forces advanced down the Malay Peninsula, Bowden's cables warned Canberra of the impending disaster. Also in Singapore was Ian Morrison, the eldest son of his famous father, who was working as a journalist at the Ministry of Information. He escaped in one of the last freighters to leave the city and when he reached Melbourne began work on a scarifying condemnation of British colonial incompetence in his book *Malayan Postscript*. The Australian government ordered Bowden to stay until the last moment. His final cable read, 'Our work completed. We will telegraph from another place at present unknown.'

According to Peter Thompson, 'In the early hours of 15 February 1942 Bowden and his two colleagues [Norman Wooten and John Quinn] left Singapore in the motor launch *Mary Rose* which ran into the Japanese Navy at the entrance to Banka Strait. The men were taken to Muntok Harbour where Bowden was involved in an altercation with a Japanese guard. He was led outside and half an hour later two shots were heard. Gordon Bowden had been forced to dig his own grave and was then executed.'[8]

CHAPTER TWENTY-EIGHT

ONE WAR ENDS . . .

In the Philippines, Bill Donald and Ansie Lee were captured by the Japanese invaders and interned with 400 other foreigners at Sulphur Springs in the hills outside Manila. Several internees recognised Donald and greeted him as a celebrity but he asked them to keep his identity a secret and they agreed. The camp commandant, a decent old German named Dahlan who had fought against the British in World War I, registered him as 'William Donald of Edinburgh', rather than 'W.H. Donald of Chungking'. He also stored Donald's papers and diaries in a locked shed and looked after them until the end of the war.[1]

Donald was later moved to the huge Santa Tomas University internment camp in Manila and then to a new internment camp which was being set up in an agricultural college at Los Banos on the southern tip of the Philippines' largest lake, Laguna de Bay. And there he would see out the war under conditions debilitating to his physical and mental health.

While the Australian legation at Chongqing had been witness to several Japanese bombing raids in the early days, from 1942 the Japanese concentrated their efforts on the drive south to the islands at Australia's north. According to the First Secretary, Keith Waller, the attacks which 'had made physical conditions almost unbearable virtually ceased'. Waller, a graduate of Melbourne's Scotch College and Melbourne University, habitually wore spats and affected a patronising air. He joined the Department of External Affairs in 1936 and would remain within its confines throughout his career as a member of the 'old school' of Anglo-Australian bent.

In Chongqing, Waller resented the Chinese attitude to British colonial policies and their undisguised disdain at the collapse of British defences in the face of the Japanese advance. He treated Charles Lee with unabashed racism. In a dispatch to the department, he wrote, 'In Canberra Lee was a neat and scrupulously clean little fellow, but once he was among his own people he began reverting to type with astonishing rapidity. [He] uses the Chinese privy which is so extraordinarily dirty and smelly that no European would dream of using it for a moment. He has to be driven to baths by elaborate and rather primitive jests and now eats completely *au Chinoise* with his mouth open and shovels his food in as if he were eating rice. The poor wretch does not speak English let alone Chinese.'[2]

Waller's superior, Sir Frederic Eggleston, was much less in the thrall of the British. Indeed, he had conceived a particular loathing for Winston Churchill that had its beginnings in World War I when, as First Lord of the Admiralty, he withdrew all British naval vessels from the Pacific to confront Germany and pressured Australia to contribute its own ships as well. Churchill had added insult to injury with the disastrous Gallipoli adventure and was now virtually abandoning the Pacific theatre to the Japanese. Eggleston found him 'fallacious and self-serving'. After a particularly Eurocentric Churchill speech, he reported with barely disguised fury to Canberra, 'We have been striving to build up the belief that . . . the British countries are interested in China and sympathetic with her difficulties; Churchill's speech undoes in a few moments the work of months.'

British operations in China during World War II were uniformly unsuccessful. In Burma on 16 April 1942, almost 7000 British soldiers were encircled by an equal number of Japanese troops and had to be rescued by the Chinese 38th Division under General Sun Li Jen. While the rescue mission was successful, Britain's 1st Burma Division lost nearly all its heavy equipment and was exhausted and disorganised. Most of its Burmese troops took the opportunity to desert.

Churchill's government had earlier promised to assist Chinese resistance with a Special Forces contingent raised from their British garrison in the Burmese colony together with elements of the Australian 8th

Division in Singapore. Dubbed Mission 204 and better known as 'Operation Tulip', two Australian officers and 43 men joined an initial force of six British commando units for training at the Bush Warfare School in Burma. In the event, three of the British units dropped out, two for other operations and the third was disbanded because of 'ill-discipline'.

While their British compatriots were being rescued by General Sun, the Australian and British commandos drove their trucks for nearly three weeks more than 2000 kilometres up the Burma Road toward Yunnan province. They then travelled another 800 kilometres by train before trekking across a mountain range to join up with the Chinese 5th Battalion. Eggleston made the effort to visit them at their Kiyang base in Hunan province in May 1942. By then they had been in the country for six months and though they had trained some Chinese troops in demolition work, they had yet to fire a shot in anger.

Eggleston reported, 'This inactivity has naturally produced great dissatisfaction among the men who have become thoroughly discontented.' Indeed, it seems that many had wanted to return to Burma to conduct guerrilla actions against the Japanese forces and permission was given. But they had travelled no more than 150 kilometres before they were ordered back to camp. According to the diplomat, 'The Australians were returned, much to their dissatisfaction.'

Their camp in the hills was in pleasant country, undulating and well timbered, with nearby mountain ranges up to 1000 metres. 'A feature of the district is a number of very large, substantially built family houses [that] have been taken over by the military and serve as Headquarters and barracks,' Eggleston wrote while lodging with a former Chinese consul-general, Dr Chien, at the encampment. 'The Australians have the reputation of not only being the most powerful but the keenest and most interested in the country and the people.'

There was 'a good deal of sickness' in the ranks, he said, but a well-equipped hospital had been established in an old Chinese temple. 'The men have a feeling of frustration because the Chinese show little disposition to accept their advice,' he wrote. In fact, the Chinese leadership had little respect for the Westerners' fighting prowess and no inclination whatever to permit them to operate independently on Chinese soil. And the longer they remained the more embarrassing the situation became.

The Chinese response was to remove them even further from the action – to a poverty-stricken district on the borders of Hunan, Hubei and Kiangsi provinces. There they quickly fell prey to cholera, malaria and other debilitating diseases, and were finally withdrawn to Australia. Though Eggleston was personally gratified that the officers were 'vigorous and capable' and 'the other ranks are the same typical "diggers" I used to know twenty-five years ago', his conclusion was as accurate as it was sombre: 'I have the greatest doubt whether the whole scheme as it was devised was one worth trying.' The only consolation was that the Australians escaped the fate of their mates in the 8th Division who had been forced to surrender to the Japanese at the fall of Singapore and who died in their thousands in POW camps and on the Burma Death Railway.

In 1943 a second contingent of British commandos was assigned to Chinese 'Surprise Troops' but they were withdrawn before the Chinese went into action against the Japanese. Of the 180 soldiers involved in both operations, there were only three fatalities – two British and one Australian who succumbed to cholera.

No further British fighting missions were attempted, though the Americans continued to resupply Chinese forces and provide air cover against the Japanese air force throughout the war.

Back in his legation on the more salubrious heights of Chongqing, Eggleston was engaged in a series of testing diplomatic initiatives. He had arrived determined to end the insidious extra-territoriality which the Europeans had imposed on the Qing dynasty starting with the British Opium Wars of the 1840s. Britain was also prepared to end this practise, which made Europeans immune to prosecution under Chinese law, and to sign a treaty that recognised China and its people as having the same rights as any other self-governing territory. Moreover, they urged the dominions to join in the diplomatic initiative and the Canadians were prepared to do so.

But when Eggleston saw the British draft agreement, he was appalled. It conferred the rights of 'travel, trade and residence' on the Chinese, whose foreign minister, Mayling's brother, Dr T.V. 'Paul' Soong, made it plain that he regarded these measures as simple basic rights between equals. Outright rejection of the pact would constitute a 'slap in the face' of a valued ally. Yet neither the Australian minister nor his government could possibly sign a document that swept away the White Australia policy, especially at a time when the 'yellow hordes' were on his nation's doorstep.

Dr Soong understood the problem and was prepared to be accommodating. He assured Eggleston that he was 'not trying to steal a march, and the matter of immigration could be left till after the war'. But the Australian remained suspicious, as did his foreign minister Dr H.V. Evatt who counselled 'utmost caution' in dealing with the issue.[3] There followed a series of inconclusive discussions with Chinese officials and to handle the increased activity the government upgraded the legation.

Keith Waller had married his fiancée Alison Dent in Bombay in early 1943 and brought her back to the legation, but only until he moved on to more congenial postings in Europe and the United States. He was replaced as First Secretary by Keith Officer, a Gallipoli veteran and 'a thorough and methodical worker who liked order and routine'.[4] He had attended annual assemblies of the League of Nations and in 1937 was appointed Australian counsellor attached to the British embassy in Washington, which permitted an easy transition to becoming Australia's first minister there in 1940. Officer then transferred to Tokyo and was *Chargé d'Affaires* there at the outbreak of war.

A mid-level diplomat, Malcolm Booker, also joined the team and the following year the Australian government would send two young graduates from their Canberra intake, Barry Hall and Bill Bray, for their first overseas postings, as well as the first woman in the legation, Maris King, who was plucked from the typing pool and would go on to a notable diplomatic career. The young diplomats were said to be 'well known and well liked' in Chongqing and 'in true Australian style, referred to their rotund Minister as "The Egg".'[5]

The legation in which they all lived and worked was a two-storeyed roughly square mud-brick building painted blue-grey, with a tiled roof that leaked during summer storms. It sat in a narrow block behind a high wall on the north bank of the Yangtse. In front was a flagpole, a coat of arms and a Chinese police guard.

In his unpublished recollections, Barry Hall described the building in detail: 'Upstairs were the Head of Mission's study and bedroom on one side and bedrooms for two senior staff on the other. In between were the common sitting and dining rooms with a tiny screened balcony in front. The sitting room held the Legation's library and a few ornaments collected by Sir Frederic. The dining room was dark and cheerless but could seat twelve.'

The ground floor was made up of a large entrance hall-cum-waiting room which also housed the locally engaged clerk, typists and *tingchais* who ran messages, stoked the stoves, delivered mail and cleaned the offices. Hall and Bray had their offices and bedrooms on the ground floor. The domestic staff lived behind the main building where they played mah-jong late into the night. Hall recollected: 'Keith Officer was convinced a pig was being kept there, fed on our scraps, and wanted it removed in spite of denials from all concerned.' If so, it was never discovered and Officer was forced to take out his frustration on the hens who were 'scratching up the miserable little garden that he was trying to establish in the front'.[6]

There was no piped water or sewerage. 'Water was brought in from an outside well in buckets by the "chair coolies" employed to carry Sir Frederic's sedan chair. Bath water was heated in the kitchen and carried to the bathrooms. There was no way of cooling it if it came too hot!,' Hall said. 'Thunder boxes, somewhat unnerving if you met them being carried downstairs while escorting an important visitor up, were taken out and their contents disposed of to a farmer for his fertilizer pit.'

The building had electric light but insufficient power for any appliances. According to Hall, 'After 5 pm on the long dark winter evenings reading was usually impossible and sometimes we had to play bridge to fill in the time before dinner.'

He added that, 'Drink for entertaining was a problem. Our main reliance was on a variety of gin, brewed up in the hills allegedly by two Germans who had escaped internment for that reason, and delivered in great earthenware jars labelled "Mountain Dew". Drowned in juice, it served its purpose.'

What struck Hall most forcefully was the role now played by the remarkable Charles Lee. In addition to his childhood Cantonese, Lee had acquired a fluency in Mandarin and was 'the principal interpreter, translator, office manager and political contact man'. But that was just the beginning. 'He was highly respected and well known throughout Chungking,' Hall said. 'He could communicate with everyone, high and low. If a subject had to be followed up, Charles would take his walking stick, set off on foot for a round of his official, media and other contacts, many at very senior levels, and bring back the answers. Without him, the Head of Mission and the rest of us would have been relatively isolated and ineffective.'

Malcolm Booker became good friends with his Chinese-Australian colleague. 'His Cantonese had given him access to the inner circles of the Kuomintang Government, as many officials were from the south,' he said. 'He was treated almost as a member of the family of Sun Fo, the president of the Legislative Yuan and son of Sun Yatsen. He knew everything there was worth knowing about what was going on in the regime, about its conduct of the war with the Japanese and about its continuing conflict with the communists. At the same time he gathered intelligence from the "other side" through Zhou Enlai, then the official representative of the Communist Party in Chongqing.'[7]

Lee frequently entertained his fellow diplomats, much to Hall's delight: 'Charles had contacts in theatrical circles and took us sometimes to modern plays in which his friends were performing, as well as to traditional Chinese opera performances. I can recall a number of cheerful parties in restaurants, usually instigated by Charles, forcing me, inter alia, to raise a laugh with my limited and painfully acquired repertoire of Chinese.

'Our Legation's relations were closest with the Canadians, with whom we alternated Christmas dinners, the Dutch and of course the British Embassy [as] we were dependent on the British for a range of assistance including King's Messenger service bags, organisation of supplies from India, inoculations and a visiting dentist.'

However, none of these friendships could solve Eggleston's White Australia dilemma. Britain and America signed treaties with China on 11 January 1943 to finally end the extra-territorial rights on 22 March. Eggleston suggested Australia might simply associate itself with the British treaty. But the Australian government, through foreign minister 'Doc' Evatt, argued that since it had never been a party to the system, it was 'illogical to discuss the ending of rights which had already ended'.

The Chinese, however, were anxious to have a treaty to clarify the issues and also a promise of trade negotiations. They raised the stakes by engaging other European countries in similar treaties. After Belgium signed in November, Eggleston sent a grim cable to Canberra: 'When they have completed their list, we shall be confronted with a situation in which we are among a very few dissidents.'[8] And when their closest friends, the Canadians, confided that they, too, were considering a treaty, Eggleston appealed to Evatt to intervene. The foreign minister duly sent an 'emotional' letter to his Canadian counterpart Mackenzie King (who was also his country's prime minister), explaining that the Chinese actions were 'calling into question such a fundamental national policy as White Australia'. Undeterred, Canada signed their treaty with China in April 1944.

By then Eggleston was back in Australia on leave before taking up his new post as minister in Washington. He became concerned that China might use Australia's recalcitrance against it in any peace conference after the war and feared a replay of Billy Hughes's racist stand against Japan at Versailles. He met with Evatt and proposed a compromise which retained the essence of the White Australia policy but offered travel, trade and full rights to those Chinese who were already 'lawfully resident' in Australia – at the time a mere 13,000, including 'half-castes'. The Chinese demurred and, without a treaty, relations between the two countries could not advance to a full-fledged embassy but would remain at legation level throughout the war.

★ ★ ★

Bill Donald survived his captivity, though by the time his Los Banos camp was liberated by General MacArthur's troops on his much-vaunted return to the Philippines in February 1945, he was little more than a walking skeleton. He had lost contact with Ansie, who had remained at Santo Tomas where she became engaged to an American banker. Donald had not only lost his health but all his worldly possessions. 'I ought to get to China to try to rescue something,' he said.[9]

He headed first to San Francisco on the SS *Noordam* where he reunited with his daughter Muriel who was working as a newsreader on a radio and television station. His former wife Mary was also in the city and Muriel was supporting her, but the two didn't meet. Donald was anxious to get to New York where Mayling had established herself and was said to be estranged from Chiang. However, he delayed briefly in San Francisco when contacted by the Australian delegation attending the drafting of the Charter of the United Nations. He told Muriel, 'They want me to go back to Australia and be their Far Eastern Adviser.' He declined.

When he finally reached Mayling's Manhattan hotel, he was overwhelmed by the reunion and her wish that he resume his former role as adviser to herself and her brother T.V. Soong, the Nationalist government's foreign minister. But as his strength returned, the prospect of a reprise to his old job faded and he had 'a lurking wish to go back to New Zealand'. However, he remained in New York while across the Pacific the American bomber *Enola Gay* delivered the atomic knockout punch to the imperial Japanese war machine.

When the war in China ended, Keith Officer, who had succeeeded Eggleston at the Australian legation, recalled the euphoria: 'Within a few moments Chungking was in a state of hysteria: shouting, singing, parading the streets and, as on every possible occasion in China, letting off strings of firecrackers. A US Army camp near the Legation appeared to celebrate the occasion by the almost continuous firing of revolver shots – one hoped well into the air, but even then wondered where the spent bullets were falling! When the police guard at our gate commenced to discharge their rifles I felt the fun had gone far enough and should be checked!'

The Chinese had played their part in tying up more than a million Japanese troops who would otherwise have been available for Japan's drive south to Australia. In this, it fulfilled much the same role as did Russia for Britain and the nations of Western Europe, and at a similar toll of perhaps 20 million military and civilian deaths, to say nothing of the terrible cost to the women and children at the hands of the enemy. Australia had reaped the benefit while maintaining the purity of its European bloodlines. White Australia survived and prospered. Not surprisingly, perhaps, Chiang Kai-shek's speech on the defeat of Japan would contain no thanks to the Allies and made no mention of Australia.

In the wake of Emperor Hirohito's surrender, peace negotiations between Chiang Kai-shek and Mao Zedong opened in Chongqing in August 1945 and Australia's Charles Lee used his contacts on both sides to keep Keith Officer informed. But there was more show than substance to the talks and Officer had decided that whatever the outcome, the Asian leviathan and its diaspora in most South-East Asian countries represented a potential threat to Australia.

Indeed, the Labor government in Canberra was disturbed by the 'fascist tendencies' of the Nationalist regime. Reports of Chiang's methods, including 'wide powers of search, arrest, imprisonment and intimidation, the murder of political opponents and the power of landed and financial interests', continued to arrive in Canberra from security and diplomatic sources.[10]

Donald, too, became aware of the tense and repressive political climate, but at 70 he felt his options were limited. His health was poor and he believed an extended sea voyage would provide the rest and resuscitation needed to get him back on his feet. In October he sailed for New Zealand, via Tahiti, intending to make his way eventually to Australia and then China. But he fell ill in Tahiti and at the French hospital his attending physician gave him the bad news: one lung had collapsed and the other was full of fluid; the specialised treatment required was not available at the island resort.

He cabled Mayling who by then had returned to China where the American General George Marshall was attempting to mediate between the Nationalist and Communist forces. She arranged with Marshall for an American flying boat to take the Australian to Honolulu where he was admitted to the Aiea Naval Hospital. There Donald learned that the French doctor's diagnosis had erred on the side of optimism. In fact, he was suffering from terminal lung cancer.

He cabled the Chiangs that he wanted to die in China and they responded by sending a Nationalist aircraft to return him to Shanghai. He wrote to his daughter Muriel, 'I am still here, looking forward to going back to Shanghai to see how things are there.' Of his death sentence, he said, 'To tell you the truth I feel nothing. I never did feel anything in the way of sensation and I feel no more or less today.'

He was admitted to the Country Hospital where Mayling visited him from Nanjing several times and made a car available to him for short drives in the hinterland. He discovered that his house in Beijing had survived the war and made arrangements to sell it with the funds going to Muriel. His visitors included George Morrison's middle son,

Alastair, who recalled, 'He was a frail and gentle man who could joke about the solemn way a group of doctors told him he had terminal lung cancer.'[11]

In November as the nights drew in, his strength began to fail and he cried out for Mayling. When she heard the end was near, she ordered a plane to take her to Shanghai but there was a delay and it seemed she would not arrive in time. When she finally reached the hospital, she hurried to his room. His breathing was laboured but he was still conscious. She sat beside the bed, picked up the Bible and read the 23rd Psalm. His last words to her were, 'We'll meet again in the next world.' Bill Donald died at 1.15 a.m. on 9 November 1946.

In the following days the *China Press* editorialised in terms that might well have come from Mayling herself: 'Australia can be proud of Donald who served as a better Ambassador of Goodwill than could have any career diplomat, for in his every word, in his every deed, Donald showed the marks of the tradition of democracy which has made Australia what she is today. Yet Donald was more than an Australian, more than a man of "European" background. He was something far greater, far finer – a citizen of the world.'

PART THREE
AFTER WORLD WAR II

CHAPTER TWENTY-NINE
CHALLENGES AND OPPORTUNITIES

The second great conflict of the 20th century had created a new world order as America asserted its growing 'superpower' status as leader of the free world in a Cold War struggle against the Soviet Union. The British Empire began its inevitable decline as its colonies asserted their independence; while in China the Communists under Mao Zadong gathered their forces for the final confrontation with Chiang Kai-shek's Nationalist regime.

By the end of 1946 Australia's career diplomats in the legation had, with great difficulty, made the journey from Chongqing to Nanjing and finally – after an unconscionable delay of more than two years – the Australian government had appointed a replacement for Frederic Eggleston. Ben Chifley had become prime minister on the sudden death of John Curtin in July 1945 and he chose a New Zealand-born academic economist, Douglas Copland, to head the Australia legation.

It was an idiosyncratic choice. Born in the tiny town of Otaio on New Zealand's South Island in 1894, Copland had migrated to Australia in 1924 after being overlooked for two professorial chairs in New Zealand. A group of local businessmen led by Sidney Myer had combined to finance a faculty of Commerce at Melbourne University and engaged Copland as the founding professor. He would occupy the post for the next twenty years and would rise to prominence through the Great Depression when economics assumed a more influential role in the public discourse. When he failed in his application to become the university's vice-chancellor, he turned his attention to Canberra and in 1939 became the Commonwealth prices commissioner throughout the war. He was generally regarded to have been a 'great success' in the post and until 1945 was also an economic consultant to succeeding prime ministers.

While Copland had visited Japan in 1935 as a guest lecturer and had travelled to Britain, Europe and the United States, he had shown no particular interest in China or the Asian region. But he was delighted with the offer and the Department of External Affairs assured him that they would be upgrading the status of the China post to ambassadorial level. While his wife visited her family in New Zealand, Copland arrived in Chongqing in March 1946 with his own personal secretary Sylvia Brown. He was greeted by a staff headed by First Secretary Patrick Shaw, who was in the early years of a very distinguished diplomatic career. His first posting had been to Japan in 1941 where he had been interned briefly at the outbreak of war, then to New Zealand as the High Commission's Official Secretary.

Copland's early dispatches revealed an instant dislike of the Nationalists whom he found to be 'inefficient, corrupt and intractable, and destined to be replaced by the communists'.[1] And while it was a judgement based on personal talks with Zhou Enlai, and therefore widely supported and undoubtedly well founded, it revealed an entirely appropriate hostility to the Nationalists that would soon be reflected in Canberra and among the wider Australian community.

In April, the legation joined the mass diplomatic exodus from the wartime capital to Nanjing and while the arrangements were left to Third Secretary Barry Hall, Copland took the opportunity to travel to Beijing, Tientsin and Tsingtao at the invitation of the British ambassador, Horace Seymour. It would be the first of several ventures from his post. According to Copland's biographer, 'His time in China was that of an itinerant. He travelled widely, attended the first session of the United Nations General Assembly [in New York] and participated in preliminary negotiations for drafting a peace treaty with Japan.'[2]

Meantime, Hall oversaw the packing of the accumulated trappings of the Chongqing legation and worked with his friends in the Canadian embassy to secure passage on one of the dangerously overcrowded steamers heading down the Yangtse towards Nanjing. Having been rebuffed by the shipping company in favour of government officials several times, Hall finally learned of the one large steamer departing Chongqing in May after Copland returned from his trip to northern China.

Assisted by Charles Lee, he secured third-class tickets and oversaw the loading of the legation's goods and chattels. The ship was fearfully overcrowded and according to Hall, at the last minute, 'a Major General of the Nationalist Army . . . forced his way on to the ship with a drawn revolver'. Once underway they were entranced by the famous Yangtse gorges and at stops along the way were struck by the number of 'unguarded Japanese POWs in the streets, shopping and in some cases fraternising with the Chinese'. Hall noted that, 'They appeared to be well fed, cheerful and in extremely good condition, a great contrast to the schoolboy Chinese soldiery who were also much in evidence . . . We finally arrived at Nanjing on May 29th, having made a remarkably rapid journey.'[3]

Copland sent a message to Canberra complimenting Hall on his efforts.

In Nanjing the legation residence was situated on a hill in a district known as The Hall of Returning Clouds. It boasted a swimming pool and a yard large enough to host garden parties and even cricket matches with the British and visiting ships' companies. The city chancery in Peiping Road was some distance from the living quarters which the diplomats were required to share, at least in the early stages. The Shaws' young children slept in a room adjoining Copland's bedroom and other staffers were scattered through the building. Copland wrote often to his wife Ruth and daughter Rosemarie encouraging them to join him but it would be several months before they arrived.

His letters chronicle the diplomatic rituals of a legation head with only the most superficial understanding of China, its history and politics but with an abiding interest in his own career as an academic economist. Indeed, it is clear that he relied almost exclusively on Charles Lee, recently promoted to Second Secretary, for any insights into China's unfolding political turmoil.

'It is quite remarkable how many people he knows, both Chinese and European, and how popular he is with everyone,' Copland wrote on 6 July. 'Among others he was called over by Madame Sun Fo who has just returned from America. Her husband is the son of Sun Yatsen by his first wife. There is quite a joke about Charles and Madame Sun. Some two years ago she took it into her head that Charles should be married and half in jest said that she would get him a wife. To his surprise and consternation she proceeded to do so and announced that she had a young lady whom she would like Charles to meet and marry.

'If he had gone and had not married the girl, Madame Sun would have lost face. Fortunately for Charles, he was just about to return to Australia on leave and he got out of the fix by telling Mde Sun it would be very embarrassing for him just then as he was going away and didn't know how long it would be before he returned.'

More seriously, Copland said, 'If Charles should fall for a Chinese girl he would be in an awkward fix because he couldn't take her back to Australia unless he got special permission.' However, he told his wife, 'I think you will like Charles; he is certainly one of the most pleasant fellows I have had working for me for a long time. He lives all alone over the Chancery and is greatly enjoying himself because it is the first time he has really been on his own since he came to China. And he likes going out late to some obscure little Chinese café for dinner. He comes up here all the time protesting that he comes up too often, but he wants me to come out to one of his haunts with him for dinner.'

Copland seldom took up the offer but the intelligence Charles provided – together with the gossip and information received from his own dinners and receptions – allowed the minister to keep up a steady flow of despatches to Canberra. 'The department circulates a digest of despatches from all the Legations,' he wrote, 'and I notice there is far more from China than from other places. In [Keith] Officer's time the despatches from this place were pitiful. Shaw's were a vast improvement in the period in which he was acting.'

The talks between Chiang Kai-shek and Mao Zedong broke down in June as fighting between the two sides erupted in Manchuria, and the Australian diplomats could only act as a listening post to make sense of what was happening around the country. Fortunately, Lee used his contacts with the press to gather information coming into Nanjing from the provinces. He travelled to Beijing where he liaised with other diplomats, notably the Russian consul-general with whom he discussed political recognition of a Communist China should Mao's forces prevail.

The legation's finance officer and vice consul, Bill Hamilton, recalled Lee's work as 'extraordinarily valuable' in this period. 'He was able to reach sections of the central government that no one else could,' Hamilton said. 'So very often [Chinese] cabinet decisions were known in the Australian embassy before they were known anywhere else, simply because Charles had friends who would tell him within a very brief period.'[4]

As a result Copland says he was 'sounded out' by Zhou Enlai 'as to whether there was not some form of international mediation that might be adopted' to stop the evolving civil war. 'I must say that I sympathised with them,' he wrote, 'but I could only say that I would call on Zhou early next week and have a further talk. Meanwhile I'll have to send a message to Canberra about the talk. I don't expect much response.'[5]

His fears were well founded. And his work was not assisted by the news emanating from Australia where the White Australia policy was being applied in all its prejudicial insensitivity towards the Chinese population which had reached a low water mark of 12,000, of whom 7000 were registered aliens having arrived during or just before the war. The Australia–China Association appealed to Chifley to allow the merchants and families, business assistants, students and the remaining 1500 evacuees to stay. Otherwise, they said, the end of the war would see the final dissolution of Australia's Chinese community. The government was obdurate – the refugees were not welcome.

According to E.M. Andrews, 'The crisis was slow in developing. The Minister, Arthur Calwell, had close friends in the Chinese community and spoke a little Mandarin. He therefore began by being moderate, and in early 1946 persuaded the Cabinet to allow Chinese children born overseas but with an Australian-Chinese father to enter the country. In April 1947, in response to an approach by the Chinese *Chargé d'Affaires*, he tried to make the conditions of entry more liberal but was overruled in Cabinet . . . The rationale behind White Australia became confused and contradictory and the Labor Party blundered into an issue which brought it into disrepute.'[6]

The government decided to enforce the departure of the wartime refugees. Calwell came under increasing political fire for his intransigent stance, culminating in his infamous jest in parliament that 'Two Wongs don't make a White'[7]. However, elements of the Australian press, the churches, academics and an increasingly sophisticated public were expressing opposition to the policy and the apparently heartless manner in which it was administered.

In China, politicians began referring to Australian 'discrimination' and when the influential newspaper *Shanghai Xinmin Bao* gave its readers chapter and verse of the policy's sad history, Copland had great difficulty in having his reply published. Charles Lee had established a good relationship with the editor and at his request Copland's response was finally printed some weeks later. However, the effect was to revive the issue in public and government circles.

In Australia, the Chinese Nationalists were in disrepute with accusations in parliament of graft and widespread corruption in the management of funds from the UN Relief and Rehabilitation Administration (UNRRA). There were clashes over Chinese actions on Manus Island concerning their salvaging of American war surplus; and partly in response the Nationalist government led an attack on Australia's administration of New Guinea in both the Trusteeship Council and the General Assembly. Then in 1948 in the phosphate-rich Nauru, a UN trusteeship administered by an Australian-led authority,

500 Chinese labourers rioted over working conditions. Four Chinese were shot and killed while a further fifteen were wounded.

So when China called for a resumption of negotiations over the long-delayed treaty between the two countries, there was little goodwill on either side to smooth the way to a resolution. Moreover, General Marshall had declared his mission to secure a rapprochement between Nationalist and Communist forces a failure and had departed. The spreading civil war in China made a mockery of the UNRRA effort to rehabilitate the country and its economy.

CHAPTER THIRTY
MAO'S DECLARATION

The ever-ambitious Douglas Copland attended the UN General Assembly early in 1947 and before returning to Nanjing spent thirteen weeks in Australia where he complained to Ben Chifley that the lack of action on the promised upgrading of his position to ambassadorial status had 'disturbed' the Chinese. He was also concerned that 'spiralling inflation has placed a considerable burden on myself and my staff'.[1]

Chifley's response is not recorded but he no doubt mollified his former adviser.

However, on Copland's arrival back at the legation he was shocked by the changes wrought in his absence. 'It is a very different Nanking from the one I had left,' he wrote to fellow economist Bernard Foster. 'In the interim the civil war had gone wrong, as it was bound to. There was a tremendous increase in prices and no end to the inflationary movement in sight, and political unrest was boiling up to a crisis. None of my Chinese friends could offer any hope of any improvement, and very few of them actually wanted to talk about it.'

Copland's attempts to negotiate the much delayed 'friendship treaty' continued to be hampered by Canberra's unbending attitude to any concessions that might be interpreted as a weakening of the White Australia policy. While the New Zealand government was concluding its own treaty without any such concerns, the Australians would quibble and procrastinate until events in China swept it into one of history's missed opportunities.

The arrival of his wife and daughter did little to assuage Copland's morale as both found it difficult to cope with Nanjing's stifling summer heat. Frederic Eggleston was now an adviser to the Department of External Affairs and in July Copland wrote to him that he was 'not particularly well pleased with Australian relations with China. With the dead weight of a return to Kuomintang dictatorship, there is neither life nor inspiration in Nanking, and by the end of the year I certainly think I shall have exhausted all the reporting I think to be worthwhile.' He wanted to travel to the north, 'not only to the cities held by the government but out into the Communist area' but he doubted that his 'friends in Canberra' would approve.

In fact, Copland was able to visit Beijing and from there observed that, 'It is not stretching one's imagination too far to say that if the Communist campaign in Manchuria is successful, the fortunes of the Government armies to the north of the Yellow River will be seriously affected.' It was not the most courageous observation in the unfolding drama and helps explain the attitude of the professional policy-makers in the department. Clearly, Copland was no longer a valued asset in the post. And when Eggleston raised the prospect by return mail that he might be interested to apply for the vice-chancellorship of the new Australian National University (ANU), Copland leapt at the chance. Over the next few months Eggleston would guide the appointment through Canberra's corridors of power.

On 30 June 1947 Mao's communist forces had crossed the Yellow River and attacked the Nationalists on three fronts in the north and east. They mounted a six-month siege of Changchun, the capital of Jilin Province, and forced the surrender of Chiang Kai-shek's forces at a cost of 150,000 civilian deaths from starvation. They appropriated the army's tanks and heavy artillery and powered south of the Great Wall, cutting Chiang's forces off from the ancient capital of Xi'an. They followed with an all-out attack on Shandong province in September 1948 and early the following year overran east-central China.

By then Copland had returned to Canberra to take up his academic post and the government had reinstated Keith Officer and – no doubt to Copland's chagrin – upgraded his position to ambassador. However, they had withdrawn most of the staff and Charles Lee was one of the few to remain.

In April 1949 the Communists crossed the Yangtse, driving south and taking Nanjing. Chiang and his government retreated to Guangzhou but the Australian embassy remained in place. In his despatches Officer argued that the Communists would undoubtedly be the future government; they would follow the Moscow line but would modify it to their own conditions and purposes. Western nations, he advised, should do everything possible to establish and maintain relations with them so they could influence their policies.

In Canberra, Eggleston supported the thesis, referring to his report during his time in Chongqing: 'The [Chinese] Communist Party as it exists today is a radical party devoted to agrarian reform. Indeed, I never meet the members and leaders of the Party without being impressed by their unrevolutionary mildness.'

Thus encouraged, Officer cabled Foreign Minister Evatt who had now added the presidency of the United Nations to his responsibilities, recommending that he make a statement urging both sides to open negotiations without delay and without unnecessary or harsh demands.[2] Evatt responded by suggesting Officer make himself available as an 'informal mediator' between Nationalist and Communist. This, however, was beyond even the remarkable capacities of Charles Lee to engineer and it came to nothing. Evatt then made one of his long, rambling speeches in parliament that mentioned the possibility of UN mediation only to provoke a hostile rejection from the Communists, now on the brink of total victory.

On 1 October 1949 Mao Zedong proclaimed the People's Republic of China at the Gate of Heavenly Peace in Beijing. One of the guests of honour was Chingling Soong – now Madame Sun Yatsen – who Mao had met at the station together with Zhou Enlai and other Communist dignitaries. Chiang Kai-shek had built a magnificent memorial to her husband in Nanjing and now he was being embraced by Chiang's hated rivals. 'Today,' she said, 'Sun Yatsen's efforts at last bore fruit.'

Chiang Kai-shek, 600,000 Nationalist troops and about two million loyalists and sympathisers retreated like the Ming dynasty court before them to Taiwan, which until 1945 had been in Japanese hands. He also took with him the vast treasure of Chinese art and crafts that had been stored in the caves surrounding Chongqing throughout the war. Once on the island, he imposed his governance on the 11 million Formosans in a regime of martial law.

Mao took up residence in a compound next to the Forbidden City and ordered the construction of palatial quarters, replete with indoor swimming pool, as the combined office and living area from which he would control the Communist imperium.

He and Premier Zhou announced that China intended to establish diplomatic relations with all friendly nations and the Soviet Union was the first to recognise the new government. The Chifley government, on Keith Officer's advice, had been considering *de facto* recognition of the new regime since early July. It was certainly the view of the prime minister and would have been supported by Eggleston and Copland, who maintained contact with Officer from the ANU. However, the issue was complicated by Britain's insistence that it retain its Hong Kong colony and America's anti-communist belligerence.

Chifley believed that without Western relationships, particularly in trade, China would develop 'a simple hermit economy'. But his cabinet and party were split on the issue and the mercurial Evatt had a foot in both camps. Chiang Kai-shek lobbied for a regional grouping – including both Australia and New Zealand – to continue the civil war. Chifley was diplomatically non-committal; the whole China issue had become an ill-timed distraction from the post-war reconstruction, with an impending federal election.

Officer remained hopeful of a decision to recognise the regime and moved with Charles Lee to Shanghai with their bags packed for Beijing. But on 25 October, Evatt publicly sided with the American secretary of state, Dean Acheson, who demanded the Communists demonstrate that their control over China 'was supported by the free will of the majority of the people' before US recognition would be granted. Indeed, Evatt added another condition – that China give 'firm and specific assurances that it would respect the territorial integrity of neighbouring countries, the British colony of Hong Kong in particular'.

The British foreign office was appalled and advised the press 'to treat Dr Evatt's statement with the scepticism it deserves'. They cabled their 'embarrassment' to their high commissioner in Canberra, 'since it attributes to the United Kingdom Government views which they do not hold and may complicate our relations with New China'.[3] Indeed, the following month at a Commonwealth foreign ministers meeting in Singapore, the British argued strongly for recognition to counter Soviet influence.

Evatt's response was to recall Officer urgently for consultations with himself and his departmental secretary, the 32-year-old John Burton, a controversial figure who had been his private secretary prior to the appointment. Also at the meeting was Eggleston, the New Zealand high commissioner and other senior figures from the department. Evatt opened proceedings by declaring that cabinet had decided on 9 November to refuse recognition, thus calling into question the meeting's entire *raison d'être*. The response from the participants, while couched in diplomatic terms, was a mixture of surprise, despair and barely controlled anger. It was clear that all of them, including the New Zealander, strongly favoured recognition. Evatt became excited and said the final decision was therefore 'deferred' and closed the meeting. He then released a statement that they had 'agreed with the principles laid down by Acheson'.

It was not true.

By then the Labor Party was engaged in a fierce election battle with the conservative forces led by a resurgent Robert Menzies at the head of the Liberal Party he'd established in 1944. The Liberal–Country Party Coalition was running hard on an anti-communist platform and Evatt was worried they would use recognition to brand Labor 'soft on communism'. Moreover, the charge played on the divisions within

Labor whose Catholic right wing was even more anti-communist than many in the centre of the Liberal Party.

The British understood the pressures on the Australian government and diplomatically withheld their recognition until five days after the election. The gesture was purely academic by then, because on 10 December 1949 the Coalition had won a handsome majority and Menzies began his second prime ministership, which would extend across the decades until 1966. Two weeks later, the new Australian cabinet decided to withhold recognition 'at the present moment' on grounds that it would only encourage the Communists in China to foment more trouble. The government then cut all communications with the Chinese Communists, closed the embassy and recalled Keith Officer, Charles Lee and the other staff permanently.

Charles Lee returned briefly to Canberra but kept his ties to China. While Lee was in Chongqing, Mayling had introduced him to a very attractive young Chinese woman, Nancy Chow, but she married a Nationalist army officer. It was not until some years later that he learned that Nancy's husband had died. He contacted Nancy and they were reunited then married in 1958. By then he had been posted to the United Nations in New York. Other postings followed to Jakarta, Singapore, the Philippines, New Zealand, Brazil and Spain where he reached the position of counsellor, one rank down from ambassador. Lee retired in 1973 and died in November 1996, aged 83. This extraordinary man's valiant contribution to Australia–China relations has only recently been acknowledged in academic circles, though never previously among the wider public.

Douglas Copland was knighted for his services in 1950 and, as ANU vice-chancellor, he reinstated the annual G.E. Morrison lectures which, despite William Liu's best endeavours, had been suspended during the war years. Indeed, Copland gave the 1948 lecture himself on 'The Chinese Social Structure'. He also secured the services of the highly distinguished China historian C.P. Fitzgerald as chair of the Department of Far Eastern History. Eggleston, too, remained deeply involved in the development of the ANU as Australia's principal repository of Asian studies and research.

Menzies' new foreign minister, Percy Spender, a former Sydney lawyer who had entered parliament as an independent before joining the Liberal Party, was a pillar of moderation by comparison with his predecessor. He believed that 'hostility to China would be absolutely fatal to long term stability' in the region. He told the British – and his own prime minister – that he was inclined to vote to admit China to the United Nations, thereby recognising the legitimacy of the new government. And he proposed to take the same message to American secretary of state, Dean Acheson.[4]

Spender's department believed that it was only a matter of time before Australia was obliged to take the step which would help to widen the split that was rumoured to have opened up between China and the Soviets. It recommended withdrawing recognition from the Chiang Kai-shek regime as a first step and Spender cabled Menzies from New York putting forward the case. Menzies was caught uneasily between opposing policy streams. His refusal to recognise Mao's government had effectively moved Australia from his beloved British association to the American camp. And when the Korean War broke out in June 1950, Australian commanders would head the British Commonwealth forces in the US-led United Nations 'police action'. Menzies compromised by taking no action at all on Spender's recommendation.

Chiang Kai-shek saw the chance to use the Korean conflict to restart the civil war and offered his Nationalist forces to join the battle. The Australian government saw through the ploy – it was about as transparent as such ploys get – and was in the process of putting their view to President Truman when word arrived that the Americans had 'squelched' the idea. Indeed, they had placed their 7th Fleet in the Taiwan Strait to prevent either side from attacking the other.

China's premier, Zhou Enlai, warned that 'an American intrusion into North Korea will encounter Chinese resistance'. General MacArthur, the US commander, ignored the warning and sent American and Australian troops over the border. As Allied forces approached the Yalu River on the Manchurian frontier, Mao Zedong unleashed the first of his Chinese 'human waves' in a massive counter-attack. Spender made a public statement assuring the Chinese that the Allies had no intention of using Korea as a springboard for an attack on Manchuria, but his voice was lost in the cacophony coming from the US where Truman was at odds with his commander in the field.

The issue was complicated by the negotiation of an ANZUS Treaty initiated and pursued by Spender. Neither he nor Menzies wanted to rock the diplomatic boat, though in private Menzies called MacArthur a 'ham actor' who had to go. At the same time the prime minister asked Spender to quietly open negotiations with China at the UN. But the initiative, if it ever took place, was stillborn.

From his Canberra office at the ANU, Copland chose the opportunity to declare that Australia had blundered by not recognising Beijing in 1949 because of the federal election. Petty domestic politics, he said, had been 'more important in world affairs than the new force which had arisen in China'. Spender responded with a restatement of government policy and a demand that the Communists demonstrate their bona fides by their actions. According to historian E.M. Andrews, 'This provoked a most merited and annihilating retort from Sir Douglas who remarked that he had more expert knowledge of China than "the Minister for External Affairs, Mr Spender would probably ever have" and he repeated his original charge.'

Spender was particularly incensed since at the time he was recommending to the Americans a two-stage approach – first a withdrawal of recognition from Chiang Kai-shek and later the recognition of Beijing with a seat on the Security Council. But when the principal American negotiator in the ANZUS talks, John Foster Dulles, came to Canberra in February 1951, Australian and New Zealand anxieties about the 'yellow hordes' and overpowering American muscle combined to kill the Spender proposal with barely a whimper. Thereafter, all Australian overtures for recognition of its most populous and powerful regional power ceased.

Exhausted and unwell, Spender retired from politics and in sad irony accepted appointment as ambassador to Washington. Without diplomatic representation on the Chinese mainland, Australia relied on shared British reporting and US intelligence agencies for information on the evolving Communist dynasty under Mao Zedong. Conditions in the cities and provinces remained largely unknown even to the government, while the Australian public received only that information which the Communists permitted to filter through the 'Bamboo Curtain'. And as the 1950s progressed, the Coalition government and their ideological allies in the Catholic wing of the Labor Party would manipulate the flow to portray China as a growing threat to Australia's well-being and even to its territorial integrity.

CHAPTER THIRTY-ONE
INTO THE HEART OF COMMUNISM

The reality within China was very different from the caricature depicted by the Australian conservatives which would culminate in slogans like 'the downward thrust of Chinese communism'. But it was certainly not the workers' paradise of socialist theory nor even the peasants' utopia that so many had hoped for. Indeed, even before he secured power, Chairman Mao had lowered expectations with the announcement of a series of 'stages' beginning with a fifteen-year 'bourgeois democracy' that permitted certain private ownership. Only then would China move on to building a truly socialist society.

In 1950, a young Australian named Pamela Tan left her family in Melbourne and set out for Beijing excited by the prospect of joining the great adventure of this 'New China'. Her father, Tan Qi-jun of Guangdong province, had jumped ship in Perth in 1928, and her half-Chinese mother, Choon Lei, had been adopted by Chinese shopkeepers in Little Bourke Street. Pamela was born in Mildura where the family ran a small vegetable shop, but when she was ten they moved to the city where Tan Qi-jun cooked in a Chinese restaurant.

By then the Chinese café had become a feature of every Australian city and a great many country towns. They had made their first appearance as 'cook shops' on outback stations and country pubs in the late 1800s; while Melbourne's Little Bourke Street boasted Chinese restaurants from the early decades of the 20th century. In the 1930s changes to the *Immigration Restriction Act* allowed cooks and café workers into Australia but since restrictions still applied to 'family reunions', restaurateurs brought in relatives under assumed names. They had little or no cooking experience but learned on the job. During World War II 'eating out' became more common and in the post-war boom cafés and restaurants proliferated across the country. While the dishes served were often modified to the Australian taste, the eateries on Little Bourke Street had the reputation as the best and most authentic Chinese cuisine in the nation.

Pamela had grown up in a country where anti-Chinese prejudice was a fact of life. 'At the end-of-year concert all the girls in my [primary school] class were dressed up as fairies in white tulle and glittering stars,' she says. 'At our last rehearsal, I heard someone say with a laugh, "Fancy having a Chinese fairy!" It hurt and made me wish more than ever that I was a white Australian.[1]

'On another occasion I was on the tram with my father and when we went to sit inside, the conductor came up and said, "She can sit here, but you, Charlie, have to sit outside. We don't want Chinamen inside with the ladies". It was terribly embarrassing and humiliating. Everybody looked as my father and I got up and went outside to sit in the open part of the tram. There were many incidents like this. English was my first language and my cultural background from the Greek myths to Shakespeare was Australian. But in those days Australians did not recognise other ethnic groups as their own people.'

Her sense of alienation was so profound that, 'At the age of fourteen I went to the office of the Chinese Kuomintang Consulate in Melbourne and asked if they had Chinese classes. There were none but the consul and his wife invited me to study the Kuomintang primary school text books with their 11-year-old son every Saturday morning, which I did for almost three years.'

However, Pamela says, the decision to travel to China did not arrive until she matriculated to Melbourne University. 'The final blow to any real assimilation into mainstream Australian society was a backhanded compliment from a fellow student: "You know, everyone reckons you're good looking for a Chinese," he said. "It must be because you're a half-caste". To me it spelt disaster to be classed in that category like my mother, despised by many and never accepted. I resolved then and there, no matter how, I would go to China. My parents thought it a worthy cause although my father had doubts. "It is very different from Australia," he said, "a very hard life. You couldn't get used to it". I was sure I could.'

Pamela entered the country of her heritage via a 'shabby' Hong Kong but 'crossing the bridge into China and seeing the red flag with its five golden stars fluttering in the wind against the blue sky, I felt a surge of pride. The station at Shenzhen was neat and clean and the workers in their navy cotton uniforms went about their duties with some dignity.' She continued by train to Beijing where she discovered she was among hundreds of overseas Chinese returning to the motherland.

'Some had come from Japan with Japanese wives and a similar number from the United States, Europe and Britain,' she says. 'They were all highly educated people, all imbued with the ideal of working for New China.' While the doctors and other professionals were quickly assigned to jobs, Pamela and many others were boarded in a former imperial palace until they could be placed: 'It was the time of the Korean War, or the War of American Aggression in Korea as it was known in China. We were taken to a stadium for a meeting to support the Chinese Volunteers in Korea. It was my first taste of politics in China with thousands of students filling the stadium.

'Knowing little Chinese, I was unable to follow what was going on. Every now and then slogans were shouted with people raising their fists. We had sat there somewhat stunned by the vehement rhetoric, anger and hatred being whipped up. The chairman read out a note which someone had written "Why aren't the returned overseas students shouting slogans too?" From then on we raised our fists and shouted with the crowd.'

From this time Pamela was known by her Chinese name Tan Pingmei. She remained unemployed for some months until she met an Australian union official, Ernie Thornton, president of the Ironworkers Federation. He was attached to the World Federation of Trade Unions and lived with his wife Lila in Beijing. They arranged for Pingmei to live and work at his Australasian Liaison Bureau where her job was to research Australia's and New Zealand's trade union movement.

'We lived a fairly Spartan life, getting up at six when the bell rang and some would do *tai ji chuan* exercises in the garden,' Pingmei says. Breakfast was served in the canteen at seven but some of the workers, Pingmei among them, would walk to the nearby Muslim shop for fresh bean curd milk and oil cakes.

'The owner, a young man in his thirties with a little white cap, smiled broadly each time we entered,' she recalls. 'He would take a white piece of dough and, beating his rolling pin to a rhythm, roll out enough to make a square, break an egg inside if you wanted, and fry it. You could also have it just sprinkled with molasses.'

However, he was living on borrowed time. The 'stages' for the gradual implementation of the Communist agenda had been abandoned along with Mao's assurance that China would never be like the Soviet Union with a proletarian dictatorship. 'What we did not know was that Mao had sneakily withdrawn the blueprint,' Pingmei says. 'Quietly things were changing. A year later those of us who went regularly to the Muslim shop were criticised for not living a simple and plain life. Under that pressure, we stopped going.'

The Communist Party members ate in a separate canteen with 'food suitable for their status'. According to Pingmei, 'The Chinese Communist Party has never believed in equality in the social sense. Seniority was taken very seriously. Those who joined the revolution in the early stages had more privileges than those who came later – in the houses to which they were assigned, in health care, in transport and so on. To have privileges is part of Chinese culture.'

After breakfast came an hour of political study, the Communist cadres working on Stalin's *History of the Bolshevik Party* and the others on Mao's *On the People's Democratic Dictatorship*. 'I tried my best to understand it,' she says, 'but at the time it didn't mean much to me. But in political study one idea that was impressed upon us was the question of which came first – matter or consciousness. It was stressed again and again, matter came before consciousness. It was always matter over mind, not mind over matter. I could not understand this emphasis until decades later when I began to follow and study Buddhism [which] places consciousness above matter. Buddhism was fairly widespread in China and in order to replace these ideas with communist ideology and atheism, "wrong concepts" had to be nipped in the bud. This began the stunting of the mind."

Pingmei's work was mostly routine. She translated extracts from the Australian press and taught some of her colleagues the geography and history of Australia. 'I found I learned much about Australia from my teaching,' she says. In addition to a full day's work, she went to night school four times a week for two years to study Mandarin. Most of the students were illiterate but it was one place where she was not made to feel an outsider. 'We were all in the same boat, our Chinese was no good, the difference being that they only had to learn to read and write whereas I had to learn vocabulary . . . in those days everyone had a sense of humour and the communists didn't go around reading ulterior political motives into everything that was being said and laughed at.'

For the first five years, Pingmei says, she was very happy:

> Lots of new things were happening and I felt I was taking part in a great new experiment that was changing a whole society. There was a definite attempt to establish equality for women and in a feudal society like China that was no small thing. We received equal wages according to our skills. Women entered many professions and those qualified were given leading positions. However, it takes more than a few words and some legislation to overcome the male domination of 4000 years in all strata of society.
>
> Of course I only saw a small part of those changes, I was still more like an observer, not a direct participant. I hadn't taken part in land reform, in fact I hadn't even been to the countryside. The media only reported on things that were positive and being in Beijing in a sheltered organisation we knew little of the real problems in China.

Of course political manipulation, corruption and crime went on behind the scenes, but people like me were totally ignorant of that.

The bureau brought her into contact with Russian staffers who frequently treated their Chinese hosts with condescension bordering on contempt: 'They were not the new, highly moral man our Chinese press made them out to be. They were ordinary human beings, some good, some bad.' And in the war the Red Army had been almost as detestable as the Japanese. A Chinese interpreter from the northeast which the Russians occupied told Pingmei, 'My mother used to burn my eldest sister's lips with the hot tongs when she had to go out to buy things for the family. She put ashes and dirt in her hair to make her look dirty, old and stupid because the Russian soldiers would rape any nice looking girl. Lots of people did that to their daughters.'

In 1954 the new government held its first elections and they bordered on the farcical. Pingmei's group would help decide the make-up of the local People's Congress of Beijing's East City and there were hours of lectures on the blood of martyrs sacrificed to give them the vote. 'I hadn't voted in Australia,' Pingmei says, 'and the entire process was new to me [but] when it came to voting nobody had any idea who we were voting for. No one had told us who the candidates were, indeed we never saw them. They had been handpicked by a higher party committee. True, it was a secret ballot. We went into the booth, put ticks against the names listed, placed the ballot paper in the box and that was it. It felt a very empty procedure and set in place the notion that we were not in control.'

★ ★ ★

That year elections were also held in Australia but here the leading candidates at least were very well known. By then the former foreign minister 'Doc' Evatt had succeeded the late Ben Chifley as leader of the Australian Labor Party (ALP), while Prime Minister Menzies had consolidated his rule over the conservative forces of the Liberal–Country

Party Coalition. Moreover, the Russians played a significant role in the elections after the Security Services helped to engineer the defection of a Soviet spy, Vladimir Petrov, from their Canberra embassy.

The 'Petrov Affair' implicated members of Evatt's staff and he came to believe it was part of a Menzies plot to discredit him. And while subsequent analysis has shown this was not the case, it undoubtedly helped the Coalition win a thumping majority in the election. Moreover, it exacerbated the division in the Labor Party which split asunder the following year with a new, virulently anti-communist grouping brought into being under the label of the Democratic Labor Party (DLP).

The Korean War had ended in 1953 but by then China was becoming seen by the conservatives as the potential enemy. The Australian government looked askance at China's decision to supply arms and advisers to the Nationalist forces fighting the French in Indo-China. Indeed, following a trip to London and Washington, Menzies not only pursued a new 'Forward Defence' policy designed to fight any perceived enemy as far from Australia's northern shores as possible but actually named Communist China as the potential aggressor. He thereby set in train a policy with the capacity – even the likelihood – to become a self-fulfilling prophecy. Certainly it provided Australia's defence planners with a focus for their favoured 'scenarios' and the spending priorities to deal with them.

It also gave Australia's diplomatic cohort a framework for their activities and this led to a greater dependence on the United States – in Menzies' words 'our great and powerful friend' – and the development of a 'Two China' policy. This implied a *de facto* recognition of Taiwan as a legitimate national entity, a development that effectively prevented recognition of Beijing and the vital diplomatic relations that Australia might otherwise have enjoyed with the world's most populous state.

Then in 1956 the Australian trade minister, John McEwen, negotiated an agreement with Japan which would eventually turn that country into Australia's biggest trading partner. At the same time, however, as deputy leader of the Country Party he oversaw a growing export of Australian wool to Communist China. Without articulating it, he was enacting the unvarnished Australian approach to China that would be expressed by a later prime minister known for his three-word slogans: 'Fear and Greed'.[2]

★ ★ ★

China's own international activities were basically confined to its borders and the resumption of territories, such as Tibet, which had been vassal states in the past. But after Mao's split with the Soviets, which began in 1956 with Khrushchev's denunciation of Stalin, the government turned its attention inwards in a massive campaign to consolidate the Communist dynasty. And in its train Chairman Mao would surrender to Lord Acton's iron rule that 'absolute power corrupts absolutely'.

Even his private life came to resemble that of the emperors. Mao had no fewer than 50 estates, including five in Beijing alone. According to his doctor, Li Zhisui, who had worked in Australia before taking up his post with the chairman in 1954, 'he indulged his every sexual caprice'. Li often slept in a small room beside Mao's ballroom-sized bedroom and over the next 22 years noted the 'thousands' of young women – often several at once – who shared his bed.

The Communist Party and the People's Liberation Army [PLA] procured young women for the chairman. The girls staffed his villas and served as dancing companions at the leaders' exclusive parties. Describing one of the dances, Li wrote: 'I walked into the huge Spring Lotus Chamber with Mao. He was immediately surrounded by a dozen attractive young women who flirted with him and begged him to dance . . . As Mao got older he became an adherent of Taoist sexual practices which gave him an excuse to pursue sex not just for pleasure but to extend his life. He claimed he needed the waters of yin – or vaginal secretions – to supplement his own declining yang – or male essence, the source of his strength and power.'

And like emperors before him, Mao burned books across the country. 'The more books you read,' he declared, 'the more stupid you become.' Unless, of course he had written them.[3]

In 1953 Mao had launched the first 'Five-year Plan', designed to broaden China's economic base from its dependence on agriculture and lay the foundation for its rise to become a world power. He turned to the Soviet Union for assistance in building new industrial plants; and though the Soviets were not as forthcoming as he had hoped – and the plants were often inefficient and expensive to maintain – he was sufficiently encouraged to launch a second such plan in 1958.

He combined this with a policy of forced collectivisation in agriculture. It had proved disastrous in Russia in the 1930s and would be even more catastrophic in China. Indeed, Mao's 'Great Leap Forward' would devastate the countryside and result in the death by starvation of many millions of his countrymen.

The collectives, known as 'people's communes', meant that private food production was banned, livestock and farm machinery became the property of the communes and many thousands of peasants were required to work on massive infrastructure projects. And his insistence that villagers contribute scrap iron to fuel a national steel industry was calamitous.

'The media was euphoric about the Great Leap Forward,' says Tan Pingmei. 'Half out of enthusiasm, half out of fear, and not without misgivings, the peasants handed in their animals, tools and land, the iron pots and other scarce possessions, to the collective. The results were tragic. The steel proved largely unusable and as millions of peasants spent the entire summer trying to turn it out, the grain of a bumper harvest in 1958 rotted in the fields with no one to harvest it.'

There was a 15 per cent fall in grain production in 1959 and a further 10 per cent decline the following year. But fearful cadres sent false accounts up the chain of command and when the Central Committee requisitioned rice and wheat for the cities based on their reports, the countryside was swept clean of its stores and up to 30 million peasant families succumbed to starvation. There were even suggestions that Mao was fully aware of the unfolding disaster and at a meeting in Shanghai on 25 March 1959, declared, 'When there is not enough to eat, people starve to death. It is better to let half of the people die so that the other half can eat their fill.'

At the same time the chairman launched the Hundred Flowers Campaign, ostensibly to seek different opinions on how best to manage the way forward. Liberal and intellectual Chinese responded with an array of suggestions, including criticism of the Communist Party and its leadership. Mao was outraged and his retribution was swift and deadly. He purged his defence minister, Peng Dehuai, and ordered a program of 'rectification' for party members throughout the country. Some 500,000 'dissidents' were either tortured, executed or both.

According to Pingmei, 'Everyone had to toe the Party line and declare their unswerving support. But the rectification meetings were held in secret. Non-party people like myself knew nothing of the policy struggle that was going on.' However, as the movement drew to a close, a meeting was called of the entire trade union organisation – some 2000 people – and she was required to attend:

> It was a great shock to us non-Party people to hear a resolution expelling the former Trade Union president Lai Ruo-yu (who had died of cancer not long ago) and another official close to him, branding them as right-wing opportunists. The head of the secretariat who chaired the meeting read out the resolution and asked all communists to raise their hands to vote in favour. A forest of hands went up.
>
> 'Anyone against?' he bellowed. To everyone's amazement, a young French interpreter raised his hand, stood up and said he objected. There was a stunned silence, then the meeting broke into a din as everybody started talking to each other at the same time. 'He must be out of his mind, he's not even a communist,' one of the older women interpreters sitting next to me muttered.
>
> For this he was taken to a detention centre to be ideologically remoulded, where he stayed forgotten for the next twenty years until after Mao's death and the downfall of the Gang of Four. He left a

tallish, robust and rather good-looking young man and returned in the eighties a thin, shrunken man, old for his late fifties. The punishment was outrageously unjust but who could speak up for him? Our minds had been shaped into the mindset of the Communist Party . . . only Chairman Mao was right.

'Maybe the most despicable thing was that senior Communist leaders, including Liu Shaoqi, Zhou Enlai and Deng Xiaoping, who knew the truth sided with Mao. 'These men were captives of their political culture,' she says. 'To them, Mao was the Emperor.'

CHAPTER THIRTY-TWO

FEAR OF COMMUNIST CHINA

Until then the Menzies government had chosen to ignore the continued links between the Australian Trade Union Movement and Chinese officialdom. Indeed, in 1957 they were unconcerned when the president of the Australian Council of Trade Unions (ACTU), the widely respected Albert Monk, his wife and three other union executives visited Wuhan for an international trade union conference. As it happened, Tan Pingmei was assigned to liaise with the delegation.

'Albert Monk had fallen ill and every day we visited him in hospital,' Pingmei says. 'Despite the doctor's advice that he take no alcohol, being an Australian he said he could not do without a beer in the terrible heat, so we each took turns to smuggle in a bottle. There was no air-conditioning in the hotel rooms in those days. Instead, huge wooden tubs with blocks of ice were placed in our rooms, with bottles of beer and soft drinks stacked on the ice for the Australians.'

Her parents also visited and both were active in the Australia–China Friendship Association. 'I have never seen my father so elated,' she recalls. 'The China he remembered – of beggars, disease, bandits, starvation and corruption, the opulence of the rich, the stark impoverishment of the poor – had all changed. He found a clean and healthy looking China, one without obvious corruption, without the contrast of extreme wealth and extreme poverty.

'My father insisted he pay for his and my mother's trip. I couldn't understand why, the Overseas Chinese Commission was fully prepared to pay for it. "You don't understand," he said when I asked him. "I pay for what I do and I say what I want." He was right. I really didn't understand.'

It was a lesson that would be well learned in the years ahead.

In 1958, Pingmei was transferred to the Foreign Languages Institute in Beijing to study French for two years in the belief that her English background would mean she learned the new language quickly. 'Actually, it wasn't the right time to learn anything,' she says. 'This was the era of the Great Leap Forward, the organisation of the People's Communes. There was revolution everywhere . . . two hours of French class in the morning and in the afternoons we were organised into groups to study the importance of combining education with physical labour. Then a few more French classes and we were off to the nearby Capital Iron and Steel Plant to clean up the factory yard. With all these extra-curricula activities we were unable to cover the set curriculum for the term. Some teachers mentioned this but most kept quiet as the ongoing anti-rightist movement taught them the wisdom of keeping their mouth shut.'

Soon afterwards the Australasian Liaison Bureau was dismantled and Pingmei's unit was amalgamated into the International Department of the All China Federation of Trade Unions – known as The Trade Unions – and the 'rightists' within extracted and exiled to the provinces.

The following year she married a low-ranking party member, Li Shao-hua, and they would produce two bright and healthy boys, Li Ting and Li Bin. But like so many couples they would be separated as one or other was assigned – or banished – to the countryside. 'Li Shao-hua and I didn't have much of a family life with the two of us in two different places,' she says. 'Family life was not to interfere with work, with revolution.'

By 1960 the split with Russia was complete. Khrushchev had asserted that no one could win a nuclear war and argued for 'peaceful coexistence', while Mao said that China was so populous it could survive an atomic holocaust and offered support for 'revolutionary wars'. According to Pingmei, 'In the sixties a new type of communist was rising to the forefront – radical leftists who ruled, not through the establishment of a legal system, but through the "spirit" of the documents of the

Communist Party. Some, it was said, didn't even read these, but picked up by word of mouth what the "spirit" of the Party was supposed to be.

'The Internationale was played every night on the radio to show the people that only the Chinese Communist Party upheld the principles of Marxism-Leninism. The anti-revisionist polemics with the Soviet Union lasted for almost a year, and to those of us who worked in the international field this was the central theme around which everything else revolved.'

The creation of the National Liberation Front in Vietnam and the outbreak of fighting against the American-backed Ngo Dinh Diem regime set the scene for a further deterioration in Sino-Australian relations. In 1961 Menzies himself was acting minister for external affairs in the election against the Labor opposition under Arthur Calwell. He took an aggressive stand against Chinese involvement in Indo-China. Moreover, he said, to recognise Communist China, would 'sell Taiwan into slavery'.

The result was in the balance for several days and preferences from the fiercely anti-Chinese Democratic Labor Party (DLP) were pivotal in securing Menzies the two additional seats the Coalition needed to retain office. This gave them increased influence over government policy and the new foreign minister, Sir Garfield Barwick, was himself an unyielding opponent of the Mao regime. Indeed, Barwick asserted that, 'For the present, China constitutes the greatest threat to the security of the region in which we live . . . there is no other major threat at this time.'[1]

He cited Chinese 'aggression' in Korea, Tibet and India and blamed China herself for her isolation. In doing so he caught the mood of the country.

Even Calwell's deputy, the up-and-coming Gough Whitlam, who had supported recognition since 1954, said in 1963 that, 'China represents a very great threat. She is potentially the most powerful country in the world and she seems prepared to run risks which Russia is unwilling to run.'

When Paul Hasluck succeeded Barwick the following year, he continued the hard line, contending that 'The fear of China is the dominant element in much that happens in Asia, and that fear is well founded ... the rising power of China, its aggression and subversion against its neighbours, and its political activities in other continents make it the major danger to peace today.'

Indeed the government had come to accept the Russian view of the Sino-Soviet dispute. According to E.M. Andrews, 'The nadir of this folly came in 1964 when Hasluck visited Moscow. He tried to warn the Russian leaders, to their slight bewilderment, against Chinese expansionism and asked them to restrain the Chinese in Vietnam. The theme of the "good" Russian Communists and the "bad" Chinese was taken up forcefully by the new External Affairs Secretary, James Plimsoll, and again found echoes even in the Labor Party. The Government's propaganda seems to have swayed large sections of the community.'[2]

This culminated in the decision to introduce conscription to the armed forces and in 1965 the commitment of the first Australian battalion to Vietnam. In the face of two millennia of deep-seated conflict between China and Vietnam, the government now took the remarkable view that Beijing and Hanoi were somehow joined at the hip. Menzies himself articulated the doctrine in parliament during the debate, saying: 'The takeover of South Vietnam must be seen as part of a thrust by Communist China between the Indian and Pacific Oceans.'[3]

His senior ministers enthusiastically chimed in. John McEwen, who had succeeded Arthur Fadden as leader of the Country Party and deputy prime minister, warned that 'the lessons of history' revealed by Chinese territorial ambitions meant that Australia itself was in jeopardy. McEwen stated: 'Never, back to the earliest recordings of civilisation, has any country, any nation, owned a continent. We own a continent, a rich continent with everything that you could want. We are 12 million people. What a prize. And if you go back 6000 years you couldn't find an instance where some nation or combination of nations haven't tried to seize a rich prize. We are the richest prize on earth today.' Only

America, he declared, could stand between the Chinese aggressor and Australia's northern shores.[4]

Menzies retired from his long prime ministerial labours on 26 January 1966 – Australia Day – and was replaced by his longstanding deputy, Harold Holt. And though the new prime minister was regarded as a more sophisticated and contemporary figure, his government's attitude to China was just as bellicose. Indeed, he embarrassed many in Australia with a fawning attitude to the United States, culminating in an embrace of President Lyndon Baines Johnson at a White House meeting with the promise, 'All the way with LBJ'.

His defence minister Allen Fairhall said, 'There is not the slightest doubt that the North Vietnamese are puppets of the Chinese and the whole conduct of the war, down to the last jot and tittle of it, comes out of the philosophy of Mao Zedong . . . It is perhaps only the first round of an attack by the Chinese Communists in an effort to dominate the world.'[5]

Hasluck concurred: 'What is happening in South-East Asia today is not just a local, temporary or isolated situation. It is part of the rivalry of power and the ideological contest which is taking place throughout the world. It is part of the stream of events continuing into the future. In both of these contests the most significant factor in Asia is China.'

Indeed, by 1966 China had become the overwhelming focus of Australian foreign policy. And while it had been on firmer ground in asserting a growing Chinese Communist leverage in Indonesia, the attempted coup there in October 1965 had resulted in a massive military backlash. More than 300,000 suspected sympathisers were slaughtered in an orgy of bloodletting that destroyed all semblance of Communist influence.

In spite of this Chinese existential threat, McEwen pursued every trading opportunity that favoured his agricultural constituents. Over the previous five years China had become easily the biggest customer for Australian wheat, with annual sales worth up to $300 million. Indeed, by 1966 the Chinese people ate twice as much Australian wheat as

Australians themselves. Yet the Australian community seemed barely aware of the schizophrenic nature of government policy.

The local Chinese population had been growing slowly since its nadir of about 7000 in 1947 and under the more enlightened policies of former immigration ministers Harold Holt and Hubert Opperman, the dictation test was abandoned and 'distinguished and highly qualified' Asian immigrants were allowed to settle. Non-Europeans could again be naturalised and those admitted on temporary permits would need to wait only five years before citizenship was open to them. By the end of 1966, within a total population of almost 12 million, some 18,000 Chinese had taken advantage of the new laws. Most had been born in mainland China but arrived via Hong Kong.

In June 1966 Holt's government suddenly announced that it would open an embassy in Taipei, the Nationalist capital still under the unshakeable command of Chiang Kai-shek. The Department of External Affairs was unprepared for the decision. There were well-founded rumours that Holt, after so many years in the thrall of Menzies, had made the rash commitment personally at a Canberra dinner with the charming and shrewd Nationalist Chinese ambassador Chen Zhimai.

It fell to Hasluck to make the case in parliament that Australia's trade and tourism with Taiwan made the new arrangements necessary. However, it was a retreat from reality and a measure of the tightening embrace of the 'domino' theory of the American right that foretold a collapse of the South-East Asian states to Chinese Communist pressure.

In October the same year Canada gave notice that it would recognise Beijing and simply 'take note' of its view that Taiwan was part of China. Canada's announcement would lead directly to a massive Chinese wheat contract and McEwen was forced on to the back foot in defending Australia's position and arguing that he 'fully expected' its wheat trade to bounce back. The Chinese government, he averred, would not be influenced by such political grandstanding but would base its decisions on price and availability.

The next month saw a vote in the UN General Assembly that for the first time recorded a simple majority in favour of admitting the People's Republic of China. Australia responded by joining with America to co-sponsor a revival of an old resolution making it an 'important matter' that required a two-thirds majority.[6]

Moreover, when Holt and McEwen went to a 'khaki' election in November 1966 – supported by a hugely popular visit from President Johnson himself – they won twice as many seats as Labor, a more decisive victory than ever achieved under Menzies' leadership. A month later Calwell resigned and was replaced by his deputy Gough Whitlam who by now had gained a reputation as a political dramatist with a philosophy of 'crash through or crash!'

CHAPTER THIRTY-THREE

THE CULTURAL REVOLUTION

John McEwen's prediction that China would resume its purchases of Australian wheat would prove correct but only because once again Mao was creating havoc in the cities, towns and rural villages of the empire. In 1966 he launched what became known as the Cultural Revolution to reassert his authority over the government. By now he had surrendered totally to Lord Acton's inescapable equation – his interests and that of his nation were inseparable. All notions of administrative probity and good governance were subsumed by raging self-interest.

In Beijing Pingmei Tan was caught in the middle of the chaos:

> The cult of Mao began with a vengeance. He was extolled like a god and *The East is Red,* a large-scale musical depicting the Long March and how Chairman Mao took the right decisions, always at the right time, was performed in the Great Hall of the People.
>
> To the ordinary people the fast recovery from famine and food shortages was the direct result of the policies of Liu Shaoqi and Deng Xiaoping, and no one openly blamed Mao for the failures and mistakes of the Great Leap Forward. The term simply disappeared and a new phrase – 'the three years of natural disasters' – came into being.
>
> In May he appointed his secretary Chen Boda to take over the *People's Daily* and in June it trumpeted in an editorial, "Sweep Away All Cow Demons and Snake Monsters" (class enemies). The targets were those in power following the capitalist road. The Cultural Revolution was launched. As it gathered pace the rampage of the Red Guards knew no bounds. Mao urged them on with slogans like

'Revolution is not a dinner party' and 'To rebel is justified'. They donned khaki uniforms, leather belts and red armbands and stormed around the streets of Beijing.

They dragged out 'bourgeois authorities' in the universities, colleges and hospitals, paraded them around with paper dunce caps on their heads and gave others, such as actresses, academics and writers, a 'yingyang haircut', shaving off half a head of hair so that all would know there was something politically wrong with them.

Others had placards reading 'landlord element' put around their necks and were made to walk the streets. They used thin wire which cut into their necks in the hot Beijing summer. Most people who saw them kept well away, pitying their plight and probably relieved it wasn't themselves.

In August a mammoth rally was held in Tiananmen Square and Pingmei attended with her colleagues in the Trade Unions. 'We were given a place very close to the rostrum,' she recalls. 'Lin Biao [the defence minister] spoke and urged the youth to greater heights, to break the "four olds" – old ideas, old culture, old customs, old habits – thus spurring them on to more rampages.' Mao then paraded with his ministers waving his *Little Red Book*.

Despite her Australian upbringing, Pingmei says, 'The hysterical cries of "Chairman Mao, Chairman Mao" carried by a million voices reverberated throughout the square, building emotion until I felt a choking in my throat which brought tears to my eyes . . . We were in a kind of stupor. I can only liken it to the frenzied bigotry that some extreme people show at a football match which engulfs their entire being so they become incapable of intelligent thought. Looking back, I wonder at my own stupidity.'

As the Red Guard hysteria swept through the country, an undeclared civil war erupted. Millions were persecuted in violent struggles that broke out across the empire and even today the true depth and extent of the conflict is yet to be fully documented. Accounts of all-out war using heavy artillery and well-organised citizen militias are still being uncovered in some provinces. Once again the rice harvest rotted in the fields and the central authorities were forced to turn to Australia to make up the shortfall.

The conflict actually intensified in 1967 and 1968 when young people from the cities were forcibly transferred to rural regions where they destroyed historical relics and artifacts and ransacked cultural and religious sites. But not all participants in the 'Down to the Countryside Movement' fared badly. Some educated young city dwellers actually benefited from the association with villagers and were welcomed into the rural communities where they brought literacy and numeracy to the children, and often to their parents. Moreover, Zhou Enlai operated wherever possible to conserve some of China's unique historical treasures.

However, behind the scenes the Cultural Revolution was increasingly directed by the so-called Gang of Four, led by Mao's fourth wife, the former actress Jiang Qing. She had married Mao in 1938 and despite his sexual peccadillos she had swallowed her pride and served as the inaugural First Lady of the People's Republic. She gave vent to her passions in the political arena over the next decades, with support from Mao, and in 1969 she capped her rise when she gained a seat on the politburo.

By then Jiang Qing had attacked the Trade Unions calling for an internal rebellion against the 'revisionists' within. Utter chaos followed when suddenly 2000 workers from outside descended on the building and staged a takeover. No one knew who the workers really were, but the Trade Unions soon fought back. Pingmei recalls, 'Everyone grouped themselves against them, rendering them powerless. They had to renounce their bid and leave.'

Similar conflicts arose in other party organisations and because each side refused to recognise the other, there was a stalemate. According to Pingmei, 'No one had power in the Trade Unions or any other organisation for that matter. The frenzy, the passion of politics and factions engulfed us, destroying our very ability to reason.

'One could feel the danger. In the Foreign Language Press there had been a murder and a suicide. In Beijing Normal University there were also a number of suicides but rumour had it that people had actually been pushed over balconies and out of windows.'

It was at this time that her husband Li Shao-hua returned from Henan where the fighting was intense. 'His advice to me was, "Lie low and watch the tigers fight it out".' However, towards the end of 1967, the two sides in the Trade Unions began to unite. 'It was rumoured they had exchanged lists of people they wanted locked up,' she says. 'Then I found that some of the heads of both sides who normally spoke to me began avoiding me, or looked away uncomfortably when our paths crossed. I began to feel instinctively like a hunted beast; there was nothing worse than to live by the "looks" of those in power.'

Australia had never seemed so far away . . .

* * *

Late on the Sunday morning of 17 December 1967 Harold Holt disappeared while swimming in the rough surf of Cheviot Beach on the eastern arm of Victoria's Port Phillip Bay. He had been accompanied only by a few friends who immediately raised the alarm. A contingent of police, navy divers and air force helicopters converged on the beach, but no trace of the missing prime minister was found. That afternoon Deputy Prime Minister John McEwen flew to Canberra for meetings with his Country Party colleagues and Richard Casey, who had become governor-general in 1965. By then it was clear that Holt had drowned and two days later McEwen took the oath of office as prime minister.

McEwen announced that he and his colleagues would not serve under the Liberals' deputy leader and treasurer, William 'Billy' McMahon, should they elect him in Holt's place. He and McMahon had clashed over trade policy and the nakedly ambitious McMahon had developed an association with lobbyists who used bribery and other backroom tactics to besmirch McEwen personally and undermine his tariff policies on behalf of Japanese clients.

The Country Party leader remained in office until the Liberals, as the senior party of the Coalition, elected Senator John Gorton as their leader in January 1968. McEwen then resumed his role as deputy prime minister and minister for trade and industry. McMahon transferred to the Department of Foreign Affairs but retained the deputy leadership of the Liberal Party.

Because Holt's body was never found, a number of increasingly unlikely speculations followed, the most memorable being the subject of a book by British author Anthony Grey. As a reporter in Beijing for Reuters, Grey would be held in prison by the Chinese government for 27 months from 1976 to 1979. In 1983 he would publish *The Prime Minister Was a Spy* in which he contended that Holt had not only spied for the People's Republic but had been picked up off Cheviot Beach by a Chinese submarine.

Some of Grey's later work dealt with UFOs.

Meanwhile, Gorton, a former RAAF pilot in World War II whose face had been damaged when his aircraft crash-landed, was known as a convivial partygoer and brought a freewheeling approach to the prime ministership. Most notably, he withdrew from Menzies' 'forward defence' policy to one of continental defence, and while he initially supported Australia's participation in the Vietnam War he refused US requests for any further build-up of Australian forces. And in 1970 as the tide of popular opinion turned against the conflict, his government declined to replace the 8th Battalion when it ended its tour of duty.

America, too, was becoming war weary and in the presidential campaign of 1968 Richard Nixon was elected on a policy of 'peace with honour'. At the same time Nixon and his national security adviser, Henry Kissinger, embarked secretly on a program to 'soften' its approach to China. By contrast, the Australian government maintained an unbending attitude to Beijing, caught in the net of its own electoral propaganda of the previous two decades.

* * *

In Beijing, Tan Pingmei was interrogated and branded an enemy of the people. 'Placards were hung around our necks with the crimes of which we were accused written on them,' she says. She was accused of accepting money from a 'capitalist roader' and found herself banished to rural poverty in a distant province where she worked in the fields and endured 'the life of a peasant from the Ming dynasty'. Then, with the Spring Festival of 1970 approaching, she was returned briefly to her husband in Beijing.

'Li Shao-hua and I spent ten happy days together going to our favourite haunts,' she says. 'It was so relaxing for me and seemed to be over in no time. Then we each [departed] to our respective cadre schools. His was near Wuhan and we were not sure when we could see each other again.'

Very soon Pingmei found she was pregnant with their second child, and then she contracted malaria: 'I have never felt so unwell in all my life. For the last two months of my pregnancy I worked in the threshing ground, drying out the wheat. Each day it was taken from the granary and spread out on the ground to dry in the hot sun, then in the evening raked up and put back. My other jobs were to mend hessian bags and spin hemp rope. The last ten days I was allowed to start making some clothes and bedding for the baby.'

Li Bin came into the world with the assistance of a midwife and Li Shao-hua was given two weeks leave to visit his wife and child. In the following months, she was returned to her former job and 'one by one we were rehabilitated, presumably no longer considered members of [a] conspiratorial clique'. Finally, she accepted the view of her husband who told her, 'You don't belong to the class that is going to change the world, so forget it. When all this is over, we will just keep to ourselves, look after the children and stay out of politics.'

* * *

Australian politics became increasingly turbulent when the deputy prime minister McEwen retired in January 1971. Two months later the Liberal Party fell into disarray when Defence Minister Malcolm Fraser resigned and denounced his leader. In the subsequent party meeting, a leadership contest between John Gorton and Billy McMahon saw its members split evenly; and Gorton, recognising he had lost the confidence of his party, used his casting vote to elect his opponent to the prime ministership.

It was the beginning of the end for the Coalition. In parliament McMahon was no match for an exuberant Gough Whitlam and in the lead-up to the 1972 election the Labor Party thrilled at the prospect of power after 23 years in the wilderness of political opposition.

Then in July 1971 after months of secret negotiations – and to the astonishment of his nation – Whitlam arrived in Beijing on an official visit to the leadership of the People's Republic of China. One hundred and eighty-four years since the British colonisation of the Great South Land, and 70 years since the creation of the Australian Commonwealth, the leadership of the two countries that dominated their respective hemispheres finally met in mutual respect. The meeting's significance in the history of Australia–China relations could hardly be overstated.

CHAPTER THIRTY-FOUR

RELATIONS THAW

By now the lofty, erudite and immaculately groomed Gough Whitlam was a towering figure in Australia's political landscape. Born in the leafy Melbourne suburb of Kew in 1916, his father Fred was a federal public servant who would rise to become the Commonwealth crown solicitor. Young Gough had a comfortable childhood in the Sydney harbourside suburb of Mosman and then in Canberra where he was a prize-winning student at the local Grammar School. He attended Sydney University where he secured a Bachelor of Arts and began his law studies before volunteering for the RAAF in 1942, the same year he married the equally imposing Margaret Dovey who had swum for Australia in the 1938 Empire Games.

Whitlam's relatively privileged upbringing generated an abiding resentment from the more traditional of his colleagues in the Australian Labor Party, but by 1971, with a meticulously designed program of reform in his political armoury, he was clearly destined for The Lodge. Even the radical left wing of his party, led by the idiosyncratic Dr Jim Cairns, had thrown its full support behind his leadership. However, the decision to make an official visit to Communist China – the *bête noir* of all right-wing Australians – was a serious political risk.

The move had originated with a close Whitlam ally, the new federal secretary of the party, Mick Young, who had travelled to China as a trade union official prior to the Cultural Revolution. A former shearer with a rough and tumble manner but an astute political antenna, Young had noted the continuing Chinese preference for wheat imports from the more accommodating Canadians. At the Federal Executive meeting in April, he moved that they make direct contact with the Chinese

Premier Zhou Enlai seeking an invitation for a party delegation to travel to Beijing for trade talks. And when the motion passed, Young and Whitlam broadened the approach to Zhou. Now they sought 'to discuss the terms on which your country is interested in having diplomatic and trade relations with Australia'.[1]

The response, when finally received, was favourable and the two men assembled a team that included the party president Tom Burns, the agriculture spokesman Rex Patterson, press secretary Graham Freudenberg, Young and perhaps most significantly, a former diplomat and acknowledged China expert, Stephen FitzGerald.

The 33-year-old FitzGerald had become interested in China during the second year of his arts degree at the University of Tasmania when he took a history course from a former New Zealander, George Wilson. 'He had a passionate commitment to engaging his students in this Asian world and exciting them about its extraordinary contributions to humankind,' FitzGerald says. 'It was history that discussed ideas, and human and social issues – poverty, development, colonialism, race, corruption, revolution – and how the people in these countries saw the Europeans in Asia.'[2]

In 1960 he was captivated by a publication from a group of academics attacking the White Australia policy. They asserted that the policy was 'poisoning our relations with Asia'. Australia, they said, needed at least a small flow of Asian migrants to enrich the national culture, to prepare the country for participation in the interracial counsels of the world, and concluded, 'Non-whites throughout the world regard the whole notion of White Australia as deeply insulting'. FitzGerald was, he says, 'excited by this new sense of Australianness' and went to rallies and protest marches in support of change.

On graduation he joined the Department of External Affairs where he was determined to be part of 'an Australian enlightenment' and on the first day of his diplomatic career he began to learn the Chinese language. However, the department's panjandrums – not least Keith Waller who would become department secretary in 1970 – were not interested in Australian culture. Indeed, he observes, 'It was openly disparaged by those who courted a faux British identity for themselves and their service . . . Its dominant culture still lay somewhere between its British origins and the attitudes of a client of the United States.'

He had met Gay Overton at university and they were married in 1961. The following year they were posted to Hong Kong where FitzGerald continued his studies at the university language school. Both were uncomfortable with the British colonial attitudes there and travelled twice to Taiwan – where a brutal and oppressive Chiang Kai-shek still ruled – and in 1964 to mainland China. By this time, he says, he had developed 'a strong disaffection' for the Coalition government's China policy which he considered 'illogical, delusional and unsustainable'.

In 1966 he resigned from the department and began a PhD at the Australian National University (ANU), just as Mao Zedong in China began his Cultural Revolution that set the Red Guards on the rampage. The following year FitzGerald began writing occasional articles in the metropolitan press and mixing with some of the leading Canberra journalists of the day, including Eric Walsh and John Stubbs, both of whom were committed Whitlam supporters. They organised a luncheon at which the newly minted opposition leader asked him to write a paper on Australia and Asia and appointed him an 'unofficial adviser'.

Over the next four years FitzGerald visited China at the height of the Cultural Revolution while continuing to strengthen the relationship with Whitlam. By the time they reached the Peking Hotel on 3 July (accompanied by a small but influential group of Australian journalists), they were equally excited by the potential of the political escapade. Whitlam, FitzGerald and Patterson met with senior officials on 4 and 5 July and while the Chinese were polite and friendly, the trade and diplomatic negotiations were lengthy and meticulous.

Then came an interregnum where they waited through a Beijing Sunday to hear whether Zhou Enlai would meet with the Australian opposition leader. Finally, at the end of the day, word reached them that it was 'on' and a convoy of official cars brought them to the imposing

Great Hall of the People. FitzGerald says, 'Zhou greets us, one by one. The Australian journalists are already here, and a larger number from the Chinese media. We sit in a large circle, with Zhou and Whitlam at the top, the Australians around Whitlam's side, the Chinese ministers and officials around Zhou's and the journalists directly opposite Whitlam and Zhou. The theatre now takes an unexpected and somewhat alarming turn: Zhou invites the journalists to remain throughout the meeting.'

This was unheard of in international diplomacy. Whitlam was momentarily fazed but according to FitzGerald, once over the initial surprise, his intellect, skills and knowledge made him a good match for the Chinese premier. Moreover, the hard negotiations had already taken place over the previous two days. FitzGerald recalls, 'As Whitlam and Zhou work through the issues, there's no arguing, no ideological perorations, not even any differences standing in the way of relations, just a *tour d'horizon* in which views and policies and differences are being explained and clarified.'[3]

Zhou's principal concern was the perceived 'encirclement' of China by the Soviet Union on the one side and by Japan and America on the other. Indeed, he predicted a Japanese economic and military expansion into South-East Asia 'pushed by the United States'. The Australians understood his concerns without necessarily sharing them. According to FitzGerald, 'Japan [had] form in its past occupation of China and it's true that it [had] recent security understandings with the United States and that there are right-wing Japanese who want to re-arm. Looking at it from Zhou's point of view, it wouldn't be difficult to come to his conclusions.'

Then, in a harbinger of the dramatic events to follow, Zhou asked Whitlam what he knew of President Nixon's chief foreign policy adviser, Henry Kissinger. Whitlam replied that they hadn't met and the moment passed. The meeting ended soon after; Zhou ushered the Australians out and the pressmen filed their stories.

When the news hit Australia, Prime Minister 'Billy' McMahon and leader of the Country Party, Doug Anthony – whose ancestry was said, without much supporting evidence, to be part Chinese – lambasted the Labor leader. 'It is time to expose the shams and absurdities of his excursion into instant coffee diplomacy,' McMahon said. 'We must not become pawns of the giant Communist power in our region. I find it incredible that at a time when Australian soldiers are still engaged in Vietnam, the Leader of the Labor Party is becoming a spokesman for those against whom we are fighting ... By accepting Peking as the sole capital of China, he is abandoning Taiwan ... In no time at all, Mr Zhou had Mr Whitlam on a hook and he played him as a fisherman plays a trout.'

Four days later Henry Kissinger arrived in China via Pakistan and almost immediately began talks with Zhou. Whitlam had left China on 14 July for Tokyo, where, on the morning of Friday 16 July (15 July in the US) he watched Nixon on worldwide television reveal Kissinger's secret trip and announce that he, too, would visit Beijing within a year. McMahon was dumbfounded. Freudenberg says, 'Thanks to the unlikely trio of Zhou Enlai, Richard Nixon and Henry Kissinger, Whitlam's high-risk initiative was transformed to a personal and political triumph – literally overnight.'

Pingmei Tan was working among villagers in rural Henan Province, teaching at the local school and tending some 300 hens in her off-duty hours. 'The announcement over the village school's broadcasting system that President Nixon would be visiting China came out of the blue,' she recalls. 'It seemed an achievement of the impossible, and it strengthened the credibility of Mao and the Premier for their astuteness in being able to bring about peaceful negotiations with the world's biggest and most powerful imperialist nation. It was summer and after a day's work in the fields we sat in our political study groups in little circles on the threshing ground discussing this political event. It was exciting because secretly we guessed it would mean change, including the re-opening of work in government, the Trade Unions and a gradual backtrack to normality.'

However, in September 1971 the Chinese government was again thrown into disarray when Mao's designated successor, Lin Biao, attempted to flee the country only for his plane to crash in mountainous Mongolia. The Communist Party condemned him as a traitor. 'To us it was a shock,' Pingmei says. 'Only recently had Lin Biao been Mao's best student. Standing there, leaning against a big pile of hessian bags I felt instinctively that this was the beginning of the end. In fact, the sigh of relief was almost audible.'

She was still at the school the following year when Nixon arrived in February for his grand rapprochement. Pingmei and many of her friends had transistor radios and with earphones they listened to the Nixon dinner in the Great Hall via Voice of America. 'California wine was served and one could even hear the clinking of glasses,' she says.

There was plenty of glass clinking in Australia that year as the Whitlam bandwagon rolled over the Coalition in an election campaign with the slogan, 'It's Time!' After 23 years of conservative rule, the electorate agreed and gave the Australian Labor Party a working majority of eight seats in the house of representatives. McMahon was succeeded by a former Melbourne lawyer, Billy Snedden, but remained in the parliament as a shadow minister and later backbencher.

Whitlam seized the reins of power and for two weeks before the Labor caucus elected the cabinet, he and his deputy, the long-serving Tasmanian Lance Barnard, shared the 27 ministerial portfolios. One of his first acts was to order negotiations to establish full relations with the People's Republic of China and in preparation broke those with Taiwan. He then appointed Stephen FitzGerald the first ambassador to the republic over the heated objections of the Department of Foreign Affairs who claimed that both they and the Chinese felt he was 'too young'. In fact, the Chinese merely wanted to ascertain that it was Stephen FitzGerald rather than the septuagenarian Emeritus Professor

C.P. Fitzgerald – recently retired from the ANU – who had been chosen for the task.

It was no easy task for the new ambassador, who reveals: 'There were times I felt awed at the task and how I'd come to be there. But not overawed. I had a whole collection of books by or about Australians in China. I was conscious of this history, that we had to reconnect it with the present China. With the whiting-out of Chinese history and the emptying out of China of the few Australians who'd been there at the start of the Cultural Revolution, I felt the singularity of my position. When the Embassy opened in 1973 there was almost no other Australian in China that we knew of. We knew there must be Chinese-Australians living with or visiting their families, but we didn't know who they were or where they were.'[4]

CHAPTER THIRTY-FIVE

THE FALL OF WHITLAM

In fact, Pingmei Tan had returned to Beijing where she was training primary school teachers to teach English and struggling to come to terms with yet another New Order. 'Perhaps the most important thing for China in 1973,' she says, 'was the rehabilitation of Deng Xiaoping. It filled us with hope. Deng's informal talks spoke of the conditions of the people since the Cultural Revolution, the plight of the intellectuals and teachers, housing shortages, food shortages, lack of hospitals, lack of trained staff and so on. These talks and articles were copied by hand and passed around everywhere.'

The official media was still dominated by the Gang of Four. 'But not many of us were interested in the media or even read it,' Pingmei says. 'It was even intimated that there was a Gang of Five – Mao being the fifth. Others said China was being ruled like "a husband and wife shop".' However, Jiang Qing and her cronies soon fought back. 'The Gang of Four launched a new polemic,' she says. 'The real purpose was to direct attacks at Zhou Enlai and Deng. Ordered to carry out the campaign, party committees had no option but there was so little fervor that the campaign petered out. Nevertheless, the momentum for change led by Deng stopped, and for a while everything seemed uncertain.'[1]

FitzGerald and his small team were based in temporary quarters in the old Peking Hotel with its high ceilings, dark corridors and creaky floors. 'The hotel is home for all, and office,' he said. 'Communication with Canberra is by an antique cyphering machine lugged from Australia and kept in the good care of the British Embassy. It's from this decrepit environment – the hotel not the British Embassy – that we launch Australia's new China diplomacy.'[2]

His first official meeting with Premier Zhou took place back in the Great Hall of the People but this time without the colour and movement of the Whitlam extravaganza. As he settled in, FitzGerald felt momentarily 'lost in the great expanse of this room with its thick handwoven carpet deadening the sound even of the attendants moving around dispensing the tea'. But he quickly recovered and the meeting spanned a wide range of issues, from the US actions in Vietnam, to the politics of the Indian Sub-Continent.

However, FitzGerald was continually 'harassed' by the Department of Foreign Affairs in Canberra which plainly opposed the China policy of its government: 'In our work there was stimulation and excitement and an absorption in what we did and I was buoyed by that, and undeterred. We were flying. But as we flew the department was often pulling at our wings.'[3]

Typical was a cable from Canberra in June 1973, directing him to 'close down' the discussion on South-East Asia he'd been having with top Chinese officials. This was followed by another from Secretary Keith Waller ordering him not to discuss Whitlam's idea for a new regional organisation or for regular talks at official level. His departmental division head, David Anderson, said, 'We don't want regular talks with China, now, annually or even at longer intervals.'

FitzGerald found it 'concerning that this opposition should come from the head of the department, and so calculatedly seek to subvert the intentions of the government'.

By contrast, Australians in many fields were 'lining up' to travel to China. Indeed, the Chinese foreign ministry, which had to organise each visit, whether from the Wheat Board, the ANU, the Australia Council or even swimming coaches, couldn't cope with the workload.

There were early visits from trade minister Jim Cairns who failed to impress his Chinese counterparts, and opposition leader Billy Snedden who succeeded, but for the wrong reasons. Snedden was received by senior foreign ministry officials and in talks, according to FitzGerald, 'He tried to be clever and debate them but came across as rude, and ill-informed'. Snedden then told travelling pressmen he'd had the ambassador 'sitting on the edge of his chair' at what he was learning from his discussions. FitzGerald says, 'If I was sitting on the edge of my chair it was in apprehension of what gaucherie might come next.'

Whitlam himself arrived with a gift from Australia – a prize Murray Grey bull named Saber Bogong. It was well received. However, when Wesfarmers livestock specialist Hugh Warden arrived in Beijing with a government trade mission in 1977, they visited a cattle breeding centre where Saber Bogong was on show. Warden says, 'Unfortunately, he was infertile and always had been, but they kept him there so they could say, "Prime Minister Gough Whitlam gave us this bull".'[4]

Meanwhile, at Whitlam's talks with Zhou – and with the Australian delegation led by Waller ranged alongside – the prime minister said, 'There should be consultations between Australia and China as close and significant as we have traditionally had with Britain and the United States and similar to discussions we now have annually with Japan at ministerial level and with the Soviet Union at official level.'

FitzGerald recalled, 'Keith Waller looks at the ceiling.'

Towards the end of the discussion, Zhou motioned Whitlam aside and after a brief colloquy, the prime minister and FitzGerald left to follow Zhou in his official car across the city to Mao's compound. There they engaged in a generally frustrating conversation with the ageing chairman until suddenly Mao said, 'Now let me ask the questions.'

According to FitzGerald, 'It was as though they'd given him medication during the afternoon to get him going and it's only now starting to work.'

Mao objected to the Australian protests at China's nuclear testing and the issue was batted back and forth, with Whitlam even more censorious of the French testing in the Pacific. The talks wound down with Mao asking whether Darwin was named after the great naturalist. An embarrassed Whitlam was stumped. Only later did he send FitzGerald a 'confession of error' to be passed on to the Chinese leader: Darwin had visited Sydney in 1836 but it wasn't until the *Beagle*'s next visit to Australia three years later (without the man himself) that it reached Darwin Harbour which its captain so named.

The Australian media covered the visit extensively, with television footage sent back to the major networks and replayed on the nightly news. It was compulsive viewing, not least for a fifteen-year-old Kevin Rudd in the 'bible belt' of Queensland's Sunshine Coast hinterland at Nambour High School. 'I was transfixed by Gough Whitlam's visit to China on television,' he told his biographer in 2007. In fact, he wrote directly to Whitlam: 'I want to be an Australian diplomat. What should I do?' Apparently Whitlam responded, 'You really should go to university and the study of a foreign language would be useful.'

While the Whitlam visit was a great success, FitzGerald was aware that it didn't mean that henceforth 'all doors will be open and everything will be easy'. However, with the prime minister's backing, the embassy's strength increased to more than a dozen staff with its own building in the diplomatic quarter.

Back in Australia, though, success was elusive.

★ ★ ★

By 1974 Whitlam confronted a hostile senate which had rejected nineteen government bills, ten of them twice. The prime minister called a double dissolution election of both houses and while a joint sitting of the parliament passed some of the contentious legislation, he failed to gain a senate majority and his numbers in the house were cut to the bone. More crucially, the Liberal Party replaced Snedden with the more substantial Malcolm Fraser as opposition leader, and at the same time the ill-discipline among Whitlam's inexperienced ministers raised increasing concerns in the electorate.

From May 1975 Fraser used his numbers in the senate to delay the passing of that year's budget, thus blocking the funding of all government activities. On 21 October, Whitlam told the house of representatives, 'I shall not advise the Governor-General to hold an election of either House or both Houses until this constitutional issue is settled. This government, so long as it retains a majority in the House of Representatives, will continue the course endorsed by the Australian people last year.' With supply due to expire on 30 November, the prime minister decided to end the senate's capacity to deny supply once and for all.

The Queen's representative of the day, (Sir) John Kerr, took a different view and secretly negotiated with Malcolm Fraser who agreed to pass supply and call a full election should Kerr commission him as a 'caretaker' prime minister. When Whitlam arrived at Government House on 11 November, newly prepared to advise a half-senate election to resolve the crisis, Kerr precluded any discussion by dismissing him on the spot. Fraser was waiting in a back room of the mansion and immediately after Whitlam's departure Kerr swore him in as prime minister.

A dazed Whitlam returned to The Lodge without informing his senators who eagerly voted with the opposition as it suddenly offered to pass supply. The Labor senators were cock-a-hoop believing they had scored a great victory. Only when they reported their triumph to The Lodge did they realise their mistake.

That afternoon the Coalition returned to the treasury benches while Whitlam attacked the governor-general before a shocked crowd of supporters from the steps of Parliament House.

The subsequent election was a disaster for Labor. On 13 December 1975 the Coalition won the biggest majority in Australian history, taking 91 seats to Labor's 36. Whitlam was devastated, his party shattered. The size of the victory would clearly ensure a Fraser government for at least two parliamentary terms.

In China, Stephen FitzGerald telephoned Whitlam for advice about his immediate future under the Coalition regime. Whitlam responded, 'Comrade, you must stand by your station.'[5] In fact, the new foreign minister, Andrew Peacock, and Fraser himself were supporters of stronger relations with China. And at the same time Beijing was also caught in a tumultuous changing of the guard at the top levels of government.

★ ★ ★

In January 1976, Zhou Enlai, first premier of the People's Republic of China, died. 'It left the people saddened, fearful and uncertain,' says Pingmei. 'His administration represented stability, predictability and peace, and having experienced the chaos and terror of the Cultural Revolution, stability and peace were what people wanted.' At her college some of the teachers built an altar featuring a photograph of Zhou draped in black and white silk. Teachers, staff and students paid their respects by bowing three times and signing a book of condolence. Pingmei recalls, 'When the Premier's hearse passed down Changan Street, his final journey to the crematorium, we dropped what we were doing and ran to the roadside to pay our last respects.'

However, while press photographers recorded the scene and television footage of the grieving crowds was broadcast live, next morning the official media – under the influence of the Gang of Four – gave greater prominence to criticising Deng Xiaoping. 'In charge of all of this was a senile, sick Chairman who could not control his ambitious wife,' Pingmei says. 'We teachers discussed these events among ourselves, and only with the communists we trusted. The students were no longer doing their homework but making wreaths and writing poetry.

'We took the afternoon off and rode our bikes to Tiananmen Square, the wreath lying flat on a tricycle cart. When we reached Changan Avenue it seemed half of Beijing was on its way there. We lined up to present our wreath. Suddenly my attention was caught by some people taking photographs, men in fawn raincoats, too uniform to look casual. Men with cold, indifferent faces swaggering arrogantly through the crowds, mounting the pedicarts that were standing unused and photographing everything and everyone. We all saw them – the security police. A cold dread came over me.'

Two days later there was a massive gathering in the square. And when trucks arrived to remove all wreaths, flowers and poems, the people revolted. According to Pingmei, 'So great was their anger and their sense of helplessness that they set fire to military vehicles and burnt down the command post at the end of the square.'

Police and militia armed with clubs encircled the protesters and moved in on them. 'They even clubbed innocent workers on their way home,' she says. 'Hundreds were arrested and it was said that blood flowed . . . Never since the establishment of the People's Republic had there been such a public protest and outcry, and in Beijing of all places.'

Meantime, Ambassador FitzGerald learned that both Fraser and Peacock wanted to visit and engage with the Chinese leadership. He set about writing a background briefing for transmission to the politicians via the department where Alan Renouf had succeeded Waller as secretary. He wrote that after Mao died, China would rapidly pull out of its political mess and abandon Maoist fundamentalism 'for a position more attuned to the real problems of governing, and more reform-oriented strategic development'. This, he said, 'will make China a very different proposition for us. The further extension of its power and influence will be an increasingly dominant factor in our political environment. To live within the orbit of Chinese influence requires a cultural leap on our part, to enable us both to live with and benefit from a predominant China and to protect our national interests and integrity.'

Unfortunately, Renouf shared his predecessor's Anglo-centric world view. He responded, 'The burden of your argument hinges on the belief that the next 25 years will see the extension of a dominant Chinese power and influence throughout the region. Possibly you will be proved correct but your logic does not persuade me.'[6]

CHAPTER THIRTY-SIX
CHANGING TIMES

Prime Minister Fraser and Foreign Minister Peacock arrived in Beijing for their official visit in June 1976, with Alan Renouf and John Menadue, formerly Whitlam's private secretary and now the head of the Prime Minister's Department, as their official advisers. The visit was a remarkable success. The two leading Liberal Party politicians were just as enthusiastic about the potential for Australia–China relations as Whitlam had been. Indeed, the respected Alan Ramsay wrote in *The National Times* that, 'Fraser arrived in Peking relying heavily on Peacock, Renouf and Menadue. By the time he left he was taking advice almost exclusively from Gough Whitlam's appointee, Ambassador FitzGerald.'

Whitlam himself, and his wife Margaret, returned to China the following month as a somewhat reluctant opposition leader who, according to FitzGerald, looked as though 'he had the stuffing knocked out of him'. The visit was unremarkable but for the earthquake that struck Tianjin while they were staying at a hotel in the city. Margaret suffered a cut leg but the couple were otherwise unharmed. Indeed, Australians back home chuckled at the Nicholson cartoon published in *The Age* with its rendering of the couple in bed and Gough inquiring, 'Did the earth move for you too, dear?' (He cabled the cartoonist from Tokyo asking for the original.)[1]

In fact, the quake wrought terrible carnage in northern China. In Beijing, Tan Pingmei was in bed with her younger son Bin who had been unable to sleep. 'At about half past two I awoke,' she recalls. 'Standing by the window to get some fresh air I saw a strange glow in the sky. I lay down and nodded off again only to be awakened a minute later by a horrible groaning, roaring and rushing of wind.

Then the apartment began to shake. I rushed across to Ting [in the next bedroom] and carried him to my room where I knelt over both children, terrified the roof would collapse on us. The windows were rattling and the whole building shaking violently . . . you could hear glass shattering, bottles falling, people shouting.'[2]

When the quake stopped, the family hurried out of the apartment and went to Changan Street which was wide and well away from tall buildings. 'Everyone was just standing, waiting, quietly waiting,' Pingmei says. 'Even the children were subdued. Then people began going home and bringing back stools, rugs, thermos flasks, cups and sitting down to wait. You might have thought we were waiting for the fireworks to start.' After about two hours the crowd gradually dispersed.

That evening Pingmei was surprised when the neighbourhood committee turned on the loudspeakers to broadcast the news: 'Not one word about the earthquake. Instead, for half an hour we were exhorted to "criticise Deng Xiaoping and carry the cultural revolution through to the end".'

Much later the government reported that some 242,000 people had been killed but other estimates put the casualties at 600,000.

Pingmei says, 'There were a few more aftershocks, then the rhythm of life picked up again.'

By September she was supervising some of her student teachers at a high school when an announcement was made over the loudspeakers that Chairman Mao had died. She recalls: 'The student teacher sitting next to me leant his head on the back of the seat in front of him and began to sob. I did likewise except I was not sobbing, I was breathing a sigh of relief. Mao had been a great man but he had exceeded the limit. He had created conditions to lead the Chinese people away from extreme poverty, degradation and misery. But as absolute power corrupts absolutely, he had become paranoid and manoeuvred to maintain his own power.'[3]

More than a million people filled Tiananmen Square for his memorial service. There was a surreal hush to the occasion since everyone wore cloth shoes and moved silently into their places. Pingmei and Li Shao-hua were among them. According to Pingmei, 'The meeting began late because conflict arose among the leadership as to who should be on the rostrum. From where we stood . . . Jiang Qing stood out because she wore a black scarf, which is not the colour for mourning in China . . . there was a tangible feeling of resentment to see her with that black scarf around her head.'

In the days that followed, she says, 'Beijing was buzzing with rumours. The earthquake heralded the beginning of the end of the dynasty, it was said.' Then suddenly in early October word flashed around the college that the Gang of Four had been arrested. Pingmei recalls its effect: 'Suddenly I no longer felt tired; and I could hear the birds singing. When the news was finally made official the people celebrated. In the ensuing weeks it was literally impossible to buy a bottle of wine, firecrackers and all sorts of foodstuffs . . . now when I returned from work, climbing to our apartment on the fifth floor, I would hear music, comic dialogue on the radio, voices and laughter from people's homes which all seemed strange and new. Something we hadn't heard in almost ten years.'[4]

At the Australian embassy, Stephen FitzGerald felt the change of atmosphere immediately. He found the 'deliriously happy' crowds in the streets astounding: 'Something I've not experienced in all the crowds I've seen in the years I've known China. People even dare to greet unknown foreigners; some join hands; some hug. Ministries empty and their officials march along Changan Street. I see Trade Minister Li Qiang and he waves and jumps in the air like a joyful leprechaun. The feeling in China has changed.' However, he did 'wonder about their expectations. The Gang of Four and their supporters are gone. But the system remains.'

By then his term in Beijing was ending. Both Fraser and Peacock asked him to remain in the diplomatic service and offered him the plum posting of Tokyo. However, FitzGerald felt that without the Japanese language he'd feel 'perpetually ill-equipped and less than effective'.

Instead he chose to return to Australia and begin a PhD at the ANU. He says, 'I was happy to be going back to Canberra for the family, where our daughters could go to a regular school, and run free with the grass under their feet.'

★ ★ ★

While both the Whitlam and Fraser governments had promoted stronger relations with China, the Australian public still retained a suspicion of its big regional neighbour. Polls taken in 1976 revealed that 51 per cent considered that Australia would be threatened in the next fifteen years and some 41 per cent believed the threat would come from China. However, a range of cultural exchanges were being developed to 'humanise' the Chinese people to an Australian audience.

In 1975, for example, the Shanghai Philharmonic Orchestra visited Australia, who reciprocated with an exhibition of landscape painting. In 1977 China mounted a fascinating exhibition of archaeological remains that drew more than 250,000 visitors in Melbourne alone. But perhaps the most significant initiative was the formation by the government of the Australia–China Council in 1978, designed to promote 'mutual understanding and cooperation in culture, science, education, information and sport'. Its chair might have been designed for Stephen FitzGerald, who by then had published his book, *China and the World*, from a series of ANU lectures and developed ever stronger personal ties with China. However, the conservatives in the Coalition prevailed and the chairmanship went to one of their own, Professor Geoffrey Blainey of Melbourne University.

Australia–China trade, starting from a low base, was growing rapidly and remained strongly in Australia's favour. A delegation led by Deputy Prime Minister Doug Anthony in 1978 opened up the market for Australian iron ore. In response, the Guangdong Trade Fair held in Sydney over two months in 1980 provided a substantial boost to Chinese exports. Nevertheless, two-way trade remained well below that of Japan;

indeed, in 1981–82 China ranked behind America, New Zealand, Britain, South Korea and Russia as a market for Australian goods.

However, for the Chinese community in Australia, change was in the wind. Whitlam had promised to remove racism from every aspect of government and in 1973 passed the *Racial Discrimination Act*. His flamboyant immigration minister, Al Grassby, ordered that race be disregarded when considering prospective immigrants. He instituted a points system based on occupation, family reunions, command of English and the applicant's record of behaviour. There was, however, a gaping flaw in their treatment of Vietnamese refugees fleeing from the communist takeover of their country. These 'boat people' were subject to rigid guidelines that were totally inconsistent with the grand principles enunciated by Whitlam and his ministers. The reason was undoubtedly political; the refugees were believed to be overwhelmingly anti-communist and therefore likely to be Coalition supporters.

The Fraser government was initially wary of the same 'boat people' but the prime minister had begun his remarkable epiphany from the rock-ribbed conservative of his early years in parliament to the extraordinarily enlightened statesmen of his post-prime ministerial career. He had earlier signed a Family Reunion Agreement with China, and now he opened the doors to a wave of Indo-Chinese refugees. Indeed, conservatives like Geoffrey Blainey and senior Liberals like John Howard would soon protest that the 'balance' of migrant intake was tipping dangerously towards Asia.

When Fraser won the 1977 election – also in a landslide – Whitlam retired and passed the baton of leadership to a former policeman turned economics graduate from the University of Queensland, Bill Hayden. An aggressive left-winger in his early days in parliament, Hayden had matured into a well-regarded treasurer in the last Whitlam ministry. And while he lacked personal charisma, he undoubtedly possessed a safe pair of hands with which to carry the party's fortunes.

★ ★ ★

In China, Tan Pingmei was becoming disillusioned with the 'system' that FitzGerald warned had remained in place. 'The old guard reverted to the old way of managing the country,' she says. 'Had they really learnt anything? Deng Xiaoping was simply maintaining the dictatorship of the Communist Party.'

The family's future looked more grim than ever: 'Li Shao-hua and I discussed this time and time again, and finally decided we would try and go to Australia. It would be best for the children. They would have a future there. It wasn't an easy decision to make because it is no small thing to pick oneself up and start again, not at middle age when you are not sure how things will work out. For Li Shao-hua and me, our youth was spent, our lives half over; what was important was the future of our two sons, their education and happiness. I wanted no more than to live freely in peace and quiet, with no more political disruptions, chaos or lawlessness. I wanted freedom for Ting and Bin to grow up happily. Simple as that.'

Negotiating the arrangements for her return with the family were far from simple. But finally in 1979 they reached Canberra where she was able to secure a job at the ANU while completing an arts degree there. 'Everything was so different from the way I remembered it,' she says. 'It was a time when Vietnamese boat people were being accepted into the country with a generosity and humanity by Australians which I would never have imagined possible.

'People were so polite, not as I remembered and not like in China. After the communists took over manners were hardly a priority, especially during and after the Cultural Revolution. In Australia it was respect for the individual that struck me. At the ANU the respect for lecturers and technical staff was so unlike China.'

However, while the boys soon fitted in to their schools and developed friendships with their classmates, the transition for Li Shao-hua was deeply unsettling. He had suffered a bout of depression in China where there was a stigma against anyone with mental problems so his condition went untreated. Now his depression returned with greater severity and before he could be convinced to seek help, he committed suicide in 1981.

'It was the support of my sons – who were 10 and 12 – and close and understanding friends that helped me find my balance,' Pingmei says. 'Over the next twenty years I brought up Ting and Bin. I was fortunate, for they were sensible, obedient, and well-mannered, healthy and intelligent.'[5]

PART FOUR
AUSTRALIA AND CHINA TODAY

CHAPTER THIRTY-SEVEN
TIANANMEN SQUARE

In the absence of stupendous events or exceptional personalities – or some combination of the two – Australia's political pendulum tended to swing on a fulcrum that gave each of the major parties a decade in the corridors of power, and in 1983 Bill Hayden was confident that Labor had the government's measure, despite Prime Minister Malcolm Fraser's personal standing. Indeed, he would later assert that 'a drover's dog' could have led his party to victory. However, he was equally aware that the ambitious and immensely popular former union boss, Bob Hawke, who had recently been elected to parliament as a Labor member, would trounce the Liberal leader at the polls. And in a remarkable act of self-sacrifice – albeit at the urging of his senior colleagues – Hayden stood aside for the contender.

As it happened, Fraser was even then seeking Governor-General Kerr's agreement to spring an early election on his opponents, unaware that he would be facing a much more formidable adversary in Hawke. Labor won in a trot, with a 24-seat swing, and Hawke donned the prime ministerial mantle in March 1983. Hayden became foreign minister, the price he exacted for stepping aside and one that Hawke was more than happy to pay.

By contrast, in China the diminutive Deng Xiaoping now held the reins of imperial power with a grip as firm as any emperor of dynasties past. Though he had endured the rigors of the Long March and had devoted himself to the revolutionary cause, despite being twice sent to the political wilderness by Mao, his fealty to Marxist economic doctrine had never been much in evidence. Now he felt able to make a radical break from the collectivist gospel with the assertion that, 'Whether a cat is black or white makes no difference. As long as it catches mice, it is a good cat'. The result was an economic oxymoron: 'socialism with Chinese characteristics'.

The new president opened China to foreign investment and encouraged private competition. He revolutionised the education system at home and permitted students to study abroad. He rejuvenated the agricultural sector and in 1984, with a harvest of 400 million tons of grain, China at last became self-sufficient in food. He even had the confidence to criticise the departed Mao whom he said was 'seven parts good, three parts bad'. But he refused to countenance any moves towards the so-called 'fifth modernisation': democracy.

This was the China that greeted the young Australian diplomat Kevin Rudd and his wife Therese Rein when they arrived in Beijing with their baby daughter, Jessica, towards the end of the year. Rudd had taken Whitlam's advice to heart and after matriculating from Nambour High had enrolled in an arts course at the ANU where he not only specialised in the Chinese language and culture but also met his wife to be.

Graduating with honours, Rudd joined the Department of Foreign Affairs and Trade (DFAT) and had been posted initially to Sweden. In preparation for the Beijing posting, he completed a Chinese 'refresher' course in Hong Kong. 'Their Mandarin course was designed for defence types and spooks,' he says. 'Consequently, I had a perfect vocabulary at that stage along the lines of "Is your flamethrower in good order?" and other useful things on the streets of Beijing.'[1]

When they arrived, the Chinese capital was a revelation. 'Beijing in those days was just beautiful,' Rudd recalls. 'There was one tall building, just one, the Civic Building on Changan Street – everything else was three storeys. It was the old Beijing minus the walls.'

The bicycle traffic was thick and he and Therese both joined the throng to explore the city and get some regular exercise. Therese says, 'When we were there Deng Xiaoping said you can sell any of your surplus produce and keep the profit; and overnight there were street markets. You could buy silk nightgowns, unbruised apples and by the time we left there were private cars, though not that many; and fifty per cent of the population was not wearing Mao suits.'

Rudd worked well with his ambassador, the respected Dennis Argall, and quickly mastered the Beijing accent. Therese joined with the other diplomatic wives on expeditions to such varied destinations as the Ming Tombs, the Great Wall, the Fragrant Hills and the Temple of Agriculture. 'In those situations you make some deep friendships,' she says. In their second year Rudd was promoted to First Secretary in the political section and she worked part-time in the British Council's English Language Resource Library.

Meantime, the Chinese Premier, Zhao Ziyang, visited Australia in response to Fraser's invitation, arriving only a month after the Hawke government was installed. Hawke was quick to realise the importance of the visit, as was his newly appointed economic adviser, Ross Garnaut.

Born in Perth in 1946, Garnaut took an arts degree and a PhD at the ANU. He headed the Economic Policy Division in New Guinea's Finance Department before returning to academic life at the university where the Labor leader had himself spent time prior to entering parliament. They quickly established a good working relationship and Garnaut saw the tremendous potential benefits to the Australian economy if China could be encouraged to participate fully in the international trading system. 'Hawke was able to build on the foundations of friendly relations in which his predecessors, Gough Whitlam and Malcolm Fraser, had personally invested heavily,' Garnaut says.

Hawke and Zhao quickly found a strong sense of common cause and a personal relationship developed. 'Zhao described China's ambition for reform and invited Australia's participation,' Garnaut recalls. 'Australia was a leader amongst governments in seeking to build a framework of bilateral, regional and multicultural economic relations to accommodate them.'[2]

Indeed, by then Ambassador Argall had suffered a breakdown and the head of the political section, David Irvine, became *Charge d'Affairs* until the new ambassador could be appointed. Hawke asked Garnaut to take the job and he was pleased to do so. The two men would develop what became the closest and most productive relationship between the Chinese and Australian leadership in the long history of the two nations.

Zhao invited Hawke to visit China and when he arrived in February 1984 he quickly built on the relationship with both Zhao and the General Secretary of the Communist Party, Hu Yaobang. 'There was a real chemistry between Hawke and the two Chinese leaders,' Garnaut says. 'Premier Zhao Ziyang suggested, and Bob Hawke accepted, that China and Australia should strive to make their relationship a model for countries with different social systems and at different levels of development.'

In 1985 Australia hosted the Chinese leadership a second time and Hawke took Hu on a tour of the massive iron ore developments in Western Australia. The following year Hawke returned for one of the more significant visits of an Australian leader to the People's Republic. Garnaut says he was blessed with embassy staff that were extraordinarily able to prepare for the prime ministerial cavalcade. It included David Irvine and economist Geoff Raby, both of whom would later become ambassadors to China themselves.

Also in the political section was David Ambrose, a highly respected China hand, as well as the hard-working Kevin Rudd. According to Garnaut, 'When [Rudd] didn't know something he learned something about it. He put a lot of effort into briefing himself so that he'd have a basis on which to make judgements.' It was a trait that he would later carry into his political career, many would say to excess. But in China it was an essential asset as his principal task was reporting on Chinese domestic politics and politicians. 'It was not very easy to mix with them,' Garnaut says, 'but he did it extraordinarily well.'

The Hawke visit was a remarkable success. 'Hu accompanied him on his provincial visits which was practically unknown for such a high official; and in Chengdu they talked until after midnight,' Garnaut recalls. 'It was an extraordinarily free-ranging conversation and at one stage it turned to the Pope, at which Hu Yaobang said, "The

Soviet Party thinks they're the Pope of communism!". Hu and Zhao spent more time with Hawke than with any other foreign leader. The British Ambassador Sir Richard Evans said in 1986 that "the Chinese leadership spends more time thinking about the Australian relationship than about any other country except the big three – the Soviets, the US and Japan".'

Garnaut confirms that at the Australian embassy they had access to the top leadership that no one else had at that time: 'We saw Hu Yaobang once a month, for example. The American Ambassador was Winston Lord and he was not particularly happy that we had greater access than the Americans. But Hawke always made it clear that the US alliance was central to Australia's defence policy. This was not a barrier to productive relations and at times was explicitly welcomed and used by Chinese leaders.'

It was well known that Hawke was close to the US Secretary of State, George Schultz, and after the visit the Australian embassy invited Winston Lord over for a private meeting. They talked in a room in the embassy that was lined with lead. Garnaut says, We gave him a full briefing and Lord said, "I suppose if anyone else is to have these meetings [with the Chinese leadership], I suppose we're glad it's Bob Hawke." Our view was that as China became a great power their attention would turn to the other major powers and we wouldn't be in quite the same privileged position, so let's make the most of it now.'

And so they did. During 1984–85 Australia's exports to China rose by almost 75 per cent, breaking the billion-dollar barrier for the first time. Hawke's second visit was capped by a 75-minute meeting with Deng Xiaoping. Indeed, it was of such importance that the prime minister arranged for Richard Rigby, Australia's outstanding Chinese linguist – and rising diplomat – to fly from his post in the London High Commission to interpret for him.

Rigby had been born in Melbourne in 1948 and gained his PhD at the ANU. His career included Department of Foreign Affairs and Trade postings to Beijing in 1981–84 and Tokyo before his London appointment. He would later reach ambassadorial status and become Assistant Director-General of the Office of National Assessments, the principal international intelligence conduit to the government. When he received the PM's summons to Beijing, he was on the next plane.

According to Rigby, Deng was an immensely charismatic character. 'His only official position was Chairman of the All China Bridge Association,' he says, laughing, 'and more seriously the Central Military Commission. He was such a diminutive figure that when sitting his feet barely reached the floor, but he focused the energy of the room like a Black Hole. Whatever he did – even taking a cigarette – he was the complete centre of attention.'[3]

The meeting, in the Great Hall of the People, went well over its allotted time as Deng told Hawke, 'The [economic] burdens that have been on the back of China in the past – centralization of decision making and subsidies – must be removed.' Moreover, he said, China regarded Australia 'as a country with a close identity of views and perceptions on a wide range of issues'.

The Australian prime minister was impressed. 'I think what is remarkable is not merely the magnitude of the changes which are envisaged,' Hawke said, 'but also the realism and the preparedness to admit that mistakes will have to be faced up to.' He also noted that Deng had 'great confidence' in his fellow members of the Chinese politburo: 'Occasionally, he said, he gives them some advice – but not too much, because he doesn't need to.'[4]

Hawke took some personal pride in Deng's statement since he saw his own role as the first among equals in similar terms. And he felt his admiration and sagacity justified when Hu Yaobang wrote to him in November 1986: 'Mr Prime Minister, as you know, while the economic restructuring is still going on, the political restructuring has been placed on our agenda. This is a great experiment of weeding through the old to bring forth the new and an experiment of steady self-improvement.

'China's reform not only has a bearing on the destiny of a quarter of the world's population and is changing China's outlook, but also is a contribution to the maintenance of world peace. Since it is an experiment, it cannot be entirely free from errors. We are convinced that so long as we dare to explore new ground and take prudent steps, we will be able to avoid major mistakes. And even if mistakes are made, they can be corrected [promptly] and greater results in the reform will be achieved. I appreciate very much your positive appraisal of and your warm support for our reform.'[5]

Alas, it was sent on the eve of student demonstrations demanding that political reform. The protests arose in December, starting in Hefei and quickly spreading to Nanjing and Shanghai. Deng Xiaoping responded by forcing the resignation of Hu Yaobang less than two months later. 'Hu's dismissal set the boundaries of political change,' Garnaut says. 'They stayed set. Deng believed in the untarnished authority of the Chinese Communist Party.'

The one saving grace was Hu's replacement by the moderate Zhao Ziyang who also retained his role as General Secretary of the Communist Party. However, later in 1987, the more hardline Li Peng became premier and after that relations with Australia became more routine, if still relatively productive. Garnaut returned to Canberra to become one of Australia's more influential academic and economic advisers, while the head of mission reverted to a departmental professional, David Sadleir.

At the end of 1986, Rudd had been recalled to Canberra where he was engaged in the DFAT's planning bureau, looking at likely developments in foreign policy five to fifteen years ahead. Then, after a period in management, he left the department to join the Labor opposition leader in the Queensland parliament, Wayne Goss, as his private secretary in 1988. It marked the beginning of Kevin Rudd's own political career.

★ ★ ★

By then Deng Xiaoping's economic reforms had not only resulted in massive economic growth, they continued to raise expectations for genuine democratic reform. And as the economy boomed, inflation also rose, to the detriment of people's buying power. The students Deng had encouraged to study abroad returned with demands for freedom of expression, greater official accountability and a bigger say in the political life of the nation. They triggered protests in cities around the country and were backed by workers with their own agendas for a better deal from the monolithic Communist administration.

These culminated in 1989 in a mass demonstration in Beijing and in April, the sudden death of Hu Yaobang, who had been sympathetic to their demands, brought up to a million demonstrators into Tiananmen Square. At first the Communist leadership sought to negotiate. But on 24 April, Premier Li Peng met with Deng Xiaoping and other party leaders who determined that 'firm action' was required. Two days later an editorial appeared in the *People's Daily* warning that 'It is necessary to take a clear-cut stand against disturbances' and branded the demonstration as an anti-party, anti-government revolt. The protestors were outraged and believing – with some justice – that the politburo was split on the issue became even more determined to press home their demands. In fact, Zhao Ziyang, was sympathetic to their cause but at the time he was visiting North Korea.

In May, a group of students went on a hunger strike and protests spread to some 400 cities across the empire. Deng and Li Peng were deeply concerned by the forthcoming visit of the Soviet leader, Mikhail Gorbachev, the first in three decades. But despite their best efforts, the students refused to compromise and the summit talks with the Russian leader in the Great Hall of the People were held against a backdrop of protest and commotion in the city square. This represented an excruciating loss of face for the Chinese leaders. And when Zhao pointedly told Gorbachev that Deng Xiaoping was the 'paramount authority' in China, Deng was outraged. It marked a decisive split between the country's two most senior political figures.

The hunger strikes galvanised support for the students and in Beijing even party officials, police and military officers joined the protest. The

Chinese Red Cross sent in teams of paramedics to tend the hunger strikers. Foreign journalists who had arrived in Beijing to cover the Gorbachev visit stayed on to record the chaos in Tiananmen Square. Australia's ABC team in Beijing provided a blanket coverage and Australians in the Chinese capital were drawn to the melee.

Deng wanted to declare martial law but Zhao resisted. Then on 19 May, Zhao and Wen Jiabao, chief of the Party General Office, went to the square where Zhao addressed the students, pleading with them not to sacrifice their futures. It was an emotional speech and drew applause from the crowd. But it was the Communist leader's final public appearance. That night Deng held a meeting with military and party leaders where he secured agreement for martial law and denounced Zhao who was placed under house arrest. Zhao Ziyang would be confined there until his death fifteen years later.

Those Australians in Tiananmen Square included Richard Rigby who had returned to the embassy as political counsellor, the embassy's second in command Colin Heseltine, and Kevin Rudd with his political principal, the newly elected Queensland premier Wayne Goss, on an official visit to the capital. 'I actually spent about three days walking around the square talking to the students,' Rudd says. 'It was an extraordinary and memorable experience.'

According to Goss, 'Kevin with his fluent Mandarin and knowledge of Chinese politics was able to take my understanding of what was happening to a completely different level. In addition, he knew many of the diplomats in Beijing at the time.'[6]

The Queensland premier and Rudd departed on 2 June, and the next evening television broadcasts warned Beijing residents to remain indoors. Instead, it was a signal for crowds of people to take to the streets where they found army units advancing on the city from every direction.

Rigby and Heseltine remained in the embassy and sent back to Canberra a running commentary of the growing crisis. Despite the efforts of thousands of Beijing's civilians to block their paths, the army tanks and armoured personnel carriers (APCs) forced their way towards the square, raking the people and the apartment buildings with gunfire. The killings infuriated city residents, some of whom attacked soldiers with anything at hand, from rocks and broomsticks to hastily assembled Molotov cocktails.

As darkness fell on the night of 4 June, army helicopters appeared above Tiananmen Square and students called their campuses to send reinforcements. By 10.30 the government loudspeakers blared warnings that troops would take 'any measures' to clear the square. Blood-spattered witnesses from the surrounding areas arrived with tales of horrific scenes. Some protestors departed; others refused to be intimidated and prepared to confront their military compatriots.

Shortly after midnight as battlefield flares bathed the square in a fierce light, the first APC arrived from the west, quickly followed by two others from the south. The students threw chunks of cement and tried to jam metal poles into their wheels before setting one of them on fire. Three soldiers escaped their vehicle and the students formed a protective cordon around them and escorted them to the first aid station.

At 1.30 a.m. the vanguard of the 38th Army and paratroopers from the 15th Airborne Corps arrived at the north and south ends of Tiananmen Square and hundreds more troops poured out of the Great Hall of the People and the History Museum.

The bloody confrontations, graphically captured and later transmitted to a horrified world, continued throughout the night as several hundred students were forced back to the Monument of the People's Heroes in the centre of the square. Tanks ran over the bodies of the slain until they were reduced to pulp. Then at 4 a.m. the lights in the square were suddenly turned off and the government loudspeaker announced, 'Clearance of the square begins now.'

Shortly afterward the lights returned and the troops advanced on the monument from all sides. The student leaders tried to organise a vote on whether to leave but a squad of soldiers in camouflage uniform charged up to the monument and shot out the student loudspeaker.

Other soldiers beat and kicked those remaining on the monument and more shots were fired.

Finally at about 5 a.m. there was an organised departure from the monument. But when the last cohort of students were making their way down the bicycle lane at the corner of Changan Street, three tanks from the square followed them, firing tear gas, and one tank charged through the crowd, killing eleven and injuring scores more. The numbers killed and wounded in Tiananmen Square and surrounds has never been properly accounted but undoubtedly runs into the many hundreds.

The following day the real barbarity of the 'Tiananmen incident' was driven home to the watching world by the graphic confrontation between a tank and a lone man simply dressed in white shirt and dark pants and carrying a shopping bag. As the tank driver in the bowels of the vehicle attempted to go around him, the 'Tank Man' (as he became known) moved into the leviathan's path. He remained there, unmoving, directly in front of the turret gun, as the tension rose. Then he moved forward and climbed on to the tank itself to speak to the soldiers inside. When that failed to turn them back, he returned to his position before the steel monster. And there he stood until a group of bystanders pulled him away.

The vision, both via television and still photography, instantly became one of the iconic images of the 20th century. It captured, in a manner that words never could, the power of individual defiance against the mindless, mechanical oppression of the state. The Tank Man's identity has never been revealed and while his fate is unknown his immortality is assured.

CHAPTER THIRTY-EIGHT
THE END OF WHITE AUSTRALIA

Those images, together with the unforgettable panic among the students racing their wounded comrades to aid stations, made a dramatic impact on Australian viewers, not least Prime Minister Bob Hawke who was also deeply moved by the reportage from Richard Rigby in Tiananmen Square and subsequent cables from Rigby and Minister Colin Heseltine at the Australian embassy.

'I have a deep love for the Chinese people,' Hawke said later. And at a tearful commemorative service on 16 June in the Great Hall of Parliament – without consulting his cabinet colleagues – he extended the visas of 16,200 Chinese students currently in Australia: 'When I walked off the dais, I was told: "You cannot do that, prime minister." I said to them, "I just did. It is done."' And in the weeks that followed some 42,000 Chinese nationals were granted permanent visas.

His action was the more remarkable since, at the time, Australia was in the midst of a heated debate about the rate of Asian immigration fuelled by comments from Professor Geoffrey Blainey and opposition leader John Howard. Moreover, there was internal resistance from the treasury, finance and immigration departments. However, the cabinet backed the PM and to counter the outcry from the conservatives, they authorised a 'multicultural agenda' which expanded the SBS television station, established English as the national language and urged migrants to take up Australian citizenship.

Professor James Jupp, the highly respected ANU demographer, said, 'It really broke the back of remaining support for White Australia. I think it was a wise decision and historians will see it as a very important one.'[1]

Internationally, Australia's response to Tiananmen Square was measured. Ministerial visits were put on hold for a time but the government was careful not to overreact. Ross Garnaut had been with Hawke at The Lodge on the night of the massacre. 'He was upset at what had befallen his friends,' Garnaut says. 'But it was resolved that there should be no general Western closing down of relations with China. Australia would register the seriousness of its response without taking actions that would cut across the reform process – suspend high level visits, but no sanctions in the areas of trade and cultural relations, nothing in the people-to-people area.'

Indeed, in 1989 Garnaut had produced a highly influential report entitled 'Australia and the Northeast Asian Ascendancy' that charted a long-term course for Australia to integrate with the resurgent Chinese and other Asian economies. But he says that while 'the steadiness' of Australian policy had some influence, it fell to Japan to lead the effort to moderate Western reactions, notably at the G7 Heads of Government meeting in the US the following year. Ambassador David Sadleir's speech in Hong Kong in 1990 simply assisted the process. There was some diminution of Western economic engagement with China, but it was more than compensated for by a burst of trade and investment from Japan, Korea, Taiwan and Chinese business leaders in South-East Asia.

Also in 1990 the Chinese Minister for Metallurgy, Qi Yuanjing, visited Australia to open the Channar iron ore mine in Western Australia, the first major Chinese investment in Australian mining since the goldrush days in the Northern Territory and Queensland. Later the same year, the Australian Trade Minister Neil Blewett reciprocated. Foreign Minister Gareth Evans travelled to Beijing in 1991 and, Garnaut says, 'slowly the exchanges built to a more normal pace'.[2]

However, by then it was becoming clear that the Hawke era had pretty well run its race. While the prime minister remained personally popular – and had secured a fourth election victory over the Coalition led by Andrew Peacock in 1990 – he had been around so long that he was fast being seen as yesterday's man. It was time for a change.

Moreover, he was being stalked by his deputy prime minister and treasurer, Paul Keating, with whom he had transformed the Australian economy and opened it up to the world.

★ ★ ★

Keating at 47 was one of the more unusual characters of 20th century Australian politics. Largely self-educated, he had risen from a rough-and-tumble Western Sydney background of factional Labor Party warfare to become a dapper and cultivated operator with total command of his portfolio. He also had a taste for Mahler and French antique clocks as well as a wicked tongue that could either encapsulate a complex economic concept with perfect clarity or leave an opponent gasping for air. Thus, his shadow minister, Peter Costello, became 'all tip and no iceberg', and the fastidious lightweight Andrew Peacock 'the souffle' that couldn't rise twice. And as he moved on Hawke, his description of the prime minister as 'old Jellyback' devastated the man fifteen years his senior who had taken such pride in governing by consensus.

In June 1991, Keating challenged for the leadership but a sentimental caucus supported the leader who had won and kept them in power for so long. However, the scale of the win was insufficient to end Keating's assault. By Christmas he was the new prime minister and Hawke had returned to private life while retaining an intense interest in China. Indeed, he would make a fortune over the next several years as a consultant advising Australian and Chinese businesses in various joint projects.

At the same time the Chinese leadership was also in replacement mode. Deng Xiaoping's international reputation had been shattered by Tiananmen Square and he officially retired from the political scene in 1992. After a great deal of internal debate on whether the politburo should continue economic reform, he toured the southern provinces giving very public encouragement to the free-market regime he had done so much to foster. 'To get rich is glorious,' he proclaimed and the businessmen of Shanghai, Guangzhou and Shenzhen took him at his word.[3]

The leadership in Beijing tried to ignore his brazen peregrinations but when the Shanghai media continually trumpeted his message, they had little choice but to respond; and in a factional struggle within the politburo, Jiang Zemin sided with Deng and thereby confirmed his position as the heir apparent to the Communist version of the Dragon Throne. Jiang then pursued an expansion of Deng's economic conundrum.

An idiosyncratic character, Jiang had developed a dinner party trick for visiting Australians and Americans: he could – and frequently did – recite Lincoln's Gettysburg Address word for word. But he purposefully established himself as an international figure and as Deng's health and influence waned, Jiang took ever greater control and became President of the People's Republic in March 1993.

Whether the new Australian prime minister was a beneficiary of Jiang's party trick is unlikely since he made only one official visit to China during his tenure. However, according to the new ambassador, Mike Lightowler, Keating made a powerful impact on the leadership. Another West Australian, and with a strong trade union background, Lightowler says, 'He might have spent only about 60 hours in China but during that time I developed the highest admiration for Keating. He was a man with a vision. He's incredibly personable. Many of these meetings between leaders are set pieces, but not with Keating. Whether it was with Zhu Rongji or Jiang Zemin, he could just sit down and chat and even with an interpreter he could engage the Chinese completely.'

Foreign Minister Gareth Evans, who had taken the post in 1988 when Bill Hayden became the Queen's representative at Yarralumla, also worked closely with the Chinese leadership. While international dynamics meant that he and Keating made Indonesia and Cambodia their first priority, they put enormous effort into persuading China to join the Asia-Pacific Economic Cooperation Forum (APEC) while also accepting Taiwan's membership; and in 1992 the People's Republic completed the formalities for full participation.

The annual leaders' meeting in various member capitals was a singular occasion, and not only for the embarrassing photo-ops in local dress.

The private and corridor meetings between leaders and officials often made vital progress in resolving issues that might otherwise have festered between the parties. They also helped to develop a sense of community within the regional powers and encouraged China to play its part in the international body politic.

Keating painted a 'big picture' of his vision for Australia and its place in the region as a republic that had moved on from the colonial ties with Britain and engaged in new alliances in the Asia-Pacific. 'Australia needs to seek its security in Asia, not from Asia,' he said.[4] He found common cause with China's vice-premier Zhu Rongji who visited Australia in 1992 and was himself a 'big picture' man. At the same time Gareth Evans engaged with the Chinese foreign minister Qian Qichen on at least twelve occasions at APEC and the United Nations.

The Labor Party under Keating handily won the 1993 election against John Hewson and the 'non-believers' in the ALP who resented his replacing Hawke, provoking the victor to dub it, 'the sweetest victory of all'. However, he lacked Hawke's common touch and with John Howard once more leading the Coalition, the unapologetic Keating was bundled out of office.

In the process Keating frustrated the political ambitions of the 39-year-old Kevin Rudd who had run for Labor in the marginal Brisbane seat of Griffith. He and Therese had door-knocked some 32,000 houses by the time of the poll and while he made a respectable personal showing, he fell well short of his Liberal opponent. After a period of intense disappointment and depression, Rudd decided to run in the next election. Meantime, he would use his Chinese expertise to establish a consultancy to assist Australian businesses seeking to export or invest in China.

★ ★ ★

By then John Howard had gathered the reins of government and moved into Kirribilli House, the Sydney mansion first acquired by Prime Minister Billy Hughes in 1930 but developed during Menzies' incumbency as accommodation for prime ministers when on business in Sydney. The Prime Minister's Department had it renovated for the Howard family's permanent residence.

The new prime minister's Anglocentric reputation gave pause to those in both government and opposition who had been working to develop friendly and productive relations with China. So with the electoral writing on the wall, Evans and Keating had selected a well-regarded diplomat in Ric Smith, a West Australian with a knowledge of the region and an innate ability to work with people across the political spectrum, to become the next ambassador to Beijing. Indeed, his appointment was formalised by the Executive Council in July 1995, some seven months before the position would be vacated by another West Australian, Michael Lightowler.[5]

Smith took up his post in February 1996, a week before the Howard victory. 'The Chinese Government then wondered about my status,' he says. 'Some asked whether I would have to be recalled and we explained that that wasn't the way it worked in Australia. I did feel for quite some months that the Chinese were testing me.'[6]

His situation was not improved by a series of troublesome issues beginning with his government's cancelling the Concessional Finance Facility which had been well-patronised by Australians doing business in China, as well as other cuts to the aid program. The Taiwanese leadership had begun to talk of independence and China fired several missiles in their general direction; and much to Beijing's displeasure, the new Australian foreign minister Alexander Downer applauded the American response of moving two carrier groups into the seas around the island. This was followed by Howard's clumsy decision to meet with the Dalai Lama and his ambivalent attitude to the shrill anti-Asian outcries of the newly elected Queensland reactionary, Pauline Hanson.

'The Chinese decided to put us in the deep freeze,' Smith says. 'Ministerial contacts were not approved and clearly nothing was going to happen in the relationship while they "taught us a lesson".' So with a certain *savoir faire*, the ambassador decided to take a few weeks of accumulated leave. However, he was back in harness before the APEC leaders' conference in Manila at the end of the year and helped to arrange a meeting between Howard and President Jiang Zemin.

According to Smith, the meeting went well: 'Howard stated his position on the issues and did so in suitable terms. Jiang accepted this and seemed to appreciate Howard's frankness.' He then invited the Australian Prime Minister to visit and in front of the media he said, 'It's always better face-to-face, isn't it?' That became what Smith identified as the 'leitmotif' of the relationship during his extended tenure until 2000. The Chinese ensured that John Howard had a full appreciation of the relationship as they saw it; and the invitation was the first step in the process.

The visit was scheduled for Easter 1997 and given his inexperience in the international arena – particularly after a somewhat uncomfortable meeting with President Bill Clinton in Washington – Howard was apprehensive. As it happened, Ric Smith had made a quick trip back to Australia in March when he received a call to come to The Lodge to talk through the coming event. Smith immediately called his embassy colleagues and staff in Beijing and developed suggestions for an agenda.

At The Lodge with the prime minister that Sunday evening was the Secretary of DFAT, Philip Flood, Howard's chief of staff, Arthur Sinodinos, the head of his department, Max Moore-Wilton, his media adviser Graeme Morris, and high-ranking officials from the treasury. Smith went through his points as Howard took notes. The most striking of these gave the first clear indication of the manner in which the Australia–China relationship would be transformed over the next decade: 'China's beginning an extraordinary economic take-off,' Smith said. 'We're going to see growth figures of 9–10 per cent. And more than 40 per cent of this growth, now and in the future, comes from the external sector – foreign trade or investment.'

There was a momentary silence. 'This is an extraordinary figure,' the diplomat said.

Howard looked up from his notes. 'I think you're right,' he said.

A quick exchange with the treasury official revealed that in Australia's case, foreign trade and investment represented just over 20 per cent of annual economic growth; and roughly the same applied to the US and Japan. 'So, this *is* extraordinary,' the prime minister said, 'forty plus per cent!'

'Yes,' Smith responded, 'and the point of course is it means that they're locked into the world; the path of growth they're on is inexorable; they can't and won't change it now for political reasons and because this interdependence has already begun. And their dependence on our resources is only going to grow.' Howard immediately grasped the potential for Australia. Smith said later, 'He seized on this and he saw the strategic and political dimensions, as well as the economic.'

The other important note on the diplomatic agenda was a judgement Smith had made about the political shadow play taking place in the politburo to decide the next of their number to assume real power at the apex of the party. From among the contenders he had settled upon Keating's 'big picture' collaborator, Zhu Rongji. Though still a vice-premier, Zhu had the gravitas to move up the chain of command, Smith believed, and advised Howard to engage with him. The group at The Lodge also decided it would be best for the prime minister to begin his visit in Shanghai to get the feel of the latest 'New China'.

Several weeks later he arrived at the Australian consulate, then in the charge of Richard Rigby. And when the prime ministerial party gathered before the picture window on the 25th floor of the building, they were confronted by a scene that might have been made for the occasion – everywhere they looked, tall buildings were topped by cranes deployed to make them taller; construction crews massed at every available site; the place was literally a hive of industry. A stunned Howard turned to his team with a half-smile and asked, 'How long has this been going on?!'

Rigby was the first to respond: 'About ten years, Prime Minister.'

CHAPTER THIRTY-NINE
THE TRADE BOOM

In Beijing, Howard met with Jiang Zemin, Premier Li Peng and had an extended visit with Zhu Rongji who would indeed become the premier the following year and would retain the post until 2003. While Howard might not have been particularly comfortable with their values and their mode of governance, his attitude remained very businesslike throughout. 'The Prime Minister established himself as a person the Chinese felt they could trust,' Smith says, 'And from then on things settled down. The next three years were incredibly busy.'[1]

One of Australia's most significant self-imposed tasks was to negotiate China's entry to the World Trade Organization (WTO), but running parallel was the human rights fallout from Tiananmen Square. In the previous seven years, the UN Commission on Human Rights had considered a motion co-sponsored by both the United States and Australia (among others) condemning China for the military suppression. But by 1997, it seemed clear that there was room for a diplomatic manoeuvre that could redound in Australia's favour.

Each time but one the motion had been defeated on a procedural technicality, even before it was put to the vote. And the one time a vote was held, it was easily defeated. But every time it surfaced it caused diplomatic resentment among the Chinese and another refusal to discuss human rights issues with Australia. Smith judged that this was never going to change unless Australia took the initiative. So in talks with the vice foreign minister Li Zhaoxing he floated the idea that Australia would no longer co-sponsor the motion if China would agree to an annual high level dialogue on human rights.

In practical terms, that meant Australia stood to gain real political capital with the Chinese government. The *quid pro quo* included permission to discuss – as a purely consular matter – the issue of the Chinese-Australian businessman, James Peng. After a falling out in 1993 with a highly placed Chinese business partner – the niece of Deng Xiaoping, no less – Peng had been seized in his Macao hotel, taken to Shenzhen and sentenced to eighteen years jail for theft and misappropriation.

Foreign Minister Alexander Downer took the proposal to cabinet which approved the plan. However, the US Secretary of State, Madeline Albright, learned of the decision and called Downer in a fury. The Australian stood firm and announced the decision publicly. This led to the Canadians and others also falling into line, but Australia's initiative earned the lion's share of diplomatic credit. And shortly afterwards Zhu Rongji made formal overtures for a visit to Australia in lieu of a proposed trip to Europe.

The Chinese premier arrived in May 1998, beginning with a tour of the massive West Australian iron ore and gas fields in the early stages of development. The state premier Richard Court and his wife, Jo, accompanied Zhu. According to Smith, 'He developed something of a relationship with Richard Court which was critical later when we got to the matter of LNG [liquid natural gas] contracts.'

From there, Zhu went on to Adelaide and Canberra where there was a large reception for him. 'But again John Howard did a clever thing,' Smith says. The prime minister held a lunch for Zhu with just his two senior people and the ambassador, and Australians Peter Costello, Downer and Smith: 'Perhaps ten people (plus interpreters) which by Chinese standards is intimate. Zhu is accustomed to going to events where there are hundreds of people and I think he appreciated this opportunity to talk fairly intimately. They spoke really frankly to each other.' Most of the conversation concerned trade and particularly Australian resources but it also broadened to include a range of international issues.

Zhu then continued to Queensland where he was escorted throughout by the defence minister John Moore. The result was the creation of a relationship with the Chinese premier that almost immediately afterwards would pay great dividends when in July that year the Asian financial crisis erupted. The following month Moore decided to make a visit to China and asked for a meeting with Zhu who, like most of his colleagues, was holidaying at the coastal resort of Beidaihe in Hebei Province. Nevertheless, Zhu took the train back to Beijing for the meeting and, toward the end of the luncheon, told the Australians he wanted a message conveyed to their prime minister.

Moore turned to Smith who offered to convey it to Canberra. Zhu said, 'No, I want you to write it down.'

The diplomat took the menu and on its back wrote one of the more significant communiques to be exchanged between the two nations. The actual wordage of the Chinese premier remains in departmental files but the gist of the message was etched in the memories of those present:

This is a crisis that is affecting so many of the countries in the region. We greatly appreciate what Australia has done in providing standby credits for Thailand, Indonesia and South Korea. This will greatly assist the stability of the region.

In all of this, Australia and China have to be solid bookends. I know that your banking system is strong and your credit is strong and you can stand by my word: we will be robust too. Ignore the speculation about Chinese banks going under; it won't happen. I own them, so it won't happen.

China and Australia have got to work together on this; and by the way, don't get drawn into the Japanese idea about an Asian IMF – it's just going to be a re-run of the [wartime] Greater East-Asian Co-Prosperity Sphere. Let's not even go there.

Smith cabled the message – from John Moore to the prime minister – in exactly Zhu's bald terms, at the first opportunity. 'Zhu was tough,' Smith says. 'He was clear-minded; he understood the big picture.'

Indeed, when Paul Keating came to China after losing power, though he was principally engaged on business issues on behalf of the Colonial

Mutual Insurance Group and others, he always met with Zhu Rongji. Smith confirms that, 'Zhu thought he was marvellous because they talked at the same level – big picture stuff – Paul Keating explaining how APEC is meant to work with China here and Japan there and America there and the rest of us circling around the table helping where we can. Zhu liked this and Keating was always putting a picture of world affairs that Zhu might not have thought of before but he'd go away and think about it. Paul can be light and he can be serious, and he likes music and so does Zhu, so there was a good connection there.'

While Australia was beginning to reap the financial rewards of China's economic boom, China itself was being transformed, culturally if not politically. 'It was fascinating to watch the explosion of art,' Smith says. In his first year, 1996, there was a Beijing Art Festival and Smith went along and found about 30 pieces that were 'pretty modest'. The next year there were 300, and by the time Smith left his post in 2000, there were 3000 works, as well as many art galleries.

Smith believes there were two things responsible for this: 'One is, of course, liberating the country and letting people express themselves through painting; and notwithstanding all the complaints they did that and now some Chinese artists are earning millions of dollars from their works.'

The second factor is more prosaic and practical. He believes that when millions of Chinese who lived in government housing were suddenly permitted to buy their dwellings, the pride of ownership – and the need to be different from neighbours – induced them to decorate their homes, firstly with cheap mass-produced art but then as they became more wealthy they went upmarket with both art and furnishings. Indeed, the Swedish company Ikea became a massive market leader across the country and remains so today.

★ ★ ★

Back in Australia, the 1998 election with the Labor opposition led by Kim Beazley, a former senior minister in the Hawke and Keating governments, cut Howard's majority from 40 to 12. In fact, Labor won a clear plurality of the votes but they were insufficient in the seats that would have secured them the treasury benches. And among the new members were two – Kevin Rudd and Julia Gillard – who would become Labor prime ministers in the years ahead.

Rudd had won his Brisbane seat handily and Gillard, a Victorian lawyer with strong ties to the union movement, now held the safe outer Melbourne seat of Lalor, named for the leader of the rebel miners at Eureka. They joined another relative newcomer on the government side who would rise to the same heights: Tony Abbott, who had come into the parliament in a by-election for the Sydney seat of Warringah.

Of the three, only Rudd had any engagement with China. Gillard, the proud daughter of a Welsh migrant, had never evinced any interest in the region, while the British-born Abbott would cheerfully confide that his adopted country's attitude to China was 'fear and greed'.

Gillard recalled her first meeting with Rudd as members of the house: 'There was a big class of new starters and we hung around as a group,' she says. 'We listened to each other's maiden speeches. And I have a very clear recollection of Kevin's.'[2]

Delivered on 11 November 1998 – the 23rd anniversary of his idol Gough Whitlam's sacking – Rudd confronted the 'outdated' Asian attitudes towards Australia. 'Despite the enormous changes to Australia's ethnicity since the war,' he told the house, 'we are still seen as an essentially European enclave in a region of non-European cultures. All of these [countries] have been colonised by one European state or another – some in the ugliest of fashions. When you add to that the particular overlay of the White Australia policy, it becomes easier to understand why our place in the region can sometimes be delicate. We are proudly Australian and should remain so. But as a nation we need to understand how others perceive us.'

Rudd criticised the Howard government for its 'mistakes' over the past three years. 'The damage is already great; the stakes are now too high,' he said. 'The repair work will probably take a decade.'

In fact, by 2000 the work of Australia's diplomatic, business and political founding fathers of what might be called 'the Chinese Engagement' was beginning to pay substantial dividends. In the 1999–2000 financial year, two-way trade grew by 24 per cent to $12.5 billion, of which exports – mostly of primary products – reached $5 billion. China had become Australia's third biggest trading partner, the biggest customer for wool, and one of the biggest markets for wheat, iron ore, alumina and coal.

The joint efforts of the Beijing embassy and government ministers had secured the granting of 'Approved Destination' status for Chinese tourism, while services – including education – had been growing at over 10 per cent annually for the past decade. And by now Chinese made up the fourth largest proportion of permanent migrants after the United Kingdom, New Zealand and Ireland. Patient embassy pressure had secured the release of James Peng; and after complex and exhausting negotiations, China had cleared the bar for its membership of the WTO.

In China, as in Australia, there was an extended period of steady leadership with Jiang Zemin and Zhu Rongji at the apex of power. And at the Australian embassy, an experienced China hand, David Irvine, succeeded Ric Smith as ambassador. Another West Australian, Irvine had attended the Hale School in Perth and graduated from the University of Western Australia with honours in Elizabethan history.

Since his earlier China posting under Ross Garnaut, Irvine had headed the China desk at the Department of Foreign Affairs and Trade, and had been posted to Indonesia where he fine-tuned his expertise in Bahasa and wrote two well-regarded books on Indonesian culture. He had a special interest in the intelligence area and most recently had been high commissioner to Papua New Guinea. By the time Irvine reached Beijing, the pace of Australia–China engagement was rising exponentially. And he was confronted by a single issue that would take its codependence in energy resources and their financial returns to a new level: the massive liquid natural gas (LNG) developments off the northwest coast of his home state.

CHAPTER FORTY

PRESIDENTIAL VISITS

One of the keys that would unlock the LNG treasures was now firmly in the grip of the Chinese premier Zhu Rongji. During his initial 1998 visit to Western Australia when he established a good relationship with Richard Court, they had touched on LNG as a possible future development. But during subsequent visits to Beijing from a combination of state and federal ministers – as well as the Shell, Chevron and Woodside Consortium developing the field – Zhu took a much closer interest.

David Irvine says, 'At first the Chinese really didn't know much about LNG. It wasn't a product they'd had any real experience with.'[1] But like many of China's senior officials at the time, Zhu was a trained engineer. And when the Australians came to put their case, they were not only given unusual direct access to the premier, they faced a barrage of questions designed to test LNG's technical feasibility and potential advantages.

According to one member of the Australian delegation, 'He wanted to know how it was transported; what kind of containers? It couldn't be a square box, for example, because it wouldn't stand the pressure; it had to be a sphere without welds. At what temperature did it liquefy? How much pressure was needed to push it through a pipe?'

Even more important was whether it would fit into China's draft national energy plan which was then in a late stage of development. There was a token LNG component drawn from the South China Sea off Shanghai, but in 1998 and 1999 the Australians had to persuade the Chinese goverment to re-open the draft to include a separate section on LNG. The Chinese then selected the province – Guangdong – where it would form a vital element of its energy needs and set about building the receiving terminal and power plant. However, Australia was far from the only potential supplier. In an international bidding war, Qatar, Indonesia and Malaysia were also in the running for the massive contract on offer.

Meantime, John Howard had won a second election against Kim Beazley as opposition leader in 2001. And in 2002 the prime minister returned to China for another meeting with his counterparts in Beijing. On this occasion, Ambassador Irvine (to Howard's initial surprise and subsequent delight) arranged for the prime minister to address the cadres at the central school of the Communist Party where Tan Pingmei had taught English in the 1980s. When one of the students questioned him about his meeting the Dalai Lama, Howard defended his position and his explanation was well received.

Later he met at length with Zhu Rongji. Indeed, both the embassy and the government threw their weight behind the Australian tender. They were successful. Moreover when the $25 billion contract was signed in 2002, it incorporated a 'partnership fund' of $25 million designed to 'enhance the relationship between Australia and China'.

★ ★ ★

In the wake of Labor's 2001 defeat, Beazley resigned his leadership in favour of the long-serving, if somewhat colourless, Simon Crean, who by 2003 was failing dismally in his efforts to improve the party's standing at the polls. All eyes had been on the domestic political theatre so it is understandable, perhaps, that in October the country took only passing note of perhaps the most powerfully symbolic and predictive events of Australia's 102-year history as an independent nation – the consecutive addresses to the parliament of the presidents of China and the United States, Hu Jintao and George W. Bush.

The background to their arrivals in Australia's House of Representatives made for a vivid contrast. John Howard had been in Washington on 11 September 2001 during the Al-Qaeda attacks on New York's twin towers and the Pentagon was not far from his hotel.

Only the day before, Bush and Howard had met in the Oval Office and made an immediate connection. And when Howard spoke to the Australian press contingent after the attack, the smoke was still rising from the Pentagon. He was visibly shaken. 'We knew then,' he said later, 'that this was a concerted terrorist attack on the United States.'

On his return to Canberra his cabinet invoked the ANZUS Treaty to offer Australia's assistance to a partner under attack for the first time in the 50-year history of the alliance. Australia signed up for the immediate American response to retaliate against the 9/11 mastermind, Osama bin Laden, his Al-Qaeda terrorist organisation and his willing hosts in Afghanistan, the Taliban.

America launched 'Operation Enduring Freedom' on 7 October 2001 and by the following January, Australian Special Forces had arrived in Afghanistan and joined American troops in the Helmand Valley heading for the Taliban stronghold at Kandahar. In March a combined force confronted a Taliban and Al-Qaeda mountain stronghold in the Battle of Anaconda and by the end of 2002 they were able to install an Afghan president, Hamid Karzai, as the interim leader of a new government. Australia was able to draw down its combat forces from the Afghan theatre and by December 2002 only two army officers remained with the UN and Coalition landmine clearing operation.

However, in Washington, a belligerent Bush administration decided the time was right for a massive intervention into the Middle East and used specious 'intelligence' to justify an all-out attack on the Iraqi dictator, Saddam Hussein. Indeed by mid-2002 plans were already underway to deploy Australian Special Forces as well as RAAF and Navy units to the invasion of Iraq. By then Howard and Bush had developed a political and personal friendship within the so-called 'Coalition of the Willing', and while the cabinet had not finally authorised the Australian commitment, Howard could hardly have been more supportive of the American president.

The prime minister's introduction of the American president to the parliament reflected an in-built and instinctive preference for the

Anglosphere. 'The things that unite the Australian and American people,' he said, 'are the belief that the individual is more important than the state, that competitive free enterprise is the ultimate foundation of national wealth.' He then surrendered to hyperbole, asserting that the two countries held that 'the worth of a person is determined by that person's character and hard work, not by their religion or race or colour or creed or social background,' when of course these are the qualities which lie at the very heart of both countries' notions of worth.

Howard recalled his first meeting with Bush at Washington's naval dockyard on the day before 9/11. Thereafter, he said, 'he rallied his own people and the people of the world against terrorism'. He then warned the president that 'this robust parliament has seen debates and divisions of view' on the Iraq invasion, while asserting that 'all Australians believe that the people of Iraq are better off without that loathsome dictator, Saddam Hussein'. Moreover, Bush was 'a friend and a standard bearer for the values that we hold in common'.

Labor's Simon Crean was far more measured, contenting himself with the tried and tested diplomatic clichés.

Outside the parliament an anti-war demonstration turned ugly with protestors scuffling with police. Inside, the Coalition members welcomed the president with rousing 'hear hears' while Crean's Labor colleagues remained suitably discrete. They were bemused by his reference to Howard as his 'man of steel' which, Bush said, was 'Texan for fair dinkum' but let it pass without audible comment. And all were silently reflective when he equated the Australians lost in the Bali bombings with the American tragedy of 9/11. They even accepted silently that the joint actions in Afghanistan had – for the moment at least – lifted the burden of oppression from some of that country's women.

However, when Bush claimed that 'no one who cared about human rights and democracy and stability in the Middle East' could oppose America's removing Saddam Hussein, Greens leader Bob Brown could restrain himself no longer. Referring to two Australians illegally detained in America's Guantanamo Bay detention centre for suspected Al-Qaeda sympathisers, he interjected, 'Respect Australia. Return the Australians to this nation for justice.'

The Speaker of the House ordered his removal and Brown went quietly. The interruption came just as Bush referred to China in pointed ambiguity. 'America and Australia,' he said, 'are working with Japan, the Philippines, Thailand, Indonesia and Singapore to . . . keep the peace in the Taiwan Straits.' However, he then noted that the next day Hu Jintao would be addressing the parliament and without missing a beat claimed that 'Australia's agenda with China is the same as my country's . . . We see a China that is stable and prosperous, a nation that respects the peace of its neighbours and works to secure the freedom of its own people.' He concluded with the usual warm-hearted peroration and the presumptuous, 'May God bless you all'.

The following day's event in the same setting stood in stark contrast to the bonhomie shared by Howard and Bush. The Australian's relationship with the Chinese leader was almost wholly 'transactional', if no less significant in the longer term. The Northwest Shelf LNG contract was about to be eclipsed by a $30 billion deal with Gorgon. The China National Offshore Oil Corporation had bought into the development together with joint-venture partners led by the American Chevron-Texaco group. But while the prime minister and his Coalition government welcomed the Chinese 'partnership' intellectually and commercially, his parliamentary introduction to the president contained no hint of personal sentiment.

'Ten years ago an event such as this would have been seen as not only unlikely but highly improbable,' he said. 'Equally, I would not have thought ten years ago that as Prime Minister I would have, as I did in 2002, addressed the cadres of the central school of the Chinese communist party in Beijing.' This, he said, illustrated the 'common sense character of the relationship' since both could occur 'without either of our two nations abandoning their distinctive but different traditions'.

However, he could not deny the extraordinary developments that were drawing the two countries into each other's orbits. 'The most widely spoken foreign language in Australia today [is] Chinese,' he said, 'no fewer than 550,000 Australian residents claim Chinese ancestry; and there are 34,000 students from China studying in Australia.'

After acknowledging China's help in dealing with North Korea, Howard cut to the meat of the matter: 'It is self-evident that the relationship between Australia and the United States and China [respectively] will be extremely important to the stability of our region. Our aim is to see calm and constructive dialogue between the United States and China on those issues which might potentially cause tension between them; and it will be Australia's aim, as a nation which has different but nonetheless close relationships with both of those nations, to promote that constructive and calm dialogue.'

Hu Jintao began his speech with the highly dubious claim of Zheng He's international expeditions of the 1420s reaching Australia's shores. Even less likely was his assertion that 'for centuries, the Chinese sailed across vast seas and settled down in what they called Southern Land, or today's Australia'. And then to avow that 'they lived harmoniously with the local people, contributing their proud share to Australia's economy, society and its thriving pluralistic culture' simply flew in the face of reality. It was, however, a measure of the Chinese determination to put the relationship on a firm footing and in Hu's words, 'to consolidate and develop its all-round cooperation with Australia [as] a key component of China's external relations. I am convinced,' he said, 'that China and Australia will shape a relationship of mutual trust and long-term friendship.'

The Chinese president sought to take relations to a new level. First, he said, 'The path of political development chosen by the people of each country should be respected . . . we have stepped up the building of the rule of law in China . . . we will continue to move forward our political restructuring in a vigorous and cautious manner as our national conditions merit. China and Australia are different in social systems . . . the result of different choices made by our people and the two countries' different historical evolution. So long as they understand

and treat each other as equals, countries with different social systems may very well become partners of friendly cooperation with constantly increased common ground.'

Second, he called for deepening economic cooperation and a broad exchange of knowledge, technology and managerial expertise: 'China and Australia are highly complementary economically. We see Australia as our important economic partner. By June 2003 Australia has invested in 5600 projects in China exceeding $US3.1 billion. China has invested in 218 projects with a contractual value of $US450 million.'

Third, he called for increased cultural exchanges. 'China is now the biggest source country of foreign students in Australia,' he said of the remarkable development 'with far-reaching consequences for the interaction between the two countries for the generations ahead'.

And finally, Hu stated that the security of both countries depended on closer cooperation in the region and in the fight against terrorism: 'China advocates a new security concept featuring mutual trust, mutual benefit, equality and cooperation, and strives to resolve disputes peacefully through dialogue and cooperation.'

However, while both countries had 'shared interests' in the stability of the Asia-Pacific region, Hu advised, 'Taiwan is an inalienable part of China's territory and the complete reunification of China at an early date is the common aspiration and firm resolve of the entire Chinese people . . . Let us join hands in writing a more luminous new chapter of the China–Australia relationship of all-round cooperation.'

The speech was roundly applauded, but although the sentiments were undoubtedly laudable – and opened the door to closer links between the two nations – they had the unmistakeable air of diplomatic formulation. While the Chinese government would welcome closer ties, the issues themselves would still be subject to hard bargaining behind the scenes. However, by any measure, that was an extraordinary advance on the situation that had pertained over the past two centuries.

CHAPTER FORTY-ONE

RISE AND FALL OF KEVIN RUDD

In retrospect, that remarkable conjunction of the two addresses provided an historic watershed both in Australia's domestic and international political dynamic. Thereafter, the pace and strength of change in both arenas accelerated. The following month, for example, the Labor Party discarded Simon Crean for the unbound savagery of the Sydneysider Mark Latham who took the party to a disastrous defeat in the 2004 election. Indeed, for the first time in many years, John Howard's Coalition won a majority in both houses, giving it *carte blanche* to pass legislation that would otherwise be moderated by the senate as the house of review.

Latham was discarded and a careworn Kim Beazley returned to the leadership. A triumphant Howard would drive home his advantage with a program titled 'Work Choices' designed to undermine the trade union movement and reduce the bargaining power of workers across the land. The unions retaliated with a massive media campaign. It was cleverly pitched and immediately effective. The government's polling was soon diving to its worst levels since the Coalition first gained the treasury benches. However, the union movement's initiative put the recycled Kim Beazley in the shade. And the 'Young Turks' of the 1998 intake – notably Kevin Rudd and Julia Gillard – were increasingly impatient for power.

Rudd was now the party's foreign affairs spokesman and he combined a very active parliamentary role with regular appearances on *Sunrise,* a popular breakfast television program, opposite an up-and-coming Liberal in Joe Hockey. Rudd had few close followers among his caucus colleagues – many of whom found him too gracelessly ambitious and lacking any real commitment to the party's principles and traditions – but his public profile was formidable. Julia Gillard, by contrast, had earned the firm backing of her colleagues with her work as a Labor lawyer. She also included virtually all the female caucus members among her backers. And as Labor's new guard fomented unrest in the ranks, Beazley, a sensitive man who lacked the killer instinct, became unnerved and error prone.

On 4 December 2006, Rudd and Gillard combined their forces to challenge Beazley and his deputy, the well-liked Victorian, Jenny Macklin, for the Labor leadership. Rudd out-polled Beazley 49 to 39 and Macklin declined to stand for the deputy's position, leaving the field open to Gillard. The so-called 'dream team' then set forth on countrywide journeys to spread the word of their accession.

In the international arena, the war in Iraq became increasingly unpopular as the Bush administration misread and mishandled the political demands of a country irredeemably split between contending religious dogmas. And though Howard had cleverly secured a relatively safe provincial area of command for the Australian troops, he suffered the general obloquy visited upon the Allied incompetence.

At the same time Australia's trade and commerce with China began to boom with massive exports of LNG, iron ore and coal, and imports of a vast range of relatively inexpensive manufactures. But while Howard sought to take credit for the bonanza, Rudd's background in diplomacy with China – and his undoubted Mandarin expertise – gave him the inside running. Undeterred, the prime minister made great play of his association with the Chinese leaders – Hu Jintao chief among them – at a luncheon held during the APEC meeting in Sydney the following year.

He staged a nationally televised luncheon with the Chinese leaders and according to an Australian Associated Press report, 'The Prime Minister's speech went down well. But when Mr Rudd started addressing the leader of one-quarter of the world's population – fluently in his own tongue – the effect was stunning, There was an almost audible intake of breath among the scores of Chinese political and business heavy-weights in the audience. Many sat bolt upright in their chairs, beaming at Mr Rudd's virtuosity. The effect could not have been greater had the family's precocious nine-year-old played a Chopin prelude perfectly for visiting relatives after Christmas lunch ... Mr Rudd could not have scripted a bigger occasion in which to shine.'

Then in August 2007 with the federal election only three months away, Rudd took the initiative on an issue of increasing interest to the younger voters to whom John Howard was fast becoming a figure of the past: climate change. At a presentation to the Labor faithful, he declared it 'the greatest moral, economic and security challenge of our generation'.

The election was a triumph for Rudd and a disaster for Howard who became only the second prime minister to have lost his seat in a general election. He was replaced as Liberal leader by Dr Brendan Nelson, a former president of the Australian Medical Association with a youthful predilection for flashy ear-rings. He had held the defence portfolio in the Howard cabinet but was more conciliator than political brawler.

Nelson was no match for Rudd who drove his climate-change message home by immediately signing the Kyoto protocol to reduce greenhouse gas emissions then commissioning his former diplomatic principal, Ross Garnaut, to develop what became a well-designed emissions trading scheme. He made an emotional apology to the 'stolen generation' of Aboriginal Australians and engaged Nelson in the occasion, much to the chagrin of some of the opposition leader's more conservative colleagues.

Moreover, the Liberal leader was even then being stalked by a relative newcomer, Malcolm Turnbull, a former lawyer, journalist and merchant banker who had led an unsuccessful movement for a republic prior to his entering parliament. Turnbull made no secret of his ambitions and the following year he challenged for the leadership and defeated Nelson by four votes. However, his lust for power led him into an appalling misjudgement over a forged email from an unbalanced treasury official, Godwin Grech, that falsely accused Rudd of electoral malfeasance. This seriously weakened Turnbull's position and when the conservative wing of the Coalition recoiled from his progressive stance on climate change, he was overthrown by a single vote in favour of their champion, Tony Abbott. The former Catholic seminarian soon proved himself a no-holds-barred opposition leader.

Meantime, Rudd's much vaunted engagement with China was producing decidedly mixed results. In his four-day visit in April 2008 he became the first Western leader to publicly raise human rights abuses in Tibet. His justification was the concept of *zhengyou* – the true friend who offers unflinching advice – as he urged the leadership of President Hu Jintao and Premier Wen Jiabao to make China a 'responsible stakeholder in the quest for an harmonious world' within the rules-based global order. And in his speech to students at Beijing University, he linked Chinese and Australian history through the activities of G.E. Morrison and Bill Donald, figures who had disappeared into the mists of recent Chinese history.

The Chinese leaders were taken aback by his presumption – bordering on impertinence – but were willing to give the young man credit for his frankness. However, there were other less congenial influences at work in the Rudd approach to China. Some of his principal lecturers and supervisors during his ANU studies were imbued with cold war attitudes toward the Asian powerhouse. Pierre Ryckmans, in particular, had been harassed by the Maoist left and it was he who had approved Rudd's choice of the dissident Wei Jingsheng as the subject for his honours thesis. Wei had been tried by the Deng Xiaoping regime for posting his essay on 'The Fifth Modernisation: Democracy and Other Issues' on Beijing's Democracy Wall. Rudd uncovered the transcript of his stout – if unavailing – defence in his show trial and scored a 'first' from his examiners. But in the process he cemented his opposition to the authoritarian nature of the Chinese political system.

When his government released a 2009 Defence White Paper suggesting China's military modernisation was 'cause for concern', the Chinese were outraged.

Then in short order, Rio Tinto Australia retreated from a controversial $19.5 billion deal with China's state-owned Chinalco, and the Chinese arrested RTA's Shanghai executive Stern Hu on bribery and espionage charges. Then Australia granted a visa to the dissident Uighur World Congress president Rebiya Kadeer after Chinese diplomats tried in vain to have a documentary about her removed from the Melbourne Film Festival.

Most of the blame for this *annus horribilis* was laid at Rudd's door. Indeed, behind the scenes, Australian and Chinese diplomats developed an urgent colloquy to break through the impasse. They decided jointly that an exchange of ministers was required and nominated Foreign Minister Stephen Smith, who duly travelled to Bejing, while the Chinese proposed Vice-Premier Li Keqiang, who came to Canberra where they negotiated an 'Australia-China Statement' affirming the two countries' mutual commitment to improving ties.

By then Rudd and his government were preoccupied with the economic fallout from the Global Financial Crisis as Wall Street struggled back from the brink of total collapse and a powerful recession rippled across the world's economies. The prime minister and his treasurer, Wayne Swan, were responding with a massive spending program on Australian schools and home improvements financed largely by mining exports to China. It was a remarkably successful exercise in strategic fiscal deployment, but because Australia avoided recession, the Abbott opposition was free to focus attention on the some of the collateral failings of the home insulation program and the toll it had taken on the federal budget.

Rudd's climate-change program had also suffered a severe setback when the Greens foolishly opposed legislation establishing the emissions trading scheme proposed in the Garnaut plan, so that it failed to pass the senate. Then in December 2009 the Copenhagen conference on climate change collapsed in disarray, with Rudd blaming the Chinese as 'ratfuckers' who had undermined his best efforts to secure an agreement. However, the real damage to the prime minister arrived in early 2010 when he failed to pursue his domestic climate-change program aggressively through a double-dissolution election. When an enterprising journalist revealed that he had quietly postponed action on the emissions trading scheme indefinitely, his high-sounding claim of global warming as the 'great moral challenge of our generation' returned to haunt him.

His public popularity collapsed. Suddenly he was vulnerable to the dissidents in his party room who felt – with some justification – that he had treated their contributions and concerns with contempt. Nevertheless, in April 2010 he announced one of the more consequential achievements of his prime ministership – the creation of 'China in the World', a study centre at the ANU that would draw scholars and activists from both countries into a discussion designed to break down intellectual and political barriers between the two. His former lecturer, Geremie Barmé, would be its founding director while Richard Rigby became the associate director. It was yet another mark of the ANU's centrality in the intellectual leadership of the Australia–China relationship.

The pressure on Rudd continued when the mining industry reacted to his and treasurer Wayne Swan's poorly sold proposal for a 'super-tax' on their windfall profits with a powerful (if totally dishonest) television campaign. However, the nation at large was astonished when on 23 June the numbers men of the Labor caucus, led by former trade union organiser turned factional leader, Bill Shorten, met with Julia Gillard and urged her to move against Rudd. The party, they agreed, had reached breaking point over his erratic management style and the contemptuous attitude he'd displayed to colleagues. Gillard had independently reached the view that Rudd had 'lost his way' and had indicated to colleagues that she was willing to assume the leadership.

In a dramatic late-night meeting, she confronted the 53-year-old Rudd with the blunt message that his prime ministership was at an end. The only other person present was New South Wales senator John Faulkner who, as an honest broker, immediately understood the electoral consequences of a sudden palace coup against a first-term prime minister. Rudd pleaded to be given a second chance. He would consult with colleagues; he would engage the cabinet and the caucus in the decision-making process. Gillard wavered. Rudd begged for six months to demonstrate this new *modus operandi*.

Gillard returned to her office where she consulted again with the faction leaders. Rudd, she said, was 'personally miserable and politically paralysed' and all agreed that the situation was irredeemable. When she returned to the prime minister's office, she delivered the *coup de grace*: she had the numbers and would move against him in caucus the following day.

Rudd worked through the night in a vain attempt to retrieve his position. By morning he had so little support that he declined to contest the ballot against her. And to add insult to injury, she backed his long-time Queensland rival, Wayne Swan, as her deputy.

However, Rudd did not go quietly. A deeply religious man, he had experienced a powerful spiritual epiphany during a journey to Far North Queensland in his gap year before enrolling at the ANU to prepare himself for his Chinese avocation.[1] He regarded his rise to the prime ministership as a vital element in his religious calling. That it should be torn from his grasp by a traitorous deputy – an atheist to boot – was simply insupportable. So when Gillard went to the 2010 election seeking a mandate for her government, he felt perfectly free to undermine her campaign with damaging leaks. But at the same time he embarked on a vigorous personal campaign to secure the post of foreign minister in a returned Labor government. It would save face. It could be a springboard for his restoration to The Lodge. At the very least, it would allow him to pursue his ultimate ambition to become the UN Secretary-General.

Rudd's interventions in the campaign were so damaging to Gillard that Labor's majority was slashed to the bone and the country's first female prime minister was forced to rely on two independents to form government. And because Rudd's personal popularity remained high, she had little choice but to accede to his demands and appoint him foreign minister.

While the relationship between Gillard and her aggrieved predecessor was never close, they did conclude a working relationship. Rudd combined with his former colleague in the Beijing embassy, Geoff Raby, who was ambassador for five years from 2007, to extend and diversify relations between Australia and China. He also encouraged Gillard to develop personal ties with the Beijing leadership. And Gillard secured a commitment from China for an annual top-level meeting of the two countries' defence and foreign ministers. It was an important step forward and was strongly supported by Rudd. Indeed, it was among the very few areas where the two Australian politicians were as one.

However, Gillard was emotionally drawn to the American President Barrack Obama and during his 2011 visit to Canberra she welcomed his announcement of an American 'pivot' to Asia. And prior to Obama's address to parliament, she joined him in announcing the rotation of 1500 US marines through the Northern Territory where they would exercise with Australian Special Forces. His address to the parliament next day was one of the few genuine highlights of her difficult tenure at The Lodge. It was very different in tone and content from that of his more pedestrian predecessor:

> After a decade in which we fought two wars [in the Middle East] that cost us dearly in blood and treasure, the United States is turning to the vast potential of the Asia Pacific ... Asia will largely define whether the century ahead will be marked by conflict or cooperation, needless suffering or human progress.
>
> As President, I've therefore made a deliberate and strategic decision – as a Pacific nation, the United States will play a larger and long-term role in shaping this region and its future, by upholding core principles and in close partnership with allies and friends.

We stand for an international order in which the rights and responsibilities of all nations and people are upheld; where international law and norms are enforced; where commerce and freedom of navigation are not impeded; where emerging powers contribute to regional security, and where disagreements are resolved peacefully.

He would back this new stance with America's formidable military hardware, he said. 'I have directed my national security team to make our presence and missions in the Asia Pacific a top priority. As a result, reductions in U.S. defense spending will not – I repeat, will not – come at the expense of the Asia Pacific. We will allocate the resources necessary to maintain our strong military presence in the region. We will preserve our unique ability to project power and deter threats to peace . . . the United States is a Pacific power and we are here to stay.'

The speech was an oddly aggressive one from a president whose administration was marked by a disengagement from the wars of his predecessor and an almost total reliance on diplomacy over conflict in the international arena. However, it reflected the extraordinary growth of China's economic influence in the region since the Bush address. Indeed, Obama gave notice of a future in which China would be 'contained' by a chain of alliances from South Korea to Japan, the Philippines, Vietnam, Indonesia, Australia and to the rising power of India.

He stopped short of articulating it in those terms. But the inference was clear. 'We're already modernising America's defence posture across the Asia-Pacific,' he said. 'It will be more broadly distributed, maintaining our strong presence in Japan and on the Korean Peninsula while enhancing our presence in Southeast Asia. And our posture will be more sustainable by helping allies and partners build their capacity with more training and exercises.'

When he did name China, it was in reducing tensions with North Korea and in nuclear proliferation. But even then he noted China's initiatives in the South China Sea. And he would 'speak candidly to them about the importance of upholding international norms'.

CHAPTER FORTY-TWO

NEW LEADERS, NEW TROUBLES

In China, Xi Jinping, the man who would come to dominate his nation in the manner of Deng Xiaoping, if not Mao himself, had begun his rise through the upper ranks of the Communist dynasty in October 2007 when he joined the politburo's standing committee and central secretariat. He became vice-president in 2008 then vice-chairman of Deng's old power base, the Central Military Commission, in 2010.

Xi Jinping was born in 1953 to a senior Communist Party official who came to power with Mao in 1949. But when Xi was ten, his father was purged from his role as vice-premier and sent to work in a factory in Henan province. Three years later Xi's own secondary education was cut short by the Cultural Revolution, his father was jailed and Xi was bundled off to rural Shaanxi. Undeterred, he became the party branch secretary of his production team before returning to Beijing in 1975, where he studied chemical engineering (and Communist doctrine) at the prestigious Tsinghua University.

Thereafter Xi's future within the party was secured and he rose steadily, if not spectacularly, through the ranks. In 1985 he was part of a Chinese delegation to the United States where he stayed for several months with an American farm family in Iowa before returning to Tsinghua's law faculty where he completed his second degree. This elevated him to the next level of political power with senior appointments to Hebei and then as governor of the southern province of Fujian.

This role provided an opportunity to visit Taiwan where Xi sought investment to strengthen the private sector of his provincial economy. It was an association that would have far-reaching and little appreciated consequences in his later career at the apex of the Chinese government. It also brought him face to face with the raging corruption in the formative days of unchecked privatisation in the Special Economic Zones of the South. As the thoroughly corrupt local businessman Lai Changxing outraged the local community with his blatant villainy, Xi and an associate, Party Secretary Chen Mingyi, were called to account by national leaders Jiang Zemin, Zhu Rongji, Hu Jintao and Wei Jianxing. Lai bolted to Canada and both Xi and Chen were exonerated. But it was a lesson well learned.

In 2006 Xi rose a further step to become party chief in Shanghai where once again he was confronted by a financial scandal that saw his disgraced predecessor thrown in jail for eighteen years. These experiences had profound effects on Xi's future plans and actions when he grasped the levers of power. That time would arrive in 2013 with his election as President of the People's Republic, succeeding Hu Jintao who retired after two terms. By then Xi had developed a detailed strategy to eventually bring all aspects of China's governance within his personal control.

On his first day as president he telephoned Barrack Obama in the White House and discussed cyber security and North Korea. The issues themselves were less important than the fact that he was now engaging with the leader of the free world as his natural counterpart. Obama responded by announcing the immediate visits of Secretary of State John Kerry and Treasury Secretary Jacob Lew who would arrive in Beijing within a week. Xi confirmed his international status with visits to Russia and Africa; and he ensured that the Chinese people were aware of his peregrinations with massive television coverage from the state-owned networks.

Three months later he confronted the Third Plenum of the 18th Central Committee with far-reaching changes in economic and social policy in which market forces would play a much more significant role in the allocation of resources. Inefficient state enterprises would be 'restructured' and competition with private corporations would determine whether they sank or swam. He abolished the one-child policy and permitted parents a second offspring. At the same time he created a new National Security Commission with himself at the helm.

However, easily his most powerful and consequential initiative was a nationwide crackdown on the widespread corruption within the Communist Party regime. Indeed, it would become known as the 'new revolution' as some of the more senior party officials and functionaries were dragged from their offices and tried before the criminal courts. It was a clear response to his own experiences in Fujian and Shanghai, but it went far deeper than the usual efforts to clean up the party's image through a few show trials. Xi understood that unless the graft and embezzlement ingrained in the system were eradicated, the Communist Party would, like its dynastic predecessors, lose its Mandate of Heaven as expressed by those who suffered under its oppression.

No element of the regime was spared. Xi's 'inspection teams' fanned out over the provinces; more than 100 ministers were charged and jailed; corrupt heads of state-owned enterprises fell before the reaping hooks of Xi's cadres. And as the list of party and private miscreants grew, it became clear that none but the most scrupulous were safe from prosecution; and even they could not be sure of their fate in a country where justice jousted with political influence.

Xi reformed the bureaucracy, creating a range of supra-ministerial steering committees – known as Central Leading Groups – giving them power over the existing institutions across the economy, security, law reform and military preparedness. By the end of 2013 he had gathered all those levers of power into his personal domain, a process that would only become more manifest in the years ahead.

★ ★ ★

In Australia 2013 saw the final collapse of Labor's hold on power in Canberra. Tony Abbott's unremitting attacks on Julia Gillard combined with Kevin Rudd's unending denigration of his former deputy destroyed her public profile. And when Simon Crean berated Rudd for destabilising tactics – and Gillard failed to defend him – Rudd resigned his portfolio and threatened to stand against her. But when only a handful of supporters rallied to his cause, he declined to challenge.

Gillard chose a former New South Wales premier, Bob Carr, as his replacement as foreign minister and he filled a vacant senate seat in March 2012. Carr had coveted the foreign affairs portfolio since his earliest days in politics, but had been persuaded to become a stopgap premier of New South Wales during a Labor crisis. In the event he remained in the role for eighteen years before retiring from active politics, believing he had lost his chance to transfer to the federal arena. So when granted his deepest wish, Carr threw himself into the task. He visited China no fewer than four times during the fifteen months he held the portfolio.

However, when Labor's polling showed they would be decimated in the 2013 election, the same numbers men who conspired to replace Rudd as prime minister now turned to him to 'save the furniture'. He was more than happy to return to The Lodge, however briefly, to lead his party in the campaign while Julia Gillard retired from politics altogether. When he took the reins, the party's prospects improved, but not for long. Abbott rode to power amid the scattering of the Labor government's forces. Rudd resigned from the parliament in the wake of his defeat, but his leadership at least did what Bill Shorten and his cohorts required of it: he held the rampant Coalition to a modest 3.4 per cent swing, giving them a seventeen-seat majority in the new parliament.

Abbott's ascension introduced a new version of an old dynamic to the Australia–China relationship. The London-born prime minister was heir to the British notions of class and race that had arrived with the First Fleet, were replenished by waves of UK migrants thereafter, and given voice in the decades of Menzies' stewardship. It was Abbott who, in an aside to the German chancellor Angela Merkel, would describe Australia's attitude to the Chinese as one of 'fear and greed' without the slightest nod to their humanity. And it was Abbott who would declare China's long-time tormentor, Japan, 'Australia's best friend in Asia'. Indeed, he would make it embarrassingly clear that he wanted Australia's next fleet of submarines to be designed and built in that country.

In its 21st century incarnation, this anti-Chinese attitude was inextricably bound to America's fear that China's remarkable economic growth would challenge its primacy as the world's superpower. Obama's 'pivot to Asia' gave both motive force and intellectual cover for the forces of containment. It provided a policy framework that sat easily with the new Australian prime minister.

Nevertheless, Abbott was equally conscious of the 'greed' aspect of the three-word slogan that underlay his approach. So when Xi Jinping visited Australia in 2014 for the G20 summit in Brisbane – and with a China–Australia Free Trade Agreement to be completed – the prime minister was more than happy to offer him the opportunity to address the parliament. In fact, unbeknown to Abbott – and indeed most Australians – Xi had already visited all Australian states and territories but Tasmania.

Beginning in 1988, his five journeys Down Under had been conducted under the public radar (though no doubt quietly documented by the intelligence services). 'These visits left a great impression on me,' Xi said, 'and I still cherish vivid memories of the strange-looking kangaroo, the cute koala bear, flocks of white sheep, the ingenious Sydney Opera House, and the boundless expanses of the Outback. Everywhere I have been, I have personally experienced the goodwill of the Australian people towards the Chinese people.'

It was the classic 'soft sell' of a diplomat to the parliamentarians assembled in the house of representatives. But there is no reason to believe that Xi, a courteous and quietly spoken visitor, would have experienced the aggressive resentment his compatriots endured in years past. Australians have a natural politeness towards 'respectable' visitors, whatever their ethnic background. And certainly in a period of Islamic extremism, the Chinese would be more welcome than those encompassed in the police description, 'of Middle Eastern appearance'.

Like his predecessor Hu Jintao, in his parliamentary address Xi ranged over the historic relations between the two countries but was markedly silent on Hu's claims of 15th century discovery. While noting the fact of Chinese participation in the goldrush, he avoided its White Australia consequences, simply observing that 'some Chinese gradually integrated themselves into the local community and they made an important contribution to Australia's development'.

He was on slightly firmer ground when he claimed a practical alliance between the two countries in the world wars; and thereafter he concentrated on the extraordinary growth of the economic and official relationship with consultative links across 30 separate areas of government responsibility. China had been Australia's biggest trading partner for the past five years, he said, reaching $US136 billion in 2013. And his country was now Australia's biggest source of international students and tourist revenue.

Then, in nice contrast to President Obama's bellicosity from the same dais two years previously, he professed to take the audience into his confidence: 'Dear friends,' he said, 'we Chinese are striving to achieve the Chinese dream, which is the great renewal of the Chinese nation. The Chinese dream is about enhancing the strength and prosperity of the nation and the wellbeing of the Chinese people.'

In its pursuit, Xi said, his two goals were to double the 2010 GDP and so build a prosperous society, both urban and rural, by 2020; and to turn China into a modern socialist country that was democratic, culturally advanced and harmonious by the middle of the century. He then asked, 'What will China be like when it grows in strength?'

It produced a moment of attentive silence in the grey-green leather benches. 'After all,' he said, 'China is a large country of 1.3 billion people. It is like the big guy in the crowd. Others naturally wonder how the big guy will move and act.' As answer, he quoted Confucius's mangling of the Golden Rule that 'one should not do unto others what one does not want others to do unto oneself'. And then more practically, he added: 'In modern times China was ravaged by turmoil and war for more than a century and development and a decent life were beyond the reach of its people. Having gone through this, China will never subject any country or nation to the same ordeal. While China is big in size, our forefathers realised over 2000 years ago that a warlike state, however big it may be, will eventually fall.'

It was an idiosyncratic reading of Chinese imperial history, particularly at the fringes of the empire's north, south and west. However, the most significant aspect of Xi's speech came towards the end: 'Given China's high dependence on maritime routes for trade and energy imports, navigation freedom and safety is crucial. The Chinese Government is ready to enhance dialogue and cooperation with relevant countries to jointly maintain freedom of navigation and safety of maritime routes and ensure a maritime order of peace, tranquillity and win-win cooperation. At the same time the Chinese people will firmly uphold the core interests of China's sovereignty, security and territorial integrity.'

Behind the verbiage it was a clear precursor to one of the more sophisticated diplomatic-cum-security gambits to have been launched on the international community. Xi was preparing the ground for what became seen as China's 'aggression' over a group of rocky islets in the South China Sea known by various names including the Spratly Islands. By 2013 plans were well advanced for the transformation of the outcrops, which were claimed by no fewer than five other countries, into potential Chinese military facilities. The other claimants – Brunei, the Philippines, Taiwan, Malaysia and Vietnam – were outraged at the Chinese initiative and in January 2013 the Philippines submitted their claims to the Permanent Court of Arbitration.

The territorial seabeds surrounding the Spratlys are known to contain oil deposits and the seas themselves are traditional fishing grounds. More than half the world's supertanker traffic passes through the region's waters, as well as a quarter of the world's oil tonnage annually. More pointedly, prior to their mammoth reclamation program, the Chinese had made increasingly vocal complaints about the provocative

American naval vessels passing through the area to assert the right of freedom of navigation in international waters. And the ships undoubtedly carried sophisticated communications interceptors on both surface and submarine platforms.

The Chinese building program, which included a major runway and surface-to-air missile systems, would engage the world's attention as a potential flashpoint should the 'big guy' wield his newfound strength. And since the Americans were disinclined to press their military advantage at a time when their Middle East adventures had fallen into disarray, it allowed Xi Jinping to deal with the other claimants from a position of strength. He could also present a strong and unyielding image to a receptive domestic audience. In so doing, he had the opportunity to remove the return of Taiwan to the fold of the People's Republic from the front line of his nation's ambitions.

It was, and remains, a remarkably bold stratagem. The resumption of the island province had been an article of faith among the Chinese leadership – and the people – ever since Chiang Kai-shek and his nationalists retreated there some 70 years ago. Throughout the 1990s and the early years of the new century, the government built a colourful 'rainbow' across Changan Street with sections for Hong Kong, Macao and Taiwan to be filled as they returned to the People's Republic. But in the wake of the South China Sea gambit, the rainbow was quietly dismantled.

Xi's experience in developing investment ties with Taiwan during his gubernatorial tenure in Fujian had exposed him to the folly of any forcible attempt to reunite the island province with the mainland. As will be seen, the Spratlys provided a perfect substitute. The Chinese could not only assert their newfound strength, they could make magnanimous concessions to fellow claimants while eliminating the United States as a regional power broker. And in at least one case, they could call into serious question the loyalty of a traditional American ally.

CHAPTER FORTY-THREE
EVER CLOSER TIES

While Tony Abbott's cynical attitude towards China found expression in his leadership of the Australian cabinet and among elements of the defence and intelligence community, it was by no means the only voice to be heard from the political and intellectual establishment. Even within his own ministry there were contending views, while the Labor opposition, the foreign affairs bureaucracy, the ANU and some state universities all contained personalities prepared to take a more even-handed approach to the competition developing between China and the United States.

In his parliamentary address, for example, Xi Jinping had lauded Queensland's Griffith University Emeritus Professor Colin Mackerras for his 'tireless efforts to present a real China' to Australia and the world. 'He has visited China over 60 times,' Xi said, 'and has built a bridge of mutual understanding and amity between our people.' The author of seventeen major works on Chinese culture, Mackerras continued to work for a greater understanding between the two nations.

Indeed, behind the scenes, the annual top-level meetings between Chinese and Australian defence and foreign affairs ministers secured by Julia Gillard produced important if symbolic progress. These included a little-known military initiative – Exercise Kowari – in which troops from Australia, America and China combined in annual operations in the Northern Territory to produce 'friendship and cooperation' between the three forces.

Equipped with little more than a knife and a water bottle each, the troops were deployed on a remote, crocodile-infested cattle station by the Daly River. They spent a week being trained in bush skills before being left to fend for themselves. Australian Army Sergeant Emmaly Hall, who joined the exercise, told the *Sydney Morning Herald*, 'The Chinese are very similar to us; they just don't curse at all. They're very polite.'

US Major General Todd McCaffery said that while there was 'political tension' over the South China Sea, 'military-to-military engagement in the region remains important. We're pleased by the continuing engagement.'[1]

A highly respected defence analyst at the ANU, Professor Hugh White, explored Australia's future role as China grew to challenge American dominance in the region. 'China's growing power does not threaten Australia, but it does undermine the international order in Asia which has kept Australia safe and prosperous for a long time,' he wrote. 'Whether what follows is peaceful or turbulent does not just depend on China, but on all of us.

'The best outcome for Australia would be for America to relinquish primacy and share power with China and the other major powers . . . this is also the best outcome for the rest of Asia, and for America. But unfortunately it is the hardest to achieve. [America] has to begin the cycle of compromise if it is to gain momentum . . . The sooner the US starts the better.'[2]

White was Deputy Secretary for Strategy and Intelligence in the Defence Department from 1995 to 2000, when he became the founding director of the Australian Strategic Policy Institute (ASPI). A Howard initiative, ASPI was designed to provide the government with an alternative to the policy advice emanating from its own bureaucracy. It was funded 50 per cent by the defence department and the rest from a variety of private and intelligence agency sources. White brought a sophisticated and scholarly approach to the role. His successor, retired Major General Peter Abigail, who held the post until 2012, was universally regarded as 'a safe pair of hands'.

He was succeeded by another former defence deputy secretary, Peter Jennings, who took a much firmer stance towards China. By then

ASPI had secured substantial funding from private defence industries, including some from the United States. Jennings took a major role in a new Defence White Paper commissioned by the Abbott government. It would reflect an anxiety about China's intentions and the continuing need for a strong American presence in the region.

However, Tony Abbott's prime ministerial adventure was soon to be undone by a series of 'captain's calls' – including his conferring an Australian knighthood on Britain's Duke of Edinburgh – and his unfortunate dependence on his pugnacious private secretary, Peta Credlin. His polling figures slumped and when he was overthrown by the former Liberal leader Malcolm Turnbull, the nation breathed an almost audible sigh of relief. A moderate within the Liberal Party's 'broad church', Turnbull came to the leadership in September 2015 carrying the high hopes of many that his ascension would bring the revolving door of successive Australian prime ministers to a shuddering halt – at least for a term or two.

Like Kevin Rudd before him, Turnbull had a Chinese family connection. His son Alex, like Rudd's daughter Jessica, had a Chinese spouse. Alex at 34 was married to Yvonne Wang (Wang Yi Wen) and their first child, Ilsa, was born in May 2015. Yvonne's parents were said to have been on friendly terms with former President Jiang Zemin but neither held any senior party or military rank.[3] Certainly in the early months of his tenure, Turnbull's foreign policy returned to the traditional centrist stance of the previous two decades. His defence minister, Marisse Payne, ordered a rewrite of the Defence White Paper.

However, Turnbull's election came with conditions imposed by the Coalition's junior partner, the National Party, led by the bucolic protectionist, Barnaby Joyce, as well as conservatives within his own party. This meant that as the prime minister navigated a path between aspiration and obligation, he disappointed many of his strongest backers in the wider community. So when he went to the polls seeking a personal mandate in 2016, the Coalition barely scraped home by a single seat in the House of Representatives.

He was faced with a rejuvenated Labor Party and no fewer than eleven cross-bench senators holding the balance of power. The opposition leader, Bill Shorten – who had connived at the downfall of both Kevin Rudd and Julia Gillard – took credit for the election outcome and made the most of Turnbull's political liabilities. Moreover, a deeply resentful Tony Abbott remained in parliament and from the backbench continued to advance his own cause, whatever the cost to government solidarity.

Abbott's *amour-propre* took another blow when Turnbull and Marise Payne ignored his preference for the Japanese submarines and secured cabinet agreement for the contract to go to France. The Americans would also have preferred their Pacific ally to win the tender, both for the message it sent to China and the compatibility of weapons and communication systems. But they refrained from any public expressions of disappointment.

Economically, the Australia–China relationship continued its seemingly inevitable path to ever greater engagement. In 2015, ANU researcher Yu Sheng undertook an analysis of several future scenarios, all of which showed an extraordinary growth of trade between the two countries over the next ten years.

Australia's imports from China were projected to be about $50 billion annually by 2025, while exports, depending on China's growth rate, would range from $107 billion to $185 billion. More than 70 per cent of Australian exports to China were related to mineral and extraction industries. However, he found that 'the growth in Australia's exports to China will be driven mainly by services which will more than double as a proportion of total trade'. These would include education, tourism, telecommunications, computer and information services. 'Agriculture exports will also rise substantially,' he said. 'China will continue to be the most important exporting market for Australia but the role of Australia in China's export market will decline.'

Equally significant by 2016 were the remarkable social changes at play. Australia's cities and towns were taking on a considerably more

Asian appearance – slowly the nation seemed to be becoming defined as much by its geography as its history. China had become Australia's third biggest source of migrants and easily the biggest source of international students. Chinese tourism boomed to more than a million visitors annually. The Chinatowns in the capital cities had become a welcome asset to the multicultural vivacity of Australia.

Chinese-Australians such as brain surgeon Charles Teo and the late heart surgeon Victor Chang were not only highly regarded but their ethnicity had become unremarkable. In the arts and entertainment, popular and celebrated figures included SBS news reader Lee Lin Chin, screenwriter and director Tony Ayres, TV presenter Sam Pang, celebrity chefs Poh Ling Yeow and Kylie Kwong, *Mao's Last Dancer* author Li Cunxin, *Wiggles* performer Jess Fatt, painter Shen Jiawei, and many more. In politics, Chinese-Australians had been elected as lord mayors of Darwin, Adelaide and Melbourne. Sporting stars like Cathy Freeman were happy to acknowledge the Chinese elements of their ancestry; and Lin Jong (AFL), Melissa Wu (diving), Miao Miao (ping pong) and Cheltzie Lee (figure skating) were among many who distinguished themselves in their chosen fields.

Veteran Chinese-Australian businessman-activist and Brisbane's 'father of Chinatown', Eddie Liu, was honoured as 'a Queensland Great' by the community. He had arrived in Australia in 1937 aged sixteen and reached Brisbane during World War II. As he prospered in business, Liu devoted himself to a broad range of charities and became a leader of the multicultural movement in the 1980s. He died in 2013 aged 91 and at his passing, former immigration minister Phillip Ruddock said, 'I can speak with some authority when I say I don't believe there has been an Australian of Chinese descent who has made the same level of contribution to this nation and to his people as Eddie Liu.' And while the descendants of Quong Tart might seek to differ, in the 21st century Eddie's life and work had been intrinsic to a remarkable change in community attitudes.

But with closer ties had come greater opportunity for missteps and misunderstandings in a country where anti-Asian attitudes still lurked beneath the surface. China's new rich had invested heavily in Australia's booming real estate market and while they concentrated almost exclusively on the top end of the trade, they were regularly blamed for the difficulties facing first-home buyers in distant suburbs.

When the rising Labor senator Sam Dastyari declared in his parliamentary registry of pecuniary interests that a Chinese donor had paid some travel bills, the political outrage (much of it confected) would force his resignation from his party's front bench. Undoubtedly he showed poor political judgement, but it is highly probable that had his donor been British, the story would have caused barely a ripple, if indeed it had been written at all.

Dastyari's fall from grace triggered a spate of critical stories on Chinese donations to political parties despite similar donations from other foreign-owned corporations. The federal government had earlier blocked the sale of Ausgrid, the New South Wales power utility, to the Chinese company Cheong Kong Infrastructure (CKI) and the Chinese government-owned State Grid on national security grounds. Then it rejected a Chinese bid for the Kidman cattle station empire, despite the fact that both American and British investors controlled vastly more Australian farming country. That issue would only be resolved when a major Coalition supporter, the mining billionaire Gina Reinhardt, joined the Chinese consortium that made the winning bid.

While these anti-Chinese sentiments occasionally bubbled to the surface and became part of the general discourse, they were but a pale shadow of the vicious prejudice of the 19th and early 20th centuries. And with the enormous increase of two-way tourism, there was a growing people-to-people familiarity. But there was also a firm appreciation of the very different political climate in Xi Jinping's China from the freedom of expression and social activism enjoyed in Australia.

Indeed, Xi seemed to be on an autocratic course reminiscent of earlier occupants of the Dragon Throne. He was reducing the role of the Chinese media to that of a propaganda tool for the Communist Party. His message was clear: 'All news media run by the party must work to speak for the party's will and its propositions, and protect the party's authority and unity,' he told a group of editors on 22 February 2016. Then in an article in the official English-language *China Daily* several days later, he wrote: 'It is necessary for the media to restore people's trust in the party, especially as the economy has entered a new normal and suggestions that it is declining and dragging down the global economy have emerged. The nation's media outlets are essential to political stability, and the leadership cannot afford to wait for them to catch up with the times.'[4]

His approach to the legal system resulted in a confusing mix of advance and retreat from the universally accepted notions of the rule of law. He appointed a respected jurist, Judge Jiang Huiling, to head the Institute of Applied Jurisprudence that would undertake an ambitious remake of the country's legal system. And in 2015 it unveiled potentially significant reforms of the politicised structure that had prevailed throughout the communist dynasty. But in December that year, several of China's most prominent human rights lawyers were either tried or held under house arrest for blogging criticism of government policy or attempting to defend Christian churches whose crosses were being forcibly removed from their steeples.

Nevertheless, Judge Jiang said major changes were being applied to separate the lower-level courts from the local governments where party bosses appointed judges and controlled the flow of cases to the courts. Henceforth they would come under provincial administration. As well, they were trialling circuit courts where judges from one province heard cases from another. 'President Xi asks for two things,' he said, 'the courts should be fairer and result in more public confidence.'

Certainly the arrest of fifteen staff members of James Packer's Crown casino operation in October 2016 showed that Xi was serious in his crackdown on a gambling industry that could be used to launder the ill-gotten gains of corruption among China's Communist Party princelings and their business associates. Packer had been loud in his praise of the president and of good relations between the two countries. The arrests suggested that his protestations cut very little ice with Xi Jinping.

Indeed, the Australian community was itself becoming more discerning in its judgements. Packer's pursuit of Chinese 'whales' to finance a showy – not to say crass – high-rise development on the iconic Sydney Harbour foreshore engendered very little sympathy in his clash with the Chinese legal system. In fact, across the national spectrum the most vehement antipathy was confined within the relatively small coterie of competing defence think-tanks and lobby groups seeking to influence the government's stand on relations with the 'big guy'. And their ire was directed as much at each other as at the issues in play.

It is not a crowded field. There are perhaps seven significant contending groups. They include ASPI, the Institute for Regional Security, and the United States Study Centre which display the most concern about China's aspirations; the Lowy Institute, the ANU's National Security College and 'China in the World', together with the Australian Institute for International Affairs, which occupy the scholarly middle ground; while the Australia–China Relations Institute (ACRI) within Sydney's University of Technology boasts Bob Carr as its director and offers the most supportive attitude to the progress of relations between the two countries.

ACRI is partly financed by the Chinese businessman Huang Xiangmo and avers that its operations 'are based on a positive and optimistic view of Australia-China relations, capturing the spirit of the 2014 announcement of a Free Trade Agreement and the commitments by both countries to a Comprehensive Strategic Partnership'.

ASPI's Peter Jennings accuses ACRI of being part of China's attempt to use 'soft power' to lobby government for a more quiescent line on Beijng's activities in the South China Sea. 'This perspective has most pointedly been advanced by Bob Carr and others at the Australia China Research Institute,' he says. He accuses Huang of seeking to influence the political parties through hefty donations. 'Beijing struggled to gain true soft power influence,' he says, 'because the Chinese Communist Party's political culture is repressive and unattractive. But soft power can be exercised in a variety of forms and money transcends most political and ideological boundaries.'[5]

Bob Carr is no less emphatic in his view of ASPI. 'Tony Abbott won a free trade agreement from the Chinese, deeply distressing Jennings,' he says. 'Jennings's ASPI receives whopping funding from US defence companies including Lockheed Martin, Northrop Grumman and Raytheon, and is unhappy with the Coalition's China policy. Why has ASPI under Jennings taken on the job of trashing the relationship with China?'[6]

Their disparate perceptions of the Chinese recalls the two reporters from the *Argus* and the *Geelong Chronicle* on the Port Phillip wharf all those years ago. It is hard to believe they are both viewing the same events. Since that first interaction on Australian soil, the relationship between the oldest and the youngest nations of the region has passed through some rocky terrain, caused almost always by an Anglo-Australian prejudice firmly rooted in the racism that arrived with the British conquest. Since then, in both countries, there has been a studied ignorance of the developments between the two. And there has been almost no acknowledgement of the truly remarkable influence each has brought to bear on the other, to say nothing of the astonishing cast of characters who helped to drive it in each country.

CHAPTER FORTY-FOUR

A MATURE RELATIONSHIP

The gulf between the Dragon and the Kangaroo has narrowed perceptibly in the past decade. Chinese investment in Australian enterprises, from mining to agriculture to real estate, has doubled and redoubled. The growth of the Chinese presence in Australia's capital cities has been no less remarkable. Whole suburbs in up-market areas have been colonised by Chinese immigrants. Historian Peter Thompson visiting Australia from his London base in 2016 strolled through Sydney's Chinatown. 'On a Saturday night,' he says, 'its bars and nightspots attracted hundreds of young Australians as a matter of lifestyle choice. The place was throbbing with ear-splitting music and noisy, youthful energy. The city had become an Asia-Pacific metropolis.'

At the same time, China's own cities have been transformed by iconic western brands like Starbucks, McDonald's and the supermarket chains of Tesco and Walmart. And they service local consumers dressed in everything from casual wear to the latest creations from international designers. The days of revolutionary guards parading through the streets in shapeless Mao jackets shouting communist slogans has been consigned to a distant past.

The China–Australia relationship has always been a work in progress, and will remain so. But in the broad sweep of history, the trends strongly suggest that we will continue to develop ever closer ties, the economic dynamic providing growing opportunities for an expansion into other areas. It is a long and challenging process of mutual discovery. In August 2016, for example, the popular economics writer for the *Sydney Morning Herald* Ross Gittins travelled to China under the auspices of ACRI and was deeply impressed by the progress the country had made in the 21st century. 'So many of us have outdated perceptions about China - that it's a poor country producing cheap clothes and toys and knick-knacks in sweat shops,' he wrote. 'That used to be true, and in parts of the country still is. But these days China is a middle-income country anxious to get rich gloriously.'

His visit was the most recent in a series of exchanges from Australian writers, often sponsored by the Australia–China Council in DFAT. They began in 1981 when the novelist Nicholas Hasluck led a three-man team including the conservative Christopher Koch, author of *The Year of Living Dangerously*, and the much lesser known Hugh Anderson who Hasluck described as having 'a sincere belief in the Marxist view of history'.[1] The trio spent almost a month in a Kafkaesque nightmare travelling from deserted tourist venues like the Great Wall to mutually incomprehensible meetings with academics and editors as Koch and Anderson squabbled and Hasluck struggled with a succession of dizzy spells. Nevertheless, he, like those who followed in the 1990s and 2000s, found it a fascinating and valuable exercise.

Today, the exchanges range across nine Chinese cities in an annual Australian Writers' Week together with music, dance, art exhibitions, and theatrical performances. And just as many Chinese performers and practitioners of all artistic endeavour come to Australia. There is a constant two-way exchange between the great cultural institutions in both countries. Such events as Brisbane's huge Asia-Pacific Triennial art exhibition or the 2016 Celestial Empire display at Canberra's National Library draw record crowds from around Australia. But whether literary and art exchanges reach down to the person in the street in either country is dubious at best.

In business, hundreds of enterprising Australians have moved to China to exploit increasing opportunities in finance, retail, tourism, education and a myriad of Australian imports in areas as diverse as health and fitness, Aboriginal arts and specialist child care products. But once again the development is confined to a comparatively small cohort.

Cheap travel and accommodation in China has encouraged many thousands of Australians to lift their own personal bamboo curtain in tourist groups to the main cities and the leading attractions. But only a small proportion of them explored beneath the surface of the 'Chinglish' guide books or developed a genuine interest in the country and its people.

In sport, while there have been valuable coaching exchanges, the field is wide open for much greater mutual involvement. A handful of young Australian soccer players have found their way into the Chinese Super League and a few Chinese basketballers have won places in Australian teams. But the potential for cross fertilization in a range of sports from ping pong to badminton, volleyball, swimming and athletics has yet to be exploited.

Some Australian primary schools are now teaching Chinese – and in some schools by Year 6 all instruction for pupils is in Mandarin. But the proportion is telling – in South Australia, for example, of more than 700 primary schools only nineteen teach Mandarin and some of those confine the more advanced elements to pupils with a Chinese background.

Nevertheless, Prime Minister Malcolm Turnbull told a Shanghai audience in April 2016, 'Today more than one million people in Australia have Chinese ancestry. And half a million people were born in China. More Australians are learning the Chinese language, understanding Chinese history and culture.

'The growth in our region, and especially in China, reflects the hard work of hundreds of millions of people forging a brighter future for themselves. It is a story of human ingenuity and tenacity. And it's a story about how our two countries have changed, and changed each other, in ways that are leading to all Australians and all Chinese to be better able to realise their dreams. As you say here in China, the flames rise high when everybody adds wood to the fire.'

However, the quest for a peaceful and productive meeting of the several branches of the human family in the Great South Land remains in the balance.

The accession of the mercurial and inexperienced Donald Trump to the Oval Office disrupted the comforting sense of continuity in international statecraft. One of his first acts as President was abandoning the Trans-Pacific Partnership (TPP), an economic and trading agreement designed to consolidate and extend American influence in the region.

When Turnbull phoned him after Trump's inauguration the American leader angrily cut the call short on learning of the deal Australia had negotiated with his predecessor to accept Muslim refugees from Nauru and Manus Island.

Paul Keating found cause for optimism. Australia, he said, could now develop an independent foreign policy that incorporated the ANZUS Treaty without restricting the country's freedom to develop a businesslike relationship with China. 'We've got this almost crazy situation where the American alliance, instead of simply being a treaty where the United States is obliged to consult with us in the event of adverse strategic circumstances, has now taken on a reverential, sacramental quality,' he said.

'What we have to do is make our way in Asia ourselves. There's no geo-strategic problems with China, but we're being hounded by American Admirals to run ships through the South China Sea.' In fact, other regional powers – notably Indonesia – have also sought Australian involvement in provocative naval exercises in the area. All have been diplomatically rebuffed.

Against decades of precedent, Trump took a call from Taiwan's independence-minded president, Tsai Ing-wen, then threatened to use America's long-standing One China policy as a bargaining chip in US-China relations. 'I don't know why we have to be bound by a One China policy unless we make a deal with China having to do with other things,' he said. Beijing's response was deliberately restrained. The last thing Xi Jinping wanted was the elevation of the Taiwan issue to the forefront of the international agenda. It ran counter to his whole long-term strategy.

Whether by chance or design, Turnbull took the opportunity to assert Australia's continuing adherence to the One China policy; while Labor's Shadow Foreign Affairs Minister, Senator Penny Wong, followed two days later with a similar declaration. Then, after a flurry of diplomatic activity behind the scenes, President Trump changed his stance and in an orchestrated phone call with Xi Jinping, re-affirmed the United States' acceptance of Beijing's primacy.

While China's militarisation of the Spratly Islands in the South China Sea might well have diverted attention from Taiwan, it remained an irritant with the potential to spin out of control. When China refused to accept the Court of Arbitration's ruling in favour of the Philippines in the Spratly case, ASPI's Peter Jennings warned that 'There's clearly an attempt underway to see if the Philippines' new president Rodrigo Duterte can be induced to negotiate over Manila's claims in the Spratly Islands in return for economic assistance.'[2]

Sure enough, Duterte travelled to Beijing soon afterward and promised to abandon the US alliance for closer ties with China. Washington was irritated and bemused but on his return to Manila, the volatile Filipino leader contradicted himself and made supportive noises to the US . . . and then backtracked once more. Meantime, China quietly withdrew its naval units which had been chasing Filipino fishermen off their traditional grounds.

The following month the Malaysian Prime Minister, Najib Razak, travelled to Beijing where he began talks to buy a fleet of Chinese patrol boats that can carry missiles, a new development in Malaysia's military relationship with China. Xi Jinping's pre-emptive gambit appeared to have scored a second notable success; and as other claimants also find an accommodation with the 'big guy' of the neighborhood, this would not play well in Trump's America.

On the other hand, in October 2016, President Xi was declared the 'core leader' of his vast domain elevating him to the dizzy imperial heights previously occupied by Deng Xiaoping and Mao himself. His rule of a massive population who have been denied the basic human rights of freedom of assembly and expression within a legal system subject to blatant political interference was already secured for a further five years. And there is no more reason to believe that Xi is immune from Lord Acton's iron law than were his predecessors in the Communist dynasty or their imperial antecedents on the Dragon Throne.

Within Australia's defence and security establishment, China remained the notional 'enemy' against which it and its 'Five-Eyes' treaty associates – the US, UK, Canada and New Zealand – continued to measure their military capacity. Australia's external Intelligence agency ASIS devoted more attention to China than to any other sovereign nation; as did the top secret Australian Signals Directorate from its Canberra headquarters where its operatives conducted both defensive and offensive cyber operations.

The disparate attitudes of Bob Carr's ACRI versus Peter Jennings' ASPI reflected those of a much wider grouping within the Australian population. Indeed, there were indications in the resurgence of One Nation and other rightwing splinter groups that echoes of Australia's racist past were with us still. And we were not alone. The nations of Europe and Scandinavia which had accepted a flood of refugees and undocumented migrants from the Middle East and North Africa were divided and disrupted by the racist right at the ballot box.

When the explosive contretemps between Trump and the volatile North Korean leader Kim Jong-un threatened to trigger a shooting war, the rest of the world shuddered at the prospect of two such unpredictable men edging towards the unthinkable horror of nuclear conflict. Xi Jinping's public intervention to 'rein in' the Korean leader earned the forthright praise of the American president. Unfortunately, there was no guarantee that his gratitude would extend beyond the latest crisis.

But beneath the raucous clamour of international politics, the global community was trying desperately to come to terms with the seismic shifts in the power ratio. Its more perceptive leaders recognised that the Trump phenomenon was a serious blow to American prestige and authority. But they understood that in the longer term America would resume a leading and respected role in the great councils of state.

In the meantime, China would no doubt take the opportunity to position itself as a responsible and progressive force in the world, a leader of action against climate change and of the global quest for increased trade and investment to raise living standards worldwide. Indeed, Chinese Premier Li Keqing underscored their intentions during a March 2017 visit to Australia. Extension of the China–Australia Free Trade Agreement, he said, 'will show the region and the world that [we] will deliver benefits to all human beings.' Turnbull and Trade Minister Steve Ciobo took the opportunity to signal their willingness to join China's alternative to the TPP, the Regional Comprehensive Economic Partnership.

Australia's conundrum was to strengthen its ties to China without offense to its security alliance with America. If successful, the result would secure Australia's future safety, security and prosperity. But whether its leadership and its multicultural population had the wit and the will to solve the conundrum depended on the response to the question that had bedeviled Australia since almost the beginning of its colonial history: could the prejudices of the past be replaced by a sense of realism, an appreciation that there was much to be gained from a growing Chinese engagement across an ever-broadening spectrum of endeavor; and much to be lost by refusing to learn from a history that until now, if seen at all, has been viewed through a glass darkly?

Time will tell.

ACKNOWLEDGEMENTS

I have been extraordinarily fortunate in having access to the work of a remarkable cohort of Australian writers and historians, many of whom have concentrated their vision on particular persons, periods and localities within the great mosaic of the Australia–China experience. Kathryn Cronin, for example, in her *Colonial Casualties* (MUP, 1982) has brought the Chinese struggle on the Victorian goldfields brilliantly to life with a remarkable attention to detail. Robert Travers has written the most engaging and insightful biography of Quong Tart in his *Australian Mandarin* (Kangaroo Press, 1981). Margaret Slocomb has captured the plight of the Chinese indentured pastoral workers in Queensland with great skill and feeling in her *Among Australia's Pioneers* (Balboa, 2014).

These and many others have been enormously helpful in providing aspects of the saga, particularly in the early days of Australia's colonial history. But no one was more generous than my frequent co-author Peter Thompson whose brilliant work on the life and times of the great journalists and political activists G.E. Morrison and, especially, Bill Donald in *Shanghai Fury* (Random House, 2011) provided a vivid insight into the China of the late 19th and early 20th centuries. The war years of the Australian mission in Chongqing and Nanjing owe much to the excellent work of the ANU scholar Will Sima; and both Pamela Tan and her Rosenberg publishers (*The Chinese Factor*, 2008) graciously permitted me to retell her story from within the Chinese mainland during the nightmarish decades from 1950.

More recently, Australia's first Ambassador to the People's Republic, Stephen FitzGerald, provided an intimate picture of the diplomatic world of Beijing in his *Comrade Ambassador* (MUP, 2015) while subsequent ambassadors Ross Garnaut, Ric Smith, David Irvine and Mike Lightowler were very generous with their time in a series of interviews. The same goes for ASPI director Peter Jennings.

I am deeply indebted to Richard Rigby, Associate Director of the Australian Centre on China in the World at the ANU, who has been extremely helpful throughout the research and writing and very kindly read the manuscript prior to publication. I am also very appreciative of my agent-cum-editor Margaret Kennedy for her guidance throughout, and my valued publisher at Hachette Australia, Matthew Kelly. However, the opinions and attitudes expressed in the work are exclusively my own.

I am surprised that this is the first time the chronicle of this most pivotal relationship has ever been attempted. The knowledge of its singularity provided a sense of responsibility in the telling. No doubt future events will bring new twists and turns to the saga. But perhaps by reflecting on the story to this crucial point in our shared history a pattern will emerge to guide decisions from both participants in the years ahead. One can but hope. As the Chinese might say, *shan yu yu lai feng man lou* – coming events cast their shadows before them.

Robert Macklin, Canberra

BIBLIOGRAPHY

Albinski, Henry S., *Australian Policies and Attitudes toward China*, Princeton University Press, 1965.
Allen, Roland, *The Siege of the Peking Legations*, Smith Elder & Co., London, 1901.
Andrews, E.M., *Australia and China: The Ambiguous Relationship*, Melbourne University Press, 1985.
Australian Centre on China in the World (ANU) and China Institutes of Contemporary International Relations, *Australia and China: A Joint Report on the Bilateral Relationship*, Canberra/Beijing, 2012.
Barmé, Geremie R. & Manuel, Ryan (Eds.), *A New Australia–China Agenda*, Australian Centre on China in the World, Australian National University, Canberra, 2014.
China Institute, *George Morrison Lectures 1932–1941*, ANU College of Asia and the Pacific, Canberra, 2007.
Cronin, Kathryn, *Colonial Casualties*, Melbourne University Press, 1982.
Crossley, Pamela Kyle, *The Manchus*, Blackwell, Cambridge, Mass., 2002.
Feiling, Keith, *A History of England*, Macmillan, London, 1950.
Fenby, Jonathan, *China: The Fall and Rise of a Great Power, 1850–2008*, Allen Lane, London, 2008.
Fitch, Don, *The Immortal Part: The Story of Edward Little, Australia's First Trade Commissioner in China*, Australian Scholarly Publishing, Melbourne, 2001.
Fitzgerald, C.P., *Revolution in China*, Cresset Press, London, 1952.
FitzGerald, Stephen, *Comrade Ambassador: Whitlam's Beijing Envoy*, Melbourne University Press, 2015.
Hasluck, Nicholas and Koch, C.J., *Chinese Journey*, Fremantle Arts Centre Press, 1985.
Hessler, Peter, *Country Driving: Three Journeys across a Changing China*, Text Publishing, 2010.
Hoyt, Edwin, *The Fall of Tsingtao*, Arthur Barker, London, 1975.
James, Lawrence, *The Rise and Fall of the British Empire*, Abacus, London, 1912.
Lary, Diana, *The Chinese People at War 1937–1945*, Cambridge University Press, 2010.
Lo Hui-Min, *The Correspondence of G.E. Morrison 1895–1912*, Cambridge University Press, 1978.
Morrison, Alistair R., *The Road to Peking*, Pandanus Press, Canberra, 2001.
Morrison, G.E., *An Australian in China*, Horace Cox, London, 1895.
Morrison, Ian, *Malayan Postscript*, Faber and Faber, London, 1942.
Preston, Diana, *The Boxer Rebellion: China's War on Foreigners, 1900*, Robinson, London, 2002.
Rolls, Eric, *Citizens: Flowers and the Wide Sea*, University of Queensland Press, Brisbane, 1996.
Selle, Earl Albert, *Donald of China*, Invincible Press, Sydney, 1948.
Sharman, Lyon, *Sun Yat-sen, His Life and its Meaning*, Stanford University Press, 1968.
Slocomb, Margaret, *Among Australia's Pioneers*, Balboa Press, Bloomington, 2014.
Spence, Jonathan & Chin, Ann-ping, *The Chinese Century*, HarperCollins, London, 1996.
Tan, Pamela, *The Chinese Factor*, Rosenberg, Sydney, 2008.
Thompson, Peter and Macklin, Robert, *Morrison of China*, Allen & Unwin, Sydney, 2004.
Thompson, Peter, *Shanghai Fury: Australian Heroes of Revolutionary China*, William Heinemann, Sydney, 2011.
Travers, Robert, *Australian Mandarin*, Kangaroo Press, Sydney, 1981.
Warner, Marina, *The Dragon Empress*, Vintage, London, 1993.
Xu Zhigeng, *Nanjing Massacre, 1937*, Chinese Literature Press, Beijing, 1995.

ENDNOTES

PROLOGUE
1 Interview with the author, December 2015

CHAPTER 1
1 Steven, Margaret, 'John Macarthur', *Australian Dictionary of Biography*, Vol. 2, Melbourne University Press, 1967.
2 *Port Phillip Herald*, 26 December 1848.

CHAPTER 3
1 Fitzgerald, C.P., *Revolution in China*, Cresset Press, London, 1952, p. 345.

CHAPTER 4
1 Spence, Jonathan, *God's Chinese Son*, HarperCollins, London, 1996, p. 325.
2 Fitzgerald, C.P., op. cit., p. 356.

CHAPTER 5
1 Gammage, Bill, *The Biggest Estate on Earth*, Allen & Unwin, Sydney, 2011.
2 Cronin, Kathryn, *Colonial Casualties*, Melbourne University Press, 1982, p. 22.
3 ibid.

CHAPTER 6
1 Preshaw, George, *Banking under Difficulties*, Dunlop, Edwards and Co., Melbourne, 1888.
2 *The Argus*, 23 April 1857.
3 Cronin, op. cit., p. 23.
4 ibid.

CHAPTER 7
1 Sometimes called Jembaicumbene.
2 Travers, Robert, *Australian Mandarin*, Kangaroo Press, Sydney, 1981, pp. 33-34.
3 *The Argus*, 21 July 1858.
4 Taylor, Howard, *Hudson Taylor and the China Inland Mission*, China Inland Mission, London, 1934, p. 490.
5 Cronin, op. cit., p. 105.
6 ibid.
7 Fitzgerald, C.P., op. cit., p. 576.

CHAPTER 8
1 Cronin, op. cit., p. 81.
2 ibid., p. 89.
3 ibid., p. 99.
4 ibid.

CHAPTER 9
1 ibid., pp. 18-19.

CHAPTER 11
1. Slocomb, Margaret, *Among Australia's Pioneers*, Balboa Press, Bloomington, 2014, p. 115.
2. ibid, p. 103.
3. ibid.
4. ibid.
5. ibid.
6. ibid.
7. Holthouse, Hector, *Gympie Gold*, HarperCollins, Sydney, 1999, pp. 107–112.

CHAPTER 12
1. Jones, Timothy G., *The Chinese in the Northern Territory*, NTU Press, Darwin, 1988, p. 1.
2. ibid.
3. ibid.
4. ibid.
5. Sowden, William, *The Northern Territory As It Is*, W.K. Thomas & Co, Adelaide, 1882.

CHAPTER 13
1. Travers, op. cit., p. 48.
2. ibid.
3. Rolls, Eric, *Citizens,* UQP, Brisbane, 1996, p. 3.
4. Jones, op. cit., p. 63.

CHAPTER 14
1. Thompson, Peter and Macklin, Robert, *Morrison of China*, Allen & Unwin, 2004, pp. 15–28.
2. Taylor, op. cit., pp. 493–499.
3. ibid., p. 502.

CHAPTER 16
1. Willard, Myra, *History of the White Australia Policy to 1920*, Augustus Kelly, New York, 1968, pp. 82–84.
2. Parkes, Sir Henry, *Fifty Years in the Making of Australian History*, Longmans, Green and Co, London, 1892, p. 475.
3. Willard, op. cit., p. 114.
4. Australia, House of Representatives, *Debates,* 1901–2, Vol. 6, p. 7335.
5. Willard, op. cit., pp. 126–127.
6. Thompson and Macklin, op. cit.

CHAPTER 17
1. ibid.
2. ibid.
3. ibid.
4. Paterson, A.B., *Happy Dispatches*, Lansdowne Press, Sydney, 1980, pp. 14–18.

CHAPTER 18
1. Deakin, Alfred, introduction to *David Syme: The Father of Protection in Australia* by Ambrose Pratt, Ward Lock & Co., Melbourne, 1908.
2. Thompson, Peter, *Shanghai Fury*, William Heinemann, Sydney, 2011, p. 93.
3. ibid.
4. ibid.
5. Morrison, G.E., 'Port Arthur From Within', *The Times,* 25 January 1905.
6. Selle, Earl Albert, *Donald of China*, Invincible Press, Sydney, 1948, p. 42.

CHAPTER 19
1. Rolls, op. cit., pp. 416–428.
2. ibid.
3. Thompson and Macklin, op. cit., p. 305.
4. Thompson, op. cit., p. 134.
5. ibid.
6. ibid.

CHAPTER 20
1. ibid.
2. ibid.
3. Thompson and Macklin, op. cit., p. 318.
4. ibid., p. 329.
5. Morrison to Brahim, 16 January 1912.

CHAPTER 21
1. Rolls, op. cit., pp. 431–434.
2. Author's interview with Alastair Morrison, June 2004.
3. Donald to Morrison, 4 July 1912, 'Morrison Papers', Mitchell Library, Sydney.
4. *Sydney Morning Herald*, 31 August 1912.
5. Thompson, op. cit., p. 177.
6. Thompson and Macklin, op. cit., p. 360.
7. ibid., pp. 362–363.
8. ibid.

CHAPTER 22
1. ibid., pp. 380–383.
2. ibid.
3. Hamilton, John, *Gallipoli Sniper*, Pan Macmillan, Sydney, 2008, pp. 39–45.
4. *The Mercury*, 13 March 1916, p. 4.

CHAPTER 23
1. Thompson, op. cit., p. 188.
2. Donald to Morrison, 4 February 1917, 'Morrison Papers' op. cit.
3. Rolls, op. cit., pp. 438–439.
4. Thompson and Macklin, op. cit., p. 426.

CHAPTER 24
1. Rubinstein, Hilary L., 'Thomas Jerome Kingston Backhap', *Biographical Dictionary of the Australian Senate*: biography.senate.gov.au/thomas-jerome-kingston-bakhap/.
2. Thompson, op. cit., p. 199.
3. ibid.
4. ibid.

CHAPTER 25
1. Andrews, E.M., *Australia and China: The Ambiguous Relationship*, Melbourne University Press, 1985, p. 57.
2. ibid.
3. 'Raid on Shanghai Reds', *The Times*, 13 April 1927.
4. Thompson, op. cit., p. 269.
5. ibid.
6. Selle, op. cit., pp. 289–290.
7. Thompson, op. cit., p. 327.

8 Fenby, Jonathan, *Generalissimo Chiang Kai-shek and the China He Lost*, The Free Press, London, 2003, p. 270.

CHAPTER 26
1 Andrews, op. cit., pp. 67–68.

CHAPTER 27
1 Thompson, Peter and Macklin, Robert, *The Big Fella*, p. 71.
2 *Sydney Morning Herald*, 16 May 1940.
3 A981 Australia 162ij AA CP290/3.
4 Andrews, op. cit., p. 94.
5 Sima, William, *China and ANU*, ANU Press, Canberra, 2015, p. 17.
6 Osmond, William, 'Sir Frederic William Eggleston', *Australian Dictionary of Biography*, Vol. 8, Melbourne University Press, 1981.
7 Andrews, op. cit., p. 99.
8 Thompson, op. cit., pp. 409–410.

CHAPTER 28
1 Thompson, op. cit., pp. 414–415.
2 Rasmussen, Amanda, 'Straddling Boundaries 1941–1950', 2001.
3 Andrews, op. cit., p. 114.
4 Dermody, Kathleen, 'Sir Frank Keith Officer', *Australian Dictionary of Biography*, Vol. 15, Melbourne University Press, 2000.
5 Bagnall, Kate, Opening the Chungking Legation Exhibition at the Department of Foreign Affairs and Trade, Canberra, December 2015.
6 Hall, Barry, *Recollections of a Junior Diplomat, 1944–46*, privately published by the author.
7 Rasmussen, op. cit., p. 3.
8 Andrews, op. cit., p. 115.
9 Thompson, op. cit., p. 429.
10 Andrews, op. cit., p. 122.
11 Alastair Morrison to Professor Lewis, 1 April 1980, Winston G. Lewis Papers. Mitchell Library, Sydney.

CHAPTER 29
1 Harper, Marjorie, 'Sir Douglas Berry Copland', *Australian Dictionary of Biography*, Vol. 13, Melbourne University Press, 1993.
2 ibid.
3 Report by Hall on journey by river steamer from Chungking to Nanking, 21–29 May 1946.
4 ibid.
5 Sima, op. cit., p. 74.
6 Andrews, op. cit., pp. 124–125.
7 His actual quotation: 'The [deportation] policy which I have just mentioned relates to evacuees who came to Australia during the war. This Chinese is said to have been here for twenty years, and obviously, therefore, is not a wartime evacuee. Speaking generally, I think there is some claim for him to be regarded as a resident of Australia, and I have no doubt his certificate can be extended from time to time as it has been extended in the past. An error may have been made in his case. The gentleman's name is Wong. There are many Wongs in the Chinese community, but I have to say — and I am sure that the Honourable Member for Balaclava will not mind me doing so — that "two Wongs do not make a White."'

CHAPTER 30
1. Sima, op. cit., p. 74.
2. Andrews, op. cit., p. 133.
3. ibid.
4. ibid.

CHAPTER 31
1. Tan, Pamela, *The Chinese Factor*, Rosenberg, Sydney, 2008.
2. Tony Abbott in an aside to German Chancellor Angela Merkel in 2015.
3. Li Zhisui, *The Private Life of Chairman Mao*, Random House, New York, 1994.

CHAPTER 32
1. Andrews, op. cit., p. 181.
2. ibid.
3. *Debates*, 29 April 1965.
4. The author was Press Secretary to McEwen from 1967 to 1971. These words and others in very similar vein were the stock in trade of McEwen's attitude throughout the 1960s.
5. *Debates*, 15 March 1966.
6. Andrews, op. cit., p. 196.

CHAPTER 34
1. FitzGerald, Stephen, *Comrade Ambassador*, Melbourne University Press, 2015, p. 69.
2. ibid.
3. ibid.
4. ibid., p. 97.

CHAPTER 35
1. Tan, op. cit., pp. 220–230.
2. FitzGerald, Stephen, op. cit., p. 1.
3. ibid., p. 103.
4. Thompson, Peter, *Wesfarmers 100*, UWA Publishing, Perth, 2014, p. 152.
5. FitzGerald, Stephen, op. cit., p. 134.
6. ibid.

CHAPTER 36
1. ibid., p. 136.
2. Tan, op. cit., p. 239.
3. ibid.
4. ibid.
5. ibid., p. 262.

CHAPTER 37
1. Macklin, Robert, *Kevin Rudd*, Penguin, Melbourne, 2008, pp. 90–97.
2. Ross Gaunaut's remarks in this section are taken from 'Sino-Australian Economic Relations 1983–95', his contribution to *Australia and China*, Colin Mackerras (Ed.) Macmillan Education Australia, Melbourne, 1996; his interview with Bob Carr in the Ambassador Series of the Australia–China Relations Institute on 23 June 2016 and personal contact with the author.
3. Interview with the author, August 2016.
4. Grattan, Michelle, *The Age*, 20 May 1986.
5. Quoted by Ross Garnaut in 'Sino-Australian Economic Relations', p. 71.
6. Macklin, op. cit.

CHAPTER 38

1 Chan, Gabrielle, *The Guardian*, 1 January 2015.
2 Garnaut, Ross, 'Sino-Australian Economic Relations', p. 82.
3 There is some doubt whether he actually said the words, but he would not deny the sense of the remark.
4 Institute of Southeast Asian Studies, 17 January 1996.
5 Ross Garnaut had been the first of six West Australians in a row to be appointed to the post.
6 Oral history interview with Garry Sturgess for the National Library of Australia.

CHAPTER 39

1 ibid.
2 Macklin, op. cit., p. 124.

CHAPTER 40

1 Interview with the author.

CHAPTER 41

1 Rudd confided the life-changing incident to his sister Loree who relayed it to the author during his research for the 2008 book, *Kevin Rudd: The Biography*. When the author confronted Rudd with the report he refused to confirm it so the author chose not to include it. But subsequent conversations with other members of the family confirmed it; as did Rudd's reactions to his loss of the prime ministership and his subsequent quest to become UN Secretary-General, also denied him in what he believed to be traitorous circumstances.

CHAPTER 43

1 Schubert, Steven, *ABC News*, 12 September 2015.
2 White, Hugh, 'Power Shift', *Quarterly Essay*, 2010, pp. 55–56.
3 Garnaut, John, *Sydney Morning Herald*, 15 September 2015.
4 Wong, Edward, 'Xi Jinping's News Alert: Chinese Media Must Serve the Party', *New York Times*, 22 February 2016.
5 ABC Radio, 5 September 2016.
6 Carr, Bob, 'I stood for US alliance as well as our China partnership', *The Australian*, 24 September 2016.

CHAPTER 44

1 Hasluck, Nicholas, *Somewhere in the Atlas*, Freshwater Bay Press, Perth, 2007, p. 39.
2 Jennings, Peter, *The Strategist*, Australian Strategic Policy Institute, 13 July 2016: www.aspistrategist.org.au/south-china-sea-will-end/

INDEX

Abbott, Tony 296, 308, 309, 316–18, 322, 324, 325, 330
Aboriginal Australians X, 3, 26–7, 63, 68
   apology to 307
   Paddy's Island massacre 63
Aboriginal Protection and Sale of Opium Act 121
Acheson, Dean 219, 220, 222
Acton, Lord 11, 232, 243, 336
Ah Ket, William 161–2, 182
All China Federation of Trade Unions 237, 244, 245–6, 255
America *see* United States of America
Anthony, Doug 254, 267–8
ANZUS Treaty 223, 300, 334
Asia-Pacific Economic Cooperation Forum (APEC) 287–8, 290, 295, 306
Asia-Pacific Triennial art exhibition 332
Asian financial crisis 294
Atherton Tableland 66, 136
Ausgrid, sale of 327
Australasian Liaison Bureau 228
Australia
   anti-Chinese prejudice *see* racism
   Australia-China relationship *see* China-Australia relationship
   Chinese delegations to 75, 276, 299–300
   Chinese immigration *see* immigration
   Chinese investment in XI, 327
   Christian missionaries in China 171
   'Forward Defence' policy 231, 247
   gold, discovery of *see* gold
   intelligence gathering 336
   multiculturalism 284, 326
   recognition of Communist government 219–21, 223–4, 231
   United States of America, and XI, 187, 231, 240, 247, 299, 312–13
   White Australia Policy *see* White Australia Policy
Australia-China Council 267, 332
Australia-China Friendship Association 236
Australia-China Relations Institute (ACRI) 329, 331–2, 336

Australian Council of Trade Unions (ACTU) 236
Australian Institute of International Affairs (AIIA) 191, 329
Australian Labor Party (ALP) 101, 169, 193, 205, 214, 220–1, 224, 230–1, 238, 239, 242, 249, 250, 254, 255, 261, 273, 275, 279, 286, 288, 295–6, 299, 301, 305–7, 310, 311, 316–17, 322, 325, 327, 335
Australian military XI
   China, in 197–8
   Exercise Kowari 322–3
Australian Strategic Policy Institute (ASPI) 323–4, 329–30, 336
Australian Trade Union Movement 236

Bakhap, Thomas J 161
Ballarat 25, 30, 33, 79
'Bamboo Curtain' 224
Barmé, Geremie 310
Beazley, Kim 295, 299, 305, 306
Beijing 16, 43, 112, 210, 213, 217–19, 225, 227, 257, 274–5, 294, 314
   Beijing Art Festival 295
   Cultural Revolution, during 244, 246
   foreign control, under 110
   Fraser, visit of 264
   Gate of Heavenly Peace 218
   Tiananmen Square incident 280–3
   Whitlam visits 249, 250–4, 259–60, 264
Bendigo 30, 33, 34, 36, 40, 47
Blainey, Professor Geoffrey 267, 268, 284
'boat people' 268, 269
Booker, Malcolm 199, 201
Bowden, I.V.G. (Gordon) 184–5, 186, 193, 194
Boxer Rebellion 102–5, 107–110
Braidwood 38–9, 40
Brennan, Inspector Martin 77–8
Britain 9, 14–15, 19, 20, 189, 198–9, 336
   China, World War II operations in 196–7, 198
   extra-territorial rights 198–9, 202
   Hong Kong, control of 219, 220
   racism X, 42, 199

recognition of Chinese Communist government 220–1
British East India Company 3, 20, 22
Bruce, Stanley Melbourne 189, 193
Buddhism 229
Burma Road 189, 194, 197
Bush, George W. 299–301, 306, 313
business interests, Australian 332

Cai Tinggan, Rear Admiral 130–1
Cairns, Dr Jim 250, 258
California 24–5
Calwell, Arthur 214, 238, 242
Carr, Bob 317, 329–30, 336
Casey, Richard 191, 246
Celestial Empire display (2016) 332
Chang, Victor 326
Changsha 167, 194
Chen Boda 243
Chen, Consul-General W.P. 182, 184
Chen Mingyi 315
Chen Zhimai 241
Chiang Kai-shek 142, 165–6, 185, 193, 204
  civil war, and 217, 219, 222
  communist activists, vicious purges of 170–1
  Communists, struggle with 175–8, 179–81, 209
  Donald, and 174, 176–7, 179–81, 193, 205
  early years 165
  Japanese Military Academy 142, 165
  Kuomintang 165, 175
  Mao Zedong, peace negotiations with 204, 213
  Mayling Soong, and *see* Mayling Soong
  Menzies, and 188, 222
  Nanjing, southern headquarters 173, 188
  National Revolutionary Army 164, 166
  opium trade 177–8
  regime, Australian recognition of 222, 223, 241
  Sun Yatsen, and 165, 168, 218
  surrender of forces 217
  Taiwan, and 219, 241, 252, 321
  World War II, during 194, 204
  Zhang Xueliang (Young Marshal), and 172, 175–8, 179
Chifley, Ben 209, 213, 216, 219, 230
China *see also* Chinese
  Australian business interests in 332
  Australian Christian missionaries in 171
  cultural transformation 295, 332
  economic growth 290–1, 295, 325, 333
  economic reforms 273–4, 278–9, 286–7, 315–16
  Exercise Kowari 322–3
  foreign investment, opening up to 274

  Manchuria, loss of control 147
  media control 328
  one-child policy, abolition of 315–16
  origin of name 9
  Outer Mongolia, surrender of authority 147
  Outer Tibet, surrender of authority 147
  Shandong, loss of control 147
  student protests 279–83
  United States, relationship with 254, 313, 315, 321, 322–3, 334–6
  'Warring States' 10
China-Australia Free Trade Agreement 318, 329, 330, 337
China-Australia relationship 6–7
  Abbott government, under 317–20, 322–4, 330
  anti-communist feeling 223–4, 225, 240, 254
  'Australia and the Northeast Asian Ascendancy' report 285
  Australian impressions of 183–4, 191, 193, 263, 267
  Australian legation in China 106–10, 191–2, 196, 198–202, 204, 209–10
  Australian Trade Union Movement 236
  Chinese consul-generals in Australia 122
  Chinese legation in Australia 1941 192
  cultural exchanges 304
  Fraser government, under 263, 264, 267–8
  Gillard government, under 312, 317, 322
  Hawke government, under 275–9, 284–5
  Howard government, under 289–91, 292–5, 299–303, 323
  investments and business interests XI, 327, 332
  Keating government, under 287–8, 289
  Menzies government, under 186–90, 222
  racism *see* racism
  recognition of Communist government 219–21, 222, 223–4, 231
  Rudd government, under 307–9
  social changes 325–6
  soft power, exercising 329–30
  threat, China perceived as 224, 238–40, 308, 318, 324
  Tiananmen Square incident, and 284–5
  trade *see* trade
  Turnbull government, under 324, 333–5, 337
  Whitlam government, under 249–54, 258, 259–60, 267
  work in progress, as 331–7
'China in the World' study centre (ANU) 310, 329
China Inland Mission 91–2
China National Offshore Oil Corporation 302

Chinalco 309
Chinese
  coolies 3–4, 28, 68, 191
  Han 12
  indentured labour 3, 61–4
  inventions 8, 14
  language teaching in Australia 333
  leadership XI, XII
  legal rights in Australia 73
  merchants 156
  returning to China 227
  tourism XII, 297, 319, 325, 326, 332, 333
Chinese-Australians 326
  soldiers 148–52, 326
  voting rights 73
Chinese gold prospectors XI, 25, 28–30
  conflict with Caucasians 30, 32–4
  court, treatment in 36, 37
  Eureka uprising 32
  opium 29
  secret societies 29, 34, 35–7
  treatment by police 36
  Victorian judiciary 37
Chinese immigration XI, XII, 4–6, 28–9, 45, 80, 199
  Christian conversion 40–1
  demands to end 98
  falls in population 155, 171
  'family reunion' restrictions 225
  increasing 241, 268, 297, 303, 325–6, 331
  landing fee or poll tax 32, 45, 48, 70, 72, 81
  legislation 32, 54, 99
  Mei Quong Tart 38–40, 76
  Natal Method 99, 101
  Northern Territory 68–74
  Ping Que 69–74
  restrictions on 80–1, 98–101
  secret societies 29, 35
  Tiananmen Square incident, response to 284
Chinese Protectorate 45–8
  Chinese headmen 46, 48
  interpreters 46, 48
  military nature of 46
  protection and landing taxes 46
  taxes, discriminatory 46–7
Chinese Revolution (1911) 128–35
Chingling Soong (Madame Sun Yatsen) 218
Chongqing 188, 189, 191–2, 209, 221
  Australian legation 191–2, 196, 198–202, 204, 209–11
Cixi, Empress Dowager 103, 110, 112, 123
climate change 307, 309–10
Cold War 209, 308
Communists (China) 201, 209, 213, 291
  collectivisation 233, 273

corruption, Xi Jinping crackdown on 316, 328–9
  elections (1954) 230
  Five-year Plans 233
  Great Leap Forward 233, 237, 243
  international recognition of Communist government 219–21, 222, 223–4, 231, 241
  Japan, relationship with 253
  life in Communist China 225, 228–30, 233–4, 248
  Nationalists, relationship with 175–8, 179, 180, 209, 214–15, 216–17
  new radical leftists (1960s) 237–8
  political study, mandatory 228–9
  privileges 228
  'rectification' program 234–5
  Soviets, relationship with 222, 230, 232, 233, 237–8, 239, 253, 280
  torture and execution of dissidents 234
Convention of Peking 52
Copland, Douglas 209–11, 214, 216–17, 219
  post-legation career 221, 223
  reports to Canberra 212, 216
  Spender, and 223
Country Party 188, 189, 220, 231, 239, 246–7, 254
Court, Richard 293, 298
Crean, Simon 299, 301, 305
Crown Casino employees, arrest of 328
Cultural Revolution 243–6, 250, 252, 257, 262, 269, 314
Curtin, John 193–4, 209

Dalai Lama 289, 299
Daoguang, Emperor 22
Darwin 68, 69, 71, 72, 73, 74, 82–3, 259–60
Dastyari, Sam 327
Deakin, Alfred 100, 112
democracy 10
  Deng's 'fifth modernisation' 274
Democratic Labor Party (DLP) 231, 238
Deng Xiaoping 6, 235, 243, 257, 262, 265, 269, 279, 293, 308, 314
  economic reforms 273–4, 278–80, 286–7
  leader, as 273–4, 277–8, 279, 336
  political reform 279–80
  retirement 286–7
  Tiananmen Square incident 280–3, 286
'domino' theory 241
Donald, Muriel 203, 206
Donald, William 119, 123–5, 127, 134, 140, 144, 163, 164, 169, 308
  Central China Economic Investigation Bureau 177
  Charlie Soong and his family 125–6, 142

INDEX

Chiang Kai-shek, and 174, 176–7, 179–81, 193, 205
China Mail 116, 118, 119, 123, 124, 125
Chinese official, adviser to high-ranking 119
Chinese Revolutionary Movement, and 120
death 206
departure from China 188–9
Dr Hu Hanmin, and 119–120
early years 115
Eggleston, and 193
Hong Kong, office in 124–5
Japanese invasion, and 173–4
Li Yuanhong, and 154–5
Manila, captivity in 196, 203
marriage 117, 119, 125, 140, 158, 163
meeting of revolutionaries and British consul 128
memoir 189, 193
Nanjing, battle of 131–2
return to China 205
Russo-Japanese war at sea, report on 118
Sun Yatsen, and 115, 134–5, 138–40
The Times 163, 164
Yuan Shikai, and 153
Zhang Xueliang ('The Young Marshal'), and 171–3, 175–8, 179–81
'Down to the Countryside Movement' 245
Downer, Alexander 289, 293

Eggleston, Sir Frederic William 209, 217, 218, 219, 220
Australian legation, head of 190–2, 197–9, 200, 202–3
Churchill, and 196
post-legation career 217–19, 220, 221
reports to Canberra 193, 202
eunuchs 14, 17–18, 123, 136
Eureka rebellion 30–1, 296
Evans, Gareth 285, 287, 288, 289
Evatt, Dr H.V. 199, 202, 203, 218, 230
recognition of Chinese Communist government 219–20
Exercise Kowari 322–3

Fadden, Arthur 189, 239
Feng Yuxiang, General 166, 167
First Emperor *see* Shi Huang
Fitzgerald, C.P. 221, 256
FitzGerald, Stephen 251–3, 267, 269
ambassador to PRC 255, 257–60, 261, 263, 264
China and the World 267
death of Mao, on 266
Five-year Plans 233
Fraser, Malcolm 249, 260, 261, 263, 264, 266–8, 273, 275

Freudenberg, Graham 251, 254
Fujian 28, 314, 316, 321

Gang of Four 234, 245, 257, 262, 266
arrest of 266
Garnaut, Ross 275–7, 279, 285, 297, 307, 309
Germany 186–8, 196
Tripartite Pact 189
Gillard, Julia 296, 305–6, 325
leadership challenge 310–11
prime minister, as 311–12, 316–17, 322
Gipps, Governor George 3, 25
Global Financial Crisis 309
gold
Australia, in XI, 24–5, 27, 28, 65–8, 82, 136
California, in 24–5, 28
Goldfields Amendment Act 74
goldrush 5, 25, 27, 48, 125, 319
Lambing Flat *see* Lambing Flat
Major's Creek goldfields 38
New South Wales goldfields 48, 77
Northern Territory 68–74
Victoria 28, 30, 33, 34, 36–7, 125
Western Australia 81
gold prospectors 30
Chinese *see* Chinese gold prospectors
Eureka rebellion 30–1
Gorbachev, Mikhail 280–1
Gordon, Major General Charles 43–4, 75
Gorton, John 247, 249
Great Hall of the People 243, 253, 255, 258, 278, 280, 282
Great Leap Forward 233, 237, 243
Great Wall 11, 173, 217, 275, 332
Great War *see* World War I
Green Gang of criminals 165
Gruzenberg, Mikhail ('Borodin')
Sun Yatsen, connection with 164–5
Guangdong 28, 124, 225, 298
Guangdong Trade Fair (Sydney 1980) 267
Guangxu, Emperor 91, 123
Guangzhou (Canton) 3, 20, 21, 22, 38, 48, 66, 69, 76–7, 124, 126–7, 164, 183, 218, 286
'Cohong' 20
viceroy of 119

Hall, Barry 199, 200, 201, 202
movement of legation to Nanjing 210–11
Hangzhou 126, 129, 185, 188
Hanson, Pauline 289
Hasluck, Nicholas 332
Hasluck, Paul 239, 240, 241
Hawke, Bob 273, 275–6, 284, 285, 288, 295
China, visits to 276–8
leadership challenge 286
Tiananmen Square incident 284, 285

Hayden, Bill 268, 273, 287
Hebei 294, 314
Henan 254, 314
Heseltine, Colin 281, 284
HMAS *Brisbane* 169–70
Holt, Harold 240, 241, 242
    disappearance 246–7
Homer Lea 133, 138
Hong Kong 23, 48, 125, 188, 227, 241, 252, 274, 285, 321
    British control 219, 220
Hong Xiuquan 23–4, 44
Howard, John 268, 284, 288–9, 296, 299–302, 305, 306–7, 323
    China, visits to 290, 291, 292, 299
    United States, relationship with 299–302, 306
Hu Jintao 299, 302–4, 306, 308, 315, 319
Hu Yaobang 276–9, 280
Huang Xing 141, 142
Huang Xiangmo 329
Hughes, Billy 159, 160, 162, 190, 203, 288
human rights issues 292–3, 301–2, 308, 328, 336
Hunan 197, 198

immigration XI
    Chinese, to Australia *see* Chinese immigration
India 238, 258
Indonesia 240, 287, 294, 299, 302, 334
Institute for Regional Security 329
Institute of Applied Jurisprudence 328
Institute of Pacific Relations (IPR) 191
intermarriage 35, 79
    Chinese-Aboriginal 65, 122
    Chinese-European 65, 78
    prejudice against 70, 122
iron ore 276, 285, 293
Irvine, David 275, 276, 297, 298, 299

Japan 259, 266, 277, 294, 295, 302, 313, 317
    Australia, pre-war relations with 186–7, 191
    Communist China, and 253
    Great War 144, 145, 149
    Manchukuo 173–5, 183–4
    Manchuria, control of 146, 147, 173–5, 179
    Port Arthur, capture of 117
    prisoners of war 211
    Russia, hostilities with 116–17
    Shanghai, attacks on 173–4, 185
    Sino-Japanse War 173–4, 185, 187–9
    Sun Yatsen 145, 146
    trading partner of Australia XI, XII, 231–2
    Tripartite Pact 189
    Tsingtao, bombing of 145
    '21 Demands' 145–8, 158
    World War II *see* World War II
    Yangtse valley, control in 146
Jehol (later Rehe) 175
Jennings, Peter 323–4, 329, 330, 336
Jiang Huiling, Judge 328
Jiang Qing 245, 257, 266
Jiang Zemin 287, 290, 292, 297, 315, 324

Keating, Paul 7, 286, 288, 289, 295, 334
    China, visits to 287, 294–5
    leadership challenge 286
Kim Jong-un 336
Kissinger, Henry 247, 253, 254
Korean War 222–3, 227, 231, 238
Kuomintang (National People's Party) 114, 140–4, 154, 164–5, 168, 171, 175, 176, 201, 210, 214, 217
    Australian chapter, secretary of 157
    Australian hostility to Nationalists 210
    businessmen, support of 157
    Chiang Kai-shek *see* Chiang Kai-shek
    Communists, relationship with 175–8, 179–81, 209, 214–15, 216–17
    formation of 140
    Mao Zedong and *see* Mao Zedong
    President Yuan Shikai, and 142–3, 145, 154
    primary school text books 226
    pro-Japanese 155
    Soviet-style communism, conversion of members to 164
    Taiwan, retreat to 219
    World War II, during 194
Kwantung Army 173
Kyoto protocol 307

Lambing Flat 48, 53, 54
    Chinese miners, violent attacks on 49–53
    quelling of uprising 53
Latham, Sir John 183–4, 186, 187, 189, 190, 191
League of Nations 199
    Japanese invasion, and 173, 174
Lee, Ansie 189, 193, 196, 203
Lee, Charles 192, 196, 201–2, 204, 211, 218
    Copland, and 211–13, 214
    international postings 221
Li Bin 237, 248, 264, 269–70
Li Keqiang 309, 337
Li Peng 279, 280
Li Shao-hua 237, 246, 248, 266, 269–70
Li Ting 237, 265, 269–70
Li Yuanhong 128, 142–3, 154–5
Liberal Party 220–2, 230–1, 234, 246, 247, 249, 260, 264, 268, 273, 288, 305, 307, 324
Lightowler, Mike 287, 290

Lin Biao 244, 255
Lin Zexu, Commissioner 22
liquid natural gas (LNG) 293, 297, 298, 302, 306
Little, Edward S 162–3, 184
Liu Bang 12, 13
Liu Shaoqi 235, 243
Liu, William 137, 156, 157, 162, 182, 193, 221
London Missionary Society (LMS) 41–2
Long March 175, 178, 243, 273
Longyu, Empress Dowager 136
Lyons, Joseph 183, 187

Macao 66, 124, 293, 321
MacArthur, General Douglas 203, 222, 223
Macarthur, John 3–6, 27
    opium drug trade, role in 20–1
McCaffrey, Major General Todd 323
McEwen, John 188, 189, 239, 242, 249
    prime minister, as 246–7
    trade agreements 231, 240, 241–2, 243
Mackerras, Professor Colin 322
McMahon, William 'Billy' 246–7, 249, 254, 255
Malaysia 299, 320, 335
    Japanese invasion 194
Manchu dynasty *see* Qing dynasty
Manchukuo 173–5, 183–4
Manchuria 213, 217, 223
    Japanese invasion 146, 147, 173–5, 179
Mandate of Heaven 9, 11, 13, 132
Mao Zedong 194, 209, 218, 240, 254, 257, 259, 273, 314, 336
    burning books 232
    Chiang Kai-shek, peace negotiations with 204, 213
    Communist Party of China (CPC) 167–8
    Cultural Revolution 243–6, 252
    death 265–6
    early years 167
    excess and corruption 232, 234–5, 265
    Five-year Plans 233
    Great Leap Forward 233, 243
    Hunan, development of fighting force in 168
    Hundred Flowers Campaign 234
    Kuomintang, and 167–8, 172, 217
    Long March 175, 178, 243
    military opportunism 167, 168
    People's Republic of China 218, 219, 225
    Soviets, split with 232, 237
    Versailles Peace Conference, outrage over 160, 167
Mayling Soong 125, 126, 142, 172, 176–8, 179–81, 185, 189, 193, 199, 203, 205–6
Mei Hwa 188, 193
Mei Quong Tart 38–40, 76–80, 113, 122, 326

    Chinese immigration, restriction of 80–1
    Crystal Button induction 80, 87
    death of 113–14, 121
    Morrison, George Ernest, friendship with 113
    opium, opposition to 76, 78, 79
Menzies, Robert 186, 193, 220–1, 223, 230, 236, 238–40, 247, 288, 317
    anti-communist stance 231, 238
    China, relationship with 186–90, 222
    Japan, on 187, 188–9
Middle Kingdom 8, 17, 87, 119
Ming dynasty 17–18, 218, 248
Morrison, George Ernest 122, 127, 133–4, 138–9, 143–4, 156, 308
    An Australian in China 96
    Boxer Rebellion 102–5, 106–110
    Deakin, and 112
    death of 160
    Donald, and 132–3, 138, 140–1, 143, 144, 147, 154–5
    early years 87–91
    expeditions 89–91, 93–6
    journalism in China 96–7, 102
    journey overland from Beijing to Moscow 123
    lecture series to honour 182, 193, 221
    Li Yuanhong, and 154–5
    marriage 139, 140, 143, 155, 160
    Mei Quong Tart, friendship with 113
    opium trade, observations on 95–6
    Qing dynasty, role in downfall of 87, 106–110, 135
    Rear Admiral Cai Tinggan, and 130–1
    reception on return to Australia 112
    revolution, comments on 129
    Song Jiaoren, killing of 141
    Stoessel, criticism of 117–18
    Sun Yatsen, meeting with 158
    The Times 89, 96–7, 109, 117, 133, 137, 138, 143–4, 147,
    trade in China 110–11
    '21 Demands', journalistic leaking of 147
    Versailles Peace Conference 158, 160
    Yuan Shikai, and 130, 131, 137–9, 141, 144, 153–4

Nanjing 173, 180, 205, 209
    Australian legation 210–13, 216
    battle of 131–2
    civil war, during 216–17
    Communist rule, under 218
    fall of 23, 43
    Japanese attack 185, 188
    student protests 279
    Treaty of 23

Nationalists *see* Kuomintang (National People's Party)
naturalisation
   certificates of Chinese immigrants 80
   Northern Territory 73–4
'New Gold Mountain' 25, 66
New Zealand XI
   treaty with China 216, 336
Ngo Dinh Diem 238
Nixon, Richard 247, 253, 254
   China, visit to 254–5
North Korea 222, 280, 303, 313, 315, 336
Northern Territory
   Chinese migration to 68–74, 81–2
   Chinese miners in 69–74, 82
   Exercise Kowari 322–3
   1900 Chinese New Year celebrations 82–3
nuclear testing/proliferation 259, 313

Obama, Barrack 312–13, 315
   'pivot to Asia' 312–13, 318
Officer, Keith 199, 200, 204, 212, 217–18
   Communist-controlled China, in 219–20, 221
One Nation Party 289, 336
Operation Tulip 197
opium 20, 23, 24
   anti-opium movement 76
   drug trade 20–2, 177–8
   goldfields, on the 29
Opium Wars 24, 43, 198
Overland Telegraph Line 68–9

Packer, James 328–9
Paddy's Island massacre 63
Pao, Dr C.J. 187–8, 189
Paris Peace Talks *see* Versailles Peace Conference
Paterson, Andrew Barton 'Banjo' 110, 112
Patterson, Rex 251, 252
Payne, Marisse 324, 325
Peacock, Andrew 261, 263, 264, 266, 285, 286
Peng Dehuai 234
Peng, James 293, 297
People's Republic of China 218
   Communist rule *see* Communists
Philippines 75, 91, 183, 195, 203, 221, 302, 313, 320, 335
Ping Que 69–74
Poh Ling Yeow 326
poll tax 81
Port Phillip 4, 8, 330
Pu Yi, Emperor 123, 136, 173

Qi Yuanjing 285
Qian Qichen 288

Qin dynasty 8, 198
   Shi Huang 11
Qing dynasty 6, 17, 135–7
   decline of 112
   downfall of 135
   opium payments 21
   slavery 6
Queensland 121, 294
   Chinese migration to 61–7, 82
   Japanese indentured labourers 100

Raby, Geoff 276, 312
Racial Discrimination Act 268
racism X, IX, 82, 196, 214, 318, 330
   aboriginals, towards 122
   anti-Chinese XII, 8, 30, 48, 54, 60, 65, 75–8, 80, 98, 100, 122, 226–7, 317–18, 327, 330, 336
   'Asian hordes', dislike and fear of XI, 75
   Chinese 8
   Chinese immigration, opposition to 80, 98–100, 203
   Intercolonial Conference 98, 99
   Middle Eastern refugees 336
   North African refugees 336
   Whitlam legislation 268
Red Army (China) 181, 230
   Long March 175
Red Army (Russia) 230
Red Guards 243, 244, 252
Regional Comprehensive Economic Partnership 337
Rigby, Richard 277–8, 291, 310
   Tiananmen Square incident 281–2, 284
Robin, Jennie 135, 137, 139, 143, 155, 160
Rudd, Jessica 274, 324
Rudd, Kevin 260, 274, 279, 288, 296, 324, 325
   climate change, on 307, 309–10
   diplomat in China 274–5, 276
   maiden speech 296
   political career 279, 288, 296, 305–12, 316–17
   prime minister, as 307–11
   Tiananmen Square incident 281
Rudd, Therese 274, 275, 288
Russo-Japanese war at sea 117–119
   Port Arthur battle 117–18

Saber Bogong (bull) 259
Sadleir, David 279, 285
Sam Poo 55–60
Shandong 217
   peace talks 154, 158–9
   peninsula, Japanese landing 145
Shang, Caleb, 149

INDEX

Shang dynasty 9, 10
   Mandate of Heaven *see* Mandate of Heaven
Shanghai 23, 43, 205–6, 286, 291
   Australian legation 219
   Japanese attacks 173–4, 185
   student protests 279
Shanghai Philharmonic Orchestra 267
Shaw, Patrick 210, 212
Shell, Chevron and Woodside Consortium 298
Shen Jiawei 326
Shenzhen 227, 286, 293, 293
Shi Huang 11, 12
Shorten, Bill 310, 317, 325
Sincere department store 125
Sing, William Edward 'Billy' 150–2
Singapore 170, 187, 194, 302
   fall of 194, 198
Sino-Japanese War 173–4, 185, 187–9
Smith, Ric 289–91, 292–4, 295, 297
Sneddon, Billy 255, 258–9, 260
Song Jiaoren 141
Soong, Dr T.V. 'Paul' 199, 203
Soong, Mayling *see* Mayling Soong
South China Sea 19, 313, 320–1, 323, 329, 334, 335
   liquid natural gas 298
South-East Asia 258, 313
   'domino' theory, and 241
Soviet Union 209, 218, 220, 228, 259, 277
   Australian elections (1954) 231
   Communist China, relationship with 222, 230, 232, 233, 237–8, 239, 253, 280
   recognition of Chinese Communist government 219
Spender, Percy 222–4
   Copland, and 223
Spratly Islands 320–1, 335
squatters, employment of Chinese 61–4
Stalin, Josef 228, 232
History of the Bolshevik Party 228
Sun Fo 201, 212
Sun Li Jen, General 196, 197
Sun Yatsen 115, 126–7, 164, 191, 201, 212
   cancer of the liver 164–5
   Chiang Kai-shek *see* Chiang Kai-shek
   Chinese Republic, provisional president of 133, 134
   Christianity 114
   death 165
   early years 114
   handover of power 137
   Homer Lea 133, 138
   Japan, flight to 142
   leadership 126
   manifesto 115
   memorial 218
   railway post 139, 142
   revolutionary, career as 114–15
Sun Yatsen, Madame *see* Chingling Soong
Swan, Wayne 309, 310, 311

Taiping 23–4
   manifesto 24
   rebellion 24–5, 28, 42–4, 64
Taiwan 238, 241, 252, 254, 302, 314, 320, 334–5
   Australian recognition of 231, 255, 287
   Chiang Kai-shek, and 219, 241, 252, 321
   Chinese aggression towards 289, 304, 321
Tan, Pamela (Tan Pingmei) 225–30, 233, 234, 237, 257, 269, 299
   ACTU visit 236
   Cultural Revolution, and 243–6, 248, 262, 269
   Nixon visit to China 254–5
   return to Australia 269–70
   Tianjin earthquake 264–5
   Zhou Enlai, death of 262–3
Tang dynasty 8, 15–16
'Tank Man' 283
Taylor, Rev Hudson 91–2
Teo, Charlie 326
Tiananmen Square 244, 262
   international response to incident 284–5, 292
   memorial for Mao 265–6
   student protests 280–3
Tianjin earthquake 264–5
Tibet 232, 238, 308
tourism XII, 297, 319, 325, 326, 332, 333
trade 20–1, 110–11, 285
   Australia–China 184–5, 187, 202, 232, 240–1, 243, 251, 252–3, 258–9, 267–8, 275, 277, 285, 292–5, 297, 298–9, 303–4, 306, 318, 319–20, 325, 334, 337
   Australia–Japan XI, XII, 231–2, 267, 285
   opium *see* opium
Trans-Pacific Partnership (TPP) 334, 337
Trump, Donald 334–7
Tsai Ing-wen 334
Turnbull, Malcolm 307–8, 324–5, 333, 334, 335, 337

United Nations
   China, admission of 222, 223, 242
   UN Commission on Human Rights 292
   UN Relief and Rehabilitation Administration (UNRRA) 214, 215
United States of America 277, 292, 295
   anti-communist stance 219, 222, 253
   Australia, and XI, 187, 231, 240, 247, 299, 312–13

United States of America *continued*
  China, relationship with 254, 313, 315, 321, 322–3, 334–7
  Exercise Kowari 322–3
  extra-territorial rights 202
  Korean War 222–3
  One China policy 334–5
  'Operation Enduring Freedom' 300
  Taiwan, and 289

Van Diemen's Land 26, 27
Versailles Peace Conference 156–161, 190, 203
Victoria 27
  gold 28, 30, 33, 34, 36–7, 125
Victoria, Queen 22, 99, 100
Vietnam War 238, 239, 240, 247, 254, 258
Vietnamese refugees 268, 269

Waller, Keith 196–7, 199, 251, 258, 259, 263
Wang, 'Henry' 6
Wang, Yvonne (Wang Yi Wen) 324
Wanrong 174
Ward, Senior Constable 56, 58, 59, 60
Wei Jianxing 315
Wei Jingsheng 308
Wellington Koo 174
Wen, Emperor 13
Wen Jiabao 281, 308
Western Australia
  gold 81
  iron ore 276, 285, 293
western brands, iconic 331
Whampoa Military Academy 164
White, Professor Hugh 323
White Australia policy 80, 120, 204, 216, 319
  Chinese population, effect on 155, 213–14
  extra-territorial rights, and 199, 202–3
  Nationality Act 133
  opposition to 251, 284, 296
Whitlam, Gough 238, 242, 249, 250, 255, 267, 275
  Beijing, visits to 249, 250–4, 258, 259–60, 264
  dismissal 261, 296
Wong, Penny 335
World Trade Organization (WTO)
  China's entry 292–3, 297
World War I 148–52
  Chinese declaration of war 1917 155
  Chinese in Australia 149, 152, 155–6
  Chinese non-combatant duties on Western Front 154
  events prior to 144
World War II 187, 196, 204, 326
  Chinese involvement 194, 196–7, 198, 204

Chinese refugees 189, 213–14
Japanese advances 194, 196–7
Wuchang uprising 127–8

Xi'an 11, 12, 16, 110, 112, 123, 178, 179, 217
  Silk Road, terminus of 12
Xi Jinping 314–16, 318–21, 327–8, 334–5
  Chinese legal system, and 328
  'core leader', as 335–6
  corruption, crackdown on 316, 328–9
  North Korea, and 336
  visits to Australia 318–19
Xiamen (Amoy) 3, 4

Yang Hucheng, General 179
Yang Xiuqing 23
Yangtse River 11, 22, 43, 93, 125, 126
Yellow River 9, 10, 11
Yongle, Emperor 17, 18
Yu Sheng 325
Yuan Shikai 103, 112, 123, 128–9, 136, 142–3, 165
  assassination attempts 123, 135
  Boxers, treatment of 104
  death of 154
  Emperor declaration 148, 153
  Newly Created Army, commander of 103, 108
  peace settlement, negotiation of 132
  power, removal from 123
  President, elected as 142–3
  prime minister, as 129–30
  republic, restoration of 153
  Song Jiaoren, killing of 141
  Tang Shaoyi, dismissal of 140

Zhang Xueliang ('The Young Marshal') 179, 184
  Donald, and 171–3, 175–8, 179–81
  Japanese invasion of Manchuria 173–5
  North China, governor of 172
  opium addiction 176
Zhao Ziyang 275–7, 279
  Tiananmen Square incident 280–1
Zheng He 17–18, 303
Zhongguo *see* Middle Kingdom
Zhou Enlai 171, 175, 178, 180, 193, 201, 210, 213, 235, 257
  death 262–3
  People's Republic of China 218, 219
  Premier, as 219, 222, 251
  Whitlam visits to China 252–3, 254, 259
Zhu Rongji 287, 288, 291, 292, 293, 294–5, 298, 297, 299, 315
  visit to Australia 293–4, 298
Zin Jin Shin see 'New Gold Mountain'